THE ENGLISH
CIVIL WAR
DAY BY DAY

To my friend and mentor
Brigadier Peter Young DSO, MC, MA,
who introduced me to
the English Civil War and
The Sealed Knot.

THE ENGLISH CIVIL WAR DAY BY DAY

WILFRID EMBERTON

FOREWORD BY DR JOHN ADAIR

ALAN SUTTON PUBLISHING LIMITED

First published in the United Kingdom in 1995
Alan Sutton Publishing Ltd
Phoenix Mill · Far Thrupp · Stroud · Gloucestershire

British Library Cataloguing in Publication Data

A catalogue record for this book is available from the British Library.

ISBN 0-7509-0959-5

Typeset in 11/14 Garamond.
Typesetting and origination by
Alan Sutton Publishing Limited.
Printed and bound in Great Britain by
Butler and Tanner, Frome, Somerset.

Contents

List of Illustrations vii

Foreword xi

Introduction xv

Personalities xvii

List of Abbreviations xxvii

Prologue 1

1642 9

1643 51

1644 93

1645 139

Events Leading up to the Second Civil War and After 177

1646 181

1647 187

1648 189

1649 197

The Third Civil War 1650–1 201

1650 203

1651 209

Epilogue 215

Select Bibliography 217

Index 221

List of Illustrations

1   'England's Royal Pattern, or the History of King Charles the First
    from his Marriage to his Death', engraved frontispiece (Ashmolean
    Museum: CI 126)   xix

2   Parliamentarian commanders (Ashmolean Museum: CII 369)   xxv

3   The Civil Wars in England and Scotland, map   xxviii

4   Charles I, by W. Hollar, 1639   3

5   Charles I in Parliament before the war began (Ashmolean Museum: CI 107) 5

6   The execution of Thomas Strafford, 1641 (Ashmolean Museum: CI 207)   7

7   John Pym (1584–1643), by Samuel Cooper   9

8   Hampton Court Palace from the River Thames, by an unknown artist, c. 1640 10

9   Henrietta Maria, after Van Dyck, c. 1635   14

10 Charles I, by G. Honthorst, 1628   15

11 The Tower of London (Paul Lewis Isemonger/Living History Photo Library) 20

12 Major-General Phillip Skippon, by an unknown engraver   23

13 Henry Ireton (1611–51), attributed to Robert Walker, after Samuel
    Cooper and Sir Anthony Van Dyck   28

14 Lord George Digby, later 2nd Earl of Bristol (1611–76), after H. Van der
    Borcht   30

15 Sir John Hotham (Ashmolean Museum: CI 486)   32

16 *Prospect of Oxforde from the East* and map of Oxford by W. Hollar
    (Ashmolean Museum: CII 87)   36

17 Reconstruction of Rupert's cavalry at Edgehill (Paul Lewis
    Isemonger/Living History Photo Library)   40

18 The manor-house at Wormleighton   41

19 The site of the Battle of Edgehill   44

20 *A True Mapp and Description of the Towne of Plymouth . . .'* (Ashmolean
    Museum: CII 304)   52

21 *The North East View of Lancaster* (Ashmolean Museum: CIII 132)   57

22 Prince Rupert, with Birmingham in flames in the background (BL: E 99
    (14) FP 9371611)   60

23 Oliver Cromwell (1599–1658), by an unknown artist   62

24 Sir Henry Vane (1613–62), by Robert Walker   70

25 Edward Massey   72

26 Digging the defences in Gloucester   73

27	Summoning Hull (Ashmolean Museum: CI 397)	76
28	The coat of arms of Gloucester	80
29	*A True Mapp and Description of the fortification of Newport pangnell*, 1644 (Bodleian Library: MS. Top. Bucks. b. 6)	81
30	Oak leaf insignia on Civil War helmet (Paul Lewis Isemonger/Living History Photo Library)	84
31	*The South View of Beeston Castle near Chester*, etching by S. and N. Buck, 1727	87
32	*Prospect of Arrundell Castle & Towne, the Westside*, by W. Hollar (Ashmolean Museum: CII 363)	88
33	Sir William Waller, 1643 (Ashmolean Museum: CII 370)	90
34	Archbishop William Laud, after A. Van Dyck, *c*. 1636	94
35	Royalist musketeer (Paul Lewis Isemonger/Living History Photo Library)	104
36	The well-equipped pikeman (Paul Lewis Isemonger/Living History Photo Library)	105
37	The ruins of Sudeley Castle, Gloucestershire	111
38	Prince Rupert, by G. Honthorst, *c*. 1641	116
39	*The Battle of Marston Moor*, July 1644, by James Ward	117
40	Restormel Castle, Lostwithiel	124
41	*The South-east prospect of Newcastle upon Tyne* (Ashmolean Museum: CIII 54)	128
42	Donnington Castle, Berkshire	129
43	A Royalist field camp, etching by W. Hollar (BM: 140567)	140
44	*The prospect of Chester the South-west Side* and *The Ground-plott of Chester*, 1653	143
45	Charles when Prince of Wales, by William Dobson (National Gallery of Scotland: PG 1244)	146
46	Oliver Cromwell	154
47	*The Retreat at Naseby*, a mezzotint by W. Giller from a painting by Abraham Cooper, mid-nineteenth century	158
48	Ludlow Castle, Shropshire	160
49	James Graham, Marquess of Montrose, attributed to Willem van Honthorst (Scottish National Portrait Gallery: PG 998)	164
50	The Phoenix or King Charles's Tower, Chester	166
51	*The Siege of Bazinge House* (Ashmolean Museum: CII 418)	169
52	The ruins at Basing House (Paul Lewis Isemonger/Living History Photo Library)	169
53	Sir William Brereton	173
54	*A Description of the Siedge of Newark upon Trent . . . 1646* (Ashmolean Museum: CII 552)	175
55	Carisbrooke Castle, Isle of Wight	179
56	Lord Byron, Royalist Governor of Chester (Ashmolean Museum: CII 20)	182
57	Title page of the terms of surrender	183
58	The pitched stone court, Raglan Castle	184

59   Pendennis Castle, Falmouth   185
60   Title page from *An Ould Ship called an Exhortation* showing Charles I
         in Carisbrooke Castle, 1648 (Bodleian Library: C.15.3.Linc(2).)   188
61   Chepstow Castle, Gwent   189
62   *A great and bloudy fight at Colchester . . .*, from a 1648 pamphlet (BL: E 453
         (18) TP 9371611)   190
63   A prospect of Colchester   191
64   James, 1st Duke of Hamilton, by an unknown artist after Van Dyck
         (Scottish National Portrait Gallery: PG 777)   192
65   Pembroke Castle, Dyfed   193
66   *The Siege of Pontefract Castle, 1648* (Ashmolean Museum: CIII 146) 196
67   The King's death warrant (Bodleian Library: folio 52 from Rawl Prints a 7.) 197
68   The Rump Parliament of 1649 satirized   198
69   Fairfax as the King's executioner, *c.* 1649 (Ashmolean Museum: CIII 195) 199
70   The execution of Charles I, a contemporary Dutch engraving
         (Ashmolean Museum: CIII 198)   199
71   John Lilburne, Leveller, 1641 (Bodleian Library: Firth.e.63(2).)   200
72   Montrose paraded through the streets of Edinburgh before his execution,
         21 May 1650 (National Gallery of Scotland: NG 624)   203
73   Berwick, from the town plan by John Speed   204
74   The Battle of Dunbar, 3 September 1650 (Ashmolean Museum: CIII 293) 205
75   George Monck, Duke of Albemarle (Ashmolean Museum BI 125)   208
76   The coronation of Charles II at Scone, 1651 (BM: 1872-10-12-1711)   209
77   *An Exact Ground-Plot of the City of Worcester . . .* (Ashmolean Museum) 210
78   *A more full Relation of the great Victory Obtained by our Forces near Worcester* 211
79   Oak chest carved with a scene of Charles II's escape at Boscobel, 1651
         (English Heritage Photographic Library, loan)   214

Illustrations are reproduced by kind permission of the following: The Ashmolean Museum, Oxford: 1, 2, 5, 6, 15, 16, 20, 21, 27, 32, 33, 41, 51, 54, 56, 66, 69, 70, 74, 75, 77; Banbury Museum: 18, 19; The Bodleian Library, Oxford: 29, 60, 67, 71; The British Library: 22, 62; Copyright British Museum: 43, 76; The British Tourist Authority: 42, 50, 59; the City Record Office, Chester: 31, 44, 53; Colchester Museums: 63; The Cromwell Museum: 23, 24, 39, 57; English Heritage Photographic Library, loan: 79; Dr P. Gaunt: 40, 55, 58, 72; Mr Humphrey Household: 48, 61, 65; Paul Lewis Isemonger/Living History Photo Library: 11, 17, 30, 35, 36, 52; the Mansell Collection: 68; National Gallery of Scotland: 45, 72; by courtesy of the National Portrait Gallery, London: 9, 10, 12, 13, 14, 34, 38; Northampton Museums and Art Gallery: 47; Dr S. Porter: 37; Scottish National Portrait Gallery: 49, 64; University of London: 4. Reproduced by gracious permission of Her Majesty The Queen is illustration 8 from The Royal Collection © 1995 Her Majesty The Queen.

Foreword

My great pleasure in writing this introduction to Wilfrid Emberton's *The English Civil War Day by Day* arises from three springs. First, like most historians or students of the Civil War my interests have tended to become local or specific: this particular campaign and battle or that particular participant. It is so easy to lose sight of what Montgomery used to call 'the big picture'.

This attempt to piece together the jigsaw puzzle of daily events and personalities is especially important in the context of the Civil War. Like a conflagration out of control it flared up in some areas and flickered uncertainly in others. Following the rise and fall of events across the board as month succeeded month is a fascinating exercise. One gets the impression that regions and even localities were rather self-contained, and that we are dealing with a concurrent series of minor civil wars, interwoven with local feuds and sometimes family tragedies as relative fought against relative. But this is not entirely true, which brings me to my second reason for welcoming this book.

Doing history is about trying to answer two questions: what happened? and why did it happen that way rather than any other? Wilfrid Emberton has done us a signal service in answering the first question – I can remember once spending no less than two days with Brigadier Peter Young and Dr Ian Roy simply trying to work out what was going on at any one time in the Civil War, a task done for us so effortlessly by this book. But what of the second question?

Two contemporary ideas of why things happen in history – conspiracy and cock-up – can be documented by this diary. The gradual, almost accidental way in which the country lurched uncertainly into this 'war without an enemy', as Sir William Waller called it, can be seen clearly as we follow the events from day to day – more cock-up than conspiracy. On the other hand, the King as an arch-schemer virtually plotted himself onto the scaffold by way of the Second Civil War – definitely more conspiracy than cock-up.

As a Parliamentarian and a Puritan, of course, I look for more than that. It is salutary to remember that our modern practice of keeping diaries stems from the Puritans of this period. Their spiritual purpose in doing so was to seek to trace the hand of God in the unfolding pattern of one's personal history. Likewise Puritan leaders such as Oliver Cromwell would ponder upon the course of events to see where God was guiding the nation under providence and to be uplifted or admonished by the victories or defeats that came their way in the ebb and flow of war.

We cannot today savour their excitement or exaltation or plumb the depths of their disappointments. Nor may many readers even share their faith that there is a pattern or purpose in history if only our eyes could be opened to see it. But 'coincidences are miracles when God wishes to remain anonymous'. You may want to interpret them as chance or luck rather than the self-effacing results of God at work, but coincidences are integral to history and make it such a fascinating subject.

Perhaps the historian is on safer ground when contemplating with the help of this most useful journal or catalogue of coincidences the impact of events in one part of the country or another. Despite what I have said about the local and often compartmentalized nature of much of the Civil War, as well as the limitations in communication – no television or radio news, no telephones and only the beginnings of daily newspapers – no campaign or battle was an island unto itself. For example, it is impossible to understand the state of mind of Sir William Waller, the Parliamentarian commander at the Battle of Cheriton in Hampshire, without knowing what he knew, namely that Prince Rupert's successes in the Midlands at Newark had acted as a magnet to Parliament's available field forces eager to stabilize the situation, leaving London virtually defenceless except for its redoubtable but inexperienced Trained Bands. Suddenly the stakes were so much higher. No wonder that his council of war urged Waller not to risk a battle, but he did.

Sir William Waller, incidentally, was a link in the chain of events that led me to meet Wilf Emberton. For Waller had unsuccessfully besieged Basing House and it was in the village of Basing, beside those forlorn and evocative ruins of the once-proud Royalist fortress that Wilf Emberton lived with his family. My third reason for the pleasure in being invited to write this foreword is that it gives me an opportunity to write briefly about an old and much-missed friend.

We first met at Basing in the context of The Sealed Knot, the society that emerged initially to re-enact the battles of the Civil War. Its founder, Brigadier Peter Young, invited me to the first event at Edgehill. 'But where are the Roundheads?' I enquired, having watched the Cavaliers attacking nothing more than a line of smouldering thunderflashes. As a result I took the field myself at the next muster of Basing, dressed in black and armed with a halberd and pistol. Over the years I came to know Wilf and his family well. Despite the fact that he rose to command Sir Marmaduke Rawdon's Regiment of Foot (named after the royalist garrison regiment of Basing House), there was always a cheery welcome and a hot cup of tea in Wilf and Susan Emberton's caravan for the 'man in black' after many a rain-sodden battle re-enactment in the shires of England.

Wilf Emberton, however, was much more than an enthusiastic amateur soldier: he had a deep and abiding interest in the Civil War, and he demonstrated once and for all that you don't need university degrees to make a real contribution – just natural historical interest and determination. Wilf showed the latter when he published his first book *Love Loyalty: The Close and Perilous Seige of Basing House* himself in 1972. His three subsequent books, *Skippon's Brave Boys*, a history of the London Trained Bands, and (with Peter Young) *The Cavalier Army* and *Sieges of the Great Civil War*, all served to cement his reputation as the first outstanding historian to arise from The Sealed Knot. He personified not only its spirit but one of its key aims, that is to stimulate interest and to promote the study of the Civil War.

Mind you, Wilf Emberton would have emerged anyway as a historian. He loved writing, and, once free from the trammels of an inherited business, he took to authorship like the proverbial duck to water. He was full of encouragement and advice to fellow authors like myself, and I shall always remember with affection his infectious enthusiasm for our trade. All true authors hope to die with their pens in their hand, and this wish was granted to Wilf Emberton. But Wilf fortunately – or providentially – lived to see this book complete, the culmination of four years intensive research. It serves as a most fitting memorial to him, for one of his dearest wishes was to share extensive knowledge of the English Civil War. You will find no better introduction, framework or reference book to these turbulent years than the lively and informative pages that follow.

Dr John Adair
1995

Introduction

When I was asked to write this book I was at once fascinated and challenged by the original concept of its approach.

In the last fifty years or so a number of historians have essayed to chronicle the troubled path of the Great Civil War of 1642–6 and its attendant short-lived revolts of 1648 and 1650–1, with greater or less success. It is my view that any author is prevented from achieving a well-rounded homogenous whole by the fact that he is of necessity limited to one facet of the action at a time. It is therefore difficult for the general reader to appreciate that while Marston Moor was being fought the King was driving into the West en route for his victory at Lostwithiel a month later, while Cropredy Bridge had been fought three days before.

The question of how the common man lived through this time of fratricidal strife, his degree of involvement, the drain made on his personal resources and so on is either not considered or is lost in the concentration on stern military matters like logistics, tactics, strategy and manpower.

The chronological aspect of this book at once frees the author from the burdensome ties of following through. He is free to explore the scene as a whole, to flit from theatre of operations to theatre of operations, to go from a meeting of the Committee of Both Kingdoms – comparable perhaps to the modern Imperial General Staff or War Cabinet – to the worries of ordinary citizen Henry Woodhouse who is concerned in obtaining proof that he has taken the oath of allegiance. In doing so, he is also free to regard both, in proportion, as equally important to the narrative.

The deliberate medley of assaults, politics, personal and public affairs is designed to give a comprehensive overall picture of how it was to be alive at that time. So that the reader shall not be stunned by the impact of so much information, at the end of the more complex years there is a summary of how far the war has progressed – 'the story so far', as the old-fashioned serial films used to proclaim.

The main battles are laid out separately to avoid breaking the text, in a simplified form with, where possible, a note on the standard work on each.

As the book progresses it will become obvious that the deep flow of everyday life, although greatly disturbed on the surface, flowed on; and that while many historians try to persuade us in their enthusiasm that the nation stood breathless on tiptoe for the result of the significant battles like Naseby or Cheriton the people as a whole were ignorant of its occurrence and even the Committee of Both Kingdoms had other things on its mind.

Inevitably some will consider that my battle accounts are over simplified and that I have omitted events that in their opinion should have been included, but such criticisms are inherent in a work of this nature. Throughout, the discerning will perceive there are countless small stories, some consisting of a single episode, some of a number that may be traced through the index or merely by following through.

A writer may conceive, construct, research and write a book but he does not do so unaided. I am indebted to the staff of the British Library who produced photostats and books with courtesy, to the staff of the Guildhall Library and the Public Record Office, the staffs of so many smaller libraries that fulfilled my requirements, not the least being the Basingstoke Central Library. Of the very many individuals who have expressed interest and given me aid, I should mention with particular gratitude Peter Young and Alison Michelli, who have made suggestions and given me photostats and other assistance, Margaret Williams, who has shown considerable patience, skill, and interest in typing the manuscript, Ann and Gordon Hesketh, whose expertise, goodwill, and understanding have smoothed the path of this book, and last but not least my wife Susan and my children Sharon and Andrew, who must at times have thought shudderingly that the ideas and material for this book were my only topic of conversation.

Wilfrid Emberton
Old Basing

Personalities

ROYALIST

Jacob, Lord Astley (1579–1652)

Astley was a professional soldier who had seen service in Denmark, the Netherlands and Germany. He was a personal friend of Elizabeth of Bohemia and tutor to Prince Rupert, nephew of Charles I. He returned to England in 1638 and was appointed Governor of Plymouth. He served at the Battles of Edgehill and Second Newbury. He was created a baron in 1644. At the Battle of Naseby he commanded the Royalist foot and in March 1646 he surrendered the last Royalist army to Sir William Brereton at Stow-on-the-Wold. He died at Maidstone in Kent in February 1652.

John, 1st Lord Byron (1603–52)

Lord Byron was the senior of six brothers who were all Royalist and achieved high ranks. He served in the Netherlands and in Scotland. In 1639 he was appointed Lieutenant of the Tower. Later he joined the King at Oxford and horsed as many students as possible. He joined Prince Rupert at Powick Bridge, commanded the cavalry reserve at Edgehill, and fought at the First Battle of Newbury. He was created a baron on 24 October 1643. He then commanded at Nantwich, served at Marston Moor, and became Governor of Chester. After Rowton Heath when Charles I left for Denbigh, he held out against Sir William Brereton until 1646. In the spring of 1648 he endeavoured to raise Wales for the King but failed. He died in France in 1652.

Arthur, Baron Capel (1610–49)

He was created a baron in 1641 and became lieutenant-general the following year, in command of North Wales. He was an energetic but unsuccessful commander, and was very active in Cheshire and Shropshire. After being defeated by Mytton at Wem in October 1643 he was sent west to join Sir Ralph Hopton. He helped with the King's escape from Hampton Court and escorted his Queen to Paris. In the second stage of the Civil War he defended Colchester when it was attacked by Fairfax. He was captured and executed on 9 March 1649.

Robert, Earl of Carnarvon (1607–43)

The Earl of Carnarvon was lieutenant-general (horse). He served at the intake of Bristol and captured Dorchester, Weymouth and Portland. He was killed at the First Battle of Newbury.

Sir Thomas Glemham (1595–1649)

Sir Thomas was an expert in defending doomed cities but he was not as highly esteemed as he deserved to be. He defended York gallantly in 1644 and also Carlisle but was compelled to surrender both. Later he was made Governor of Oxford. He was offended when the King conferred a barony on Gerrard which might more deservedly have been bestowed on him.

George, Lord Goring (1608–57)

He was a many faceted officer, who by turns was liar, rake, drunkard, visionary leader, and courageous fighter. He served in Holland during the Thirty Years War, at the siege of Breda (1637); he was appointed by Parliament to be Governor of Portsmouth at the start of the Civil War, masking his true allegiance until the last moment when he declared for the King. At Seacroft Moor he was successful against Fairfax in March 1643 but was captured at Wakefield the same year. In 1644 he achieved his freedom and his finest hour came at Marston Moor, when as general of the left wing he broke his opponents and drove them from the field. In the closing stages of the First Civil War he figured largely in the fighting in the West Country and when all was finally over he escaped to France. He died in Madrid, reportedly as a monk, in 1657.

Ralph, 1st Baron Hopton (1598–1652)

Hopton served in the Palatinate in the Thirty Years War with many of the officers who were to be colleagues or opponents in the Civil War. He formed a particular attachment to Sir William Waller whose friendship survived the rivalry they were to experience as opponents. Hopton was appointed by Charles I to be Lieutenant-General in the West, where his notable victories were Braddock Down, Stratton and Sourton Down. The marginal victory at Lansdown and his crushing defeat of Waller at Roundway Down made 1643 a vintage year for him. Waller retaliated the following year by winning the crucial Battle of Cheriton. In the closing stages of the war Hopton returned to command the Western Army but was defeated by Fairfax at Torrington and surrendered on 14 March 1646. He retired to the Continent where he died at Bruges in 1652.

'England's Royal Pattern, or the History of King Charles the First from his Marriage to his Death': an engraved frontispiece, artist unknown.

Marmaduke, 1st Baron Langdale (1598–1661)

The 1st Baron Langdale was a professional soldier, 'brave as a lion, enterprising, judicious, but with an unfortunate temper'. He was one of the most capable and dependable cavalry leaders of the war. He defeated the Scots cavalry at Corbridge in 1644, fought at Marston Moor, relieved Pontefract the following year, and in his most brilliant exploit defeated Rossiter at Melton Mowbray. At Naseby he was in charge of the left wing when his men were dispersed by the Ironsides. While escorting the King he was engaged at the ruinous Battle of Rowton Heath. In the Second Civil War he united with the Duke of Hamilton and fought at Preston. He was one of the few officers of note to continue with his military career after the war when he fought for the Venetians against the Turks. He died at Holme in 1661.

Colonel William Legge (1609–70)

Although a soldier of proven ability, he was chiefly remarkable for his fidelity to Prince Rupert. After the fall of Bristol he tried to reconcile the King and the Prince. This resulted in his removal from the governorship of Oxford.

Sir George Lisle (d. 1648)

Sir George was the son of a bookseller. He saw action in the Netherlands but returned to England at the outbreak of war. He fought at Cheriton as colonel of horse and was brigade commander at Second Newbury where he threw off his buffcoat and fought in his shirt sleeves so that his men could see their leader in the darkness. He became Governor of Faringdon Castle which he is alleged to have resigned to accommodate his friend Sir Marmaduke Rawdon. He was captured in the Second Civil War at Colchester and was shot for breaking his parole.

Sir Charles Lucas (1613–48)

Soldiering came naturally to Charles Lucas, who 'was bred in the Low Countries and always amongst the horse so that he had little conversation in that court where civility was practiced and learnt'. He fought at Powick Bridge, Edgehill, Cirencester and a score of other places where his valour was recognized, being promoted by stages from lieutenant-colonel to lieutenant-general. He was among those who surrendered with Astley at Stow-on-the-Wold and gave his parole. It was his undoing for when he was captured with Sir George Lisle at Colchester he was shot alongside him.

Prince Maurice (1621–52)

Prince Maurice was the younger brother of Prince Rupert, whom he idolized. They were the sons of the King and Queen of Bohemia. Prince Maurice served in the trenches before Breda and at the outbreak of the Civil War set sail with Rupert to offer his services to King Charles I, his uncle. He was wounded at Powick Bridge, served at Edgehill, then gained a victory over Waller at Ripple; he fought at Roundway Down, Lansdown and Chester, Second Newbury, and Naseby. During the Second Civil War he joined Rupert in his fleet of privateers in the Mediterranean and in the West Indies until his ship *The Honest Seaman* went down with all hands in a storm. Maurice's worth has never been appreciated, overshadowed as he was by his brother.

James, Marquess of Montrose (1612–50)

Following the alliance of the Scots with Parliament in 1644, Montrose raised a small army and declared for the King. Such was his talent and inspiration that against all odds he gained victory after victory until, his luck running out, his force was slaughtered at Philliphaugh on the very day that Charles I was at Chester, preparing to set out and join him. Montrose escaped to the Continent but later returned to raise troops for Charles II. In 1650 he landed at Caithness but received little support. He was betrayed to the Covenanters and was executed in Edinburgh on 21 May.

William, Duke of Newcastle (1592–1676)

Prince of Wales, governor from 1638 to 1641. Newcastle was an earl at the beginning of the war. He became marquess in 1644 and duke in 1665. He raised siege at York in 1642 and was active in the North against the Fairfaxes whom he defeated at Adwalton Moor in 1643. In 1644 he held York against three armies and was then relieved by Rupert. In the same year his alleged non-cooperation is said to have resulted in the crushing defeat of the Royalists at the Battle of Marston Moor. After defeat he left the country for Holland, unable to bear the disgrace. He returned at the Restoration.

Prince Rupert (1619–82)

Rupert was born in Prague, son of Frederick, King of Bohemia and his wife Elizabeth, sister of Charles I. His abrupt, stern and ungracious manner seems to have made him more enemies than friends in high circles, but his men and officers seem to have idolized him for his qualities as a cavalry officer. In the Thirty Years War he was captured and imprisoned for three years. At the outbreak of the Civil War he and his brother Maurice joined the King; he soon became famous for the whirlwind charges that he taught his men to deliver. In such limited space it is difficult to record his war service but his main achievements were the taking of Lichfield, Bristol and Cirencester, Chalgrove Field, Powick Bridge, Edgehill, the relief of Lathom House, Newark, and York. After quarrelling with the King over his rendering up Bristol to Fairfax in 1645 he and Maurice left the country. In the

Second Civil War he raised and commanded a small privateer fleet. After the death of Maurice by drowning, he retired from public life, returning at the Restoration.

PARLIAMENTARY

Robert Blake (1599–1657)

Blake was educated at Oxford. He travelled extensively in India, Morocco and the Netherlands. He was MP for Bridgwater in 1640. He was notable for his determined defence of Bristol, Lyme, and Taunton. He did not, however, come to the forefront until after the execution of Charles I, when as a general-at-sea he showed a latent genius. Driving Rupert's fleet headlong from the Irish coast he sailed up the River Tagus and shattered the Royalist fleet at Malaga. Among a lengthy list of achievements may be numbered the capture of the Portuguese treasure ships, the destruction of a French squadron en route to the relief of Dunkirk, the ejection of the Royalists from the Isles of Scilly and several victories over the Dutch and the Tunisian corsairs. Probably his greatest victory was the capture of Santa Cruz and the annihilation of the Spanish treasure fleet.

Sir William Brereton, Baronet (1604–61)

He was commander-in-chief for Cheshire, Shropshire and Staffordshire. He was also MP for Cheshire. A man of culture, he established his headquarters at Nantwich which he caused to be fortified. He made his first assault on Chester in July 1643. In November he collaborated with Sir Thomas Middleton on invading Wales. In the attack by Byron on Nantwich in January 1644 he joined Sir Thomas Fairfax in defeating the Royalists. After Marston Moor he marched to relieve Montgomery Castle with Meldrum and Middleton, and won the Battle of Montgomery in September 1644. After Rowton Heath he forced Byron to surrender Chester on 3 February 1646. Along with Birch and Morgan he received Astley's surrender at Stow-on-the-Wold. He spent his last year at the Archbishop of Canterbury's palace at Croydon which had been forfeited.

Oliver Cromwell (1599–1658)

Cromwell was the son of a squire in Huntingdon and he first became an MP in 1628. In the Short Parliament of 1640 he supported John Pym and his cousin John Hampden. After Edgehill, where he was a captain of horse, he began to show his astute discernment and acute grasp of military matters. He commenced to recruit a select regiment of horse whose disciplined valour and religious fervour would go down in history – they were known as the Ironsides, a name first applied to Cromwell himself at Marston Moor by Rupert but later used to describe his men.

He rose from colonel to become lieutenant-general of the Eastern Association. Under the Self-Denying Ordinance, which required that no Member of Parliament could hold rank in the army, he relinquished his rank and Sir Thomas Fairfax became commander-in-chief of the New Model Army. Cromwell was recalled by Parliament as lieutenant-general of horse in time to ensure the great victory at Naseby. In the Second Civil War he was Parliament's chief instrument in suppressing the Royalist and Scots' outbreak. In August a Remonstrance was sent by the Army to Parliament denouncing Charles as the 'grand author of the country's woes' and demanding his punishment. Cromwell sought for some other solution as an alternative to the King's execution but finding none was the architect of the trial and execution. When Fairfax resigned as commander-in-chief the post was filled by Cromwell. In the Third Civil War (1650–1) he defeated the Scots at Dunbar on 23 September 1650 and the new King, Charles II, at Worcester a year later, his 'crowning mercy' as he called it.

In failing health Cromwell spurned the kingly title but assumed the title of Lord Protector in 1653 and with it the supreme power. In 1658 he died on the anniversary of Dunbar and was buried in Westminster Abbey. His corpse was exhumed and hung on Tyburn Tree after the Restoration to the everlasting shame of Charles II.

Robert, 3rd Earl of Essex (1591–1646)

Essex was Lord General of the Armies of Parliament at the outset of the Civil War. He served in the Thirty Years War and fought his three great battles with his enemies between him and his base, proving he was no military genius. His greatest achievement without doubt was the relief of Gloucester and his victory at the First Battle of Newbury. In 1644 having split his army in two he led one half into Cornwall where he was cornered by the King at Lostwithiel and forced to leave it to its own devices while he escaped by boat. In order to form the New Model Army in 1646 the Self-Denying Ordinance was devised and he resigned his command, dying on 4 September the same year.

Sir Thomas Fairfax (later 3rd Lord) (1612–71)

Fairfax was born at Denton in Yorkshire. He saw service in the Netherlands and Scotland. At the start of the Civil War he operated with his father Lord Ferdinando Fairfax but later fought independently with great success. He was known to his men as 'Black Tom' and 'the Rider of the White Horse'. His contemporaries thought him 'religious, faithful and valiant'.

Both father and son were at Marston Moor where their horse regiments were dispersed by the fiery charge of Goring. Lord Fairfax fled but Sir Thomas removed his distinguishing sash and field sign and crossed over to join Manchester. He was elected commander-in-chief for Parliament at thirty-two years of age. He commanded at Naseby (14 June 1645) and followed up this victory with a successful campaign in the west when he became a popular hero.

In the Second Civil War he crushed the rising in the south-west. He refused to sit in judgment at the King's trial and in 1650 being reluctant to fight the Presbyterian Scots resigned his office of commander-in-chief. He broke from the extremists and helped Monck bring about the Restoration after which he retired from public life.

Colonel John Hampden (1594–1643)

Hampden was one of the outstanding figures of the Civil War. He was a man of breeding and ability yet content to lead a subordinate role. He first came into the public eye by refusing to pay Ship Money in 1635. Although the Court found against him it was a moral victory. He was one of the famous Five Members and a signatory of the Grand Remonstrance and raised a regiment of foot – the famous Greencoats – leading them at Edgehill, and at the sieges of Coventry and Reading. His life was cut short by the mortal wound he received at the skirmish at Chalgrove Field in June 1643 when he encountered Prince Rupert.

Commissary General Henry Ireton (1611–51)

A graduate trained in the legal profession he was a devout Puritan and 'of a melancholic, reserved, dark nature who communicated his thoughts to few', according to Clarendon. He became a troop commander of Cromwell's at the outbreak of the Civil War. By Marston Moor he ranked as colonel and also fought in Second Newbury. At Naseby as Commissary General he commanded the left wing and in 1645 married Cromwell's daughter Bridget.

When an agreement between the King and Parliament failed Ireton was one of the signatories of the monarch's death warrant. He went with Cromwell to Ireland and fought with Ludlow. He was appointed Lord Deputy and captured Waterford and Limerick but died of the plague on 26 November 1651. He was exhumed with Cromwell and his corpse hung on the gallows at Tyburn by Charles II.

Edward, 2nd Earl of Manchester (1602–71)

Manchester was a lethargic, unconvinced Parliament general whose name was added to that of the Five Members by Charles. He was a nominal commander at Marston Moor and at Second Newbury but his backwardness against the King irritated many of the enthusiastic Parliament officers, particularly Cromwell who violently quarrelled with him on the subject. Probably more than anything this brought about the Self-Denying Ordinance which deprived him and people like him of rank and command, resulting in the formation of the vastly successful New Model Army.

Major-General Phillip Skippon (d. 1660)

A Norfolk man, Skippon served as a pikeman under the Veres in the Palatinate. He married Maria Comes in 1622 in Germany. In 1639 he returned to England in the rank of

Parliamentarian commanders including, left to right: Sir Thomas Fairfax, Lord Fairfax, Major-General Skippon, Lieutenant-General Cromwell, Robert Essex, the Earl of Warwick, Alexander Leslie and the Earl of Manchester.

major to claim an inheritance. He was chosen to be instructor of the 'Gentlemen practicing Armes at the famous Artillery Gardens' and after the King's ill-advised attempt to arrest the Five Members he was appointed major-general of the London Trained Bands by the City authorities. Within a short time he was idolized by his command. He led them out rank after rank, regiment after regiment, to confront the King at Turnham Green.

He took a prominent part in the relief of Gloucester, and the First and Second Battles of Newbury. He was left in command of the foot at Lostwithiel when the army was abandoned by Essex, and conducted the surrender and withdrawal with dignity. When the New Model Army came into being Skippon was major-general under Fairfax, and commanded the foot in the centre, where he was seriously wounded. In the Second Civil War Skippon prevented the Kentish Royalists from entering the City. He was appointed one of the judges at the King's trial but he did not attend. Later he was one of the officers concerned during the unpopular 'rule of the Major-Generals'. He died early in 1660 leaving behind a son and three daughters.

Sir William Waller (1597–1668)

Waller was successful early and was popularly called 'William the Conqueror' but he was not altogether successful later on, being defeated by his friend Sir Ralph Hopton (with whom he had served on the Continent) at Lansdown 5 July 1643 and again at Roundway Down on 13 July. However, equipped with a new army to replace that lost at Roundway, Waller obtained his revenge by wiping out Hopton's garrison at Alton and heavily defeating him at Cheriton on 29 March 1644. After his defeat at Cropredy Bridge three months later he suggested to Parliament that it was useless to expect to achieve anything without a standing professional army. It was from this germ of an idea that the New Model sprang. Deprived of his commission by the Self-Denying Ordinance Waller did not attempt to obtain further command as Cromwell did.

Note
For further information regarding the contestants' lives see *Leaders of the Civil War 1642–1648* by Geoffrey Ridsdill-Smith and Margaret Toynbee (Roundwood Press, 1977).

List of Abbreviations

Astley:	Sir Jacob Astley, Royalist general
Brereton:	Sir William Brereton, Parliamentary commander
Committee:	The Committee of Both Kingdoms, composed of Scots and Parliamentary Commissioners responsible for the conduct of the war. All other committees are given their full title.
Culpeper:	John, First Baron Culpeper, Royalist Chancellor of the Exchequer
Digby:	George Digby, 2nd Earl of Bristol
Fairfax:	Sir Thomas Fairfax, Parliamentary general
Forth:	Patrick Ruthven, Earl of Forth and Brentford
Goring:	Lord George Goring, Royalist cavalry commander
Hopton:	Sir Ralph Hopton, Royalist general
Ireton:	Commissary General Henry Ireton
Langdale:	Sir Marmaduke Langdale, Royalist cavalry
Leslie:	Major-General David Leslie, Scots cavalry commander
Leven:	Alexander Leslie, Earl of Leven, Scots general
Massey:	Lieutenant-General Edward Massey, Parliamentary commander
Maurice:	Maurice, Prince Palatinate, brother of Rupert
Montrose:	James Graham, Marquess of Montrose, Royalist Lieutenant-General for Scotland
Ormonde:	James Butler, Marquess of Ormonde, Royalist Lord Lieutenant of Ireland
Prince, the:	Charles, Prince of Wales
Rupert:	Rupert, Prince Palatinate, the King's nephew
Waller:	Sir William Waller, Parliamentary general

The Civil Wars in England and Scotland showing the main towns and engagements.

Prologue

1625

Accession of Charles I.

The Parliaments of 1625, 1626, 1628 and 1629 were short-lived, being dismissed by the King when the subsidies voted seemed insufficient or had unacceptable conditions attached thereto.

1629

March

Charles decides to rule without Parliament, and does so for eleven years. This period is known as the 'Personal Rule'.

1632

Viscount Wentworth is appointed Lord Deputy of Ireland.

1633

William Laud becomes Archbishop of Canterbury.

1634

The first writs for Ship Money are issued.

1634–7

The Laudian Visitations.

1637

John Hampden is tried for refusing to pay Ship Money.

The New Prayer Book is introduced into Scotland by the King's order to promote uniformity of worship in England and

Scotland. It is read for the first time on 23 July at St Giles Cathedral (now the High Kirk) in Edinburgh where it causes an uproar.

1638

February

28th   The chief leaders of the Protestors sign the National Covenant at the Mercat Cross in Edinburgh.

June

12th   By a narrow margin the court gives its judgment against Hampden for non-payment of ship money in 1635.

1639

March

The first Bishops' War against the Scots arises from the King's stubborn attempts to enforce the use of the New Prayer Book but ends with the pacification of Berwick on 19 June.

1640

January

Wentworth is created Earl of Strafford.

April

The King is forced to summon Parliament to obtain a grant enabling him to repel the once-again rebellious Scots. This was known as the Short Parliament and its tenure of office was of three weeks' duration, as it refused to supply money unless its grievances were redressed, namely undue use of royal perogative and failure of Parliament to be regularly called to meet. This Parliament was notable for the emergence of John Pym as leader of the dissidents.

June

Second Bishops' War. The army raised by the King, regardless of Parliament's attitude, is little better than a rabble and is soundly thrashed by the Scots under Alexander Leslie at Newburn upon Tyne.

October

The Scots, advancing into England, occupy Durham and Northumberland forcing the king to sue for peace. Leslie

Charles I by Wenceslaus Hollar, 1639.

demands £850 per day until a treaty is signed. The King is forced to summon Parliament again.

October

21st   Treaty of Ripon.

November

3rd   The Long Parliament (duration twenty years) meets.
By force of circumstances the King agrees to make concessions.

11th   Impeachment of Strafford.
Sir Francis Windebank, Secretary of State, is accused of transactions with and for papists. Under house arrest he makes good his escape to France.

December

4th   The Earls of Bedford, Essex and Bristol, the Lords Saye, Savill and Kimbolton are made Privy Councillors, followed a few days later by the Earl of Warwick.

7th   Lord Finch, Keeper of the Great Seal, is accused of High Treason.

18th   Impeachment of Laud.

22nd   Lord Finch, under house arrest, flees the country.

1641

January

23rd   Lord Littleton, Chief Justice of the Court of Common Pleas, is made Keeper of the Great Seal.

29th   Oliver St John is made Solicitor General.

February

16th   The Triennial Act, requiring that Parliament should automatically meet every three years should the Crown fail to summon it, receives Royal Assent.

March

2nd   Charles Louis, Elector Palatinate, the King's nephew, arrives in England to claim his promised bride, the Princess Mary, who has meanwhile been matched more advantageously.

April

20th   Princess Mary (aged 9) and Prince William of Orange (aged 12) marry. The King receives his new son-in-law at Whitehall.

Charles I in Parliament before the war began. The engraving is surrounded by the insignia of members of the House.

May

3rd A Parliamentary committee is set up to investigate widespread rumours of army unrest – the so-called Army Plot.

10th The King gives assent to the Act of Attainder against Strafford, and at the same time a bill for the perpetuation of the existing Parliament.

11th The King sends the Prince of Wales to the House of Lords to plead for mercy for Strafford.

12th Strafford is executed at noon on Tower Hill.
The Prince of Orange returns home to Holland.
Oliver Cromwell and Sir Henry Vane bring in a bill for the abolition of episcopy.

June

Ship Money Tax is declared illegal.

July

The King approves of two bills by which the High Commission and the Court of Star Chamber are abolished.

August

10th The King leaves for Scotland.

14th The King enters Edinburgh.

17th The King goes in procession to the Scottish Parliament House.

October

23rd Rebellion breaks out in Ireland under Phellim O'Neill, Rory M'Guire and Lord Muskerry.

November

8th Pym pushes a request through Parliament for the King to employ only those counsellors and ministers that are approved by the House.

18th The King leaves Edinburgh.

23rd The Grand Remonstrance, a criticism of the policy in Church and State of the King's reign, is carried by 159 votes to 148 after an all-night sitting in the Commons.

25th The King arrives in London and is received with acclaim and ceremony.

29th London apprentices are cleared from the vicinity of the Commons by the Westminster Trained Bands under the Earl of Dorset for 'threatening behaviour'.
The first unofficial news-sheets reporting speeches in the

The execution of Thomas Strafford, 12 May 1641.

House appear. Soon they are so popular that competitors appear weekly and sell briskly to a news-hungry public, even reaching Edinburgh.

December

1st   A deputation from the Commons presents the Grand Remonstrance to the King at Hampton Court. Up to this time he has totally ignored it, and even now only agrees to read it in due course.

2nd   The King visits Parliament to give his consent to the Tonnage and Poundage Bill.

7th   Sir Arthur Haslerig presents a bill in the Commons for placing all naval and military appointments under Parliament's control – the Militia Bill. This passes its first reading by 158 votes to 125.

9th Three Members, Wilmott, Ashburnham and Pollard, are expelled for complicity in the Army Plot.

14th The King comes in state to the House of Lords not to answer the Remonstrance but to bid them cease all the disputing over the Militia Bill and to expedite the voting of supplies to Ireland.

15th Sir William Purefoy moves that the Great Remonstrance be printed. This is carried by a majority of almost a hundred votes.

21st John Venn and his colleagues succeed in introducing a number of Puritan members into the Common Council of London in the Annual Elections, thereby removing an equal number of Royalist supporters.

　　The King replaces Sir William Balfour as Lieutenant of the Tower with Colonel Thomas Lunsford. He also issues a declaration on religion and appoints new bishops.

26th Lunsford is replaced as Lieutenant of the Tower by Sir John Byron.

27th Parliament reassembles after Christmas. Sir William Jephson, a Munster landlord, tells the Commons that he has proof that the Queen has given authority for the rebels to rise for the defence of the Roman Catholic Church.

29th The King entertains Lunsford and his principal officers to a Christmas dinner at Whitehall. As they depart full of good cheer they are jeered at by a crowd of apprentices. They are affronted and draw swords to disperse the youngsters, resulting in some casualties.

30th Archbishop Williams of York draws up a protest against the forcible exclusion of bishops from the House of Lords which is badly received.

1642

January

1st The Commons, its members allegedly in fear of their lives, leaves Westminster and goes into Committee in the Guildhall. The King offers Pym the post of Chancellor of the Exchequer knowing well that he will have to refuse.

2nd Culpeper and Falkland are sworn in as Chancellor of the Exchequer and Secretary of State respectively.

3rd In the House of Lords Sir Edward Herbert, Attorney General, accuses Lord Mandeville, John Pym, John Hampden, Sir Arthur Haselrig, Denzil Holles and William Strode with High Treason by the King's order. Lord Digby, said to have been the instigator of the plot, was next to have moved their imprisonment but missed his cue and left the House hurriedly, leaving the Lords mystified and amazed.

4th Attempting to arrest the Five Members (Pym, Holles, Hampden, Haselrig and Strode) by force of arms in the very Commons itself, the King is thwarted by their absence. Being forewarned they have taken refuge in the City.

John Pym (1584–1643): a miniature by Samuel Cooper. Pym was the recognized leader of the House of Commons in the Long Parliament which met in November 1642.

5th The King addresses the Common Council at the Guildhall demanding the delivery of the Members to him. In a tumultuous meeting this is virtually denied. He dines with the Mayor, Sir Richard Gurney. On his return to Whitehall menacing and vociferous crowds surge round the coach.

6th   The City is in a ferment. Royalist troops are believed to be ready to descend on the City and, in effect, promote martial law. The gates are closed and a multitude of citizens turn out under arms. Parliament issues a proclamation declaring all those who help breach the Privilege of Parliament to be public enemies.

7th   The formation of a Committee of Public Safety by Common Council.

8th   The Freedom of the City is bestowed on Phillip Skippon, a veteran officer of the Dutch Wars.

9th   The Sheriffs of London are directed to provide a guard to protect the committee meeting at Guildhall and also when it returns to Westminster.

10th Parliament appoints Skippon in overall command of the London Trained Bands, with the rank of major-general. (The Trained Bands were the ancestors of the territorial army – part-time soldiers drawn from the forty city wards, and their officers from city guilds.) Mariners and lightermen flock into the City offering their services to the Parliament.

    The royal family, apprehensive of the consequences of the citizens' mood, moves from Whitehall to Hampton Court.

11th The Five Members return triumphantly by water to Westminster to a heroes' reception.

Hampton Court Palace from the River Thames, by an unknown artist, c. 1640. The Palace was given over to Parliament in December 1653 and became Cromwell's weekend retreat.

12th   The King moves from Hampton Court to Windsor Castle for safety.

13th   The King sends a conciliatory message to both Houses.

14th   Lord Digby attends a thinly disguised recruiting muster at Kingston upon Thames.

15th   Upon hearing of this the Houses accuse Digby of treasonous conduct and he flees to Holland to avoid arrest.

16th   Sir Edward Dering, a Kentish neutral, publishes his *Speeches in Parliament* with a commentary, seemingly feeling he needs to vindicate his moderate attitude.

17th   The Queen tells the Dutch ambassador, Heenvliet, that the King is well loved everywhere but in London. In a dispatch to The Hague, Heenvliet expresses his doubts of this.

     Sir Richard Onslow, Deputy Lieutenant for Surrey, raises the county Trained Bands, disperses Digby's men at Kingston and siezes the magazine for Parliament.

18th   Certain merchants request that Byron should be replaced as Lieutenant of the Tower by someone they can trust, otherwise they will not bring further bullion into the Mint.

19th   Parliament authorizes the increase in the size of the London Trained Bands and fixes the active service pay of the captains at 50*s* per day.

20th   The King again sends to both Houses, saying he is willing to conciliate but calls on God to witness that he is blameless if conciliation is not reached.

21st   The first of a series of executions of Roman Catholic priests takes place and Father Alban Roe and Thomas Greene are hanged.

22nd   The King requests that the City furnish £100,000 to prosecute the war against the Irish rebels, which task has been allotted to them by the King.

23rd   The Commons Committee sitting in Grocers' Hall directs the Common Council to elect the Militia Commanders.

24th   The Commons replies to the King's message of 20 January and ask him as an assurance of good faith if he will appoint a Parliament nominee to command the Tower. The Lords refuse to associate themselves with this motion.

25th   The Common Council refuses the loan that the King requested on 22 January on the grounds that the misunderstanding between him and Parliament makes it hardly a viable proposition.

26th   The Commons replies to the King's message stating that if he gives it surety of his good intentions they can reach an accommodation – the required surety being the rendering up of the Tower and other principal forts, as well as the whole militia.

Pym in conference with the Lords describes the flow of organized petitions which come in from all over the country denouncing the King as 'the voice of England'.

27th   The Commons speaks out against the Duke of Richmond naming him an evil counsellor, a forwarder of the Papist doctrine, and recommending that he should be removed as Lord of the Cinque Ports.

28th   The King replies to the Commons' letter, as its members knew he would, that its demands are unacceptable.

29th   After the Richmond debate the Commons recommends to the Lords that they should petition the King to remove the duke from office. The Lords amiably refuse.

30th   The Commons, alarmed at the influx of Papists from the rebellious areas of Ireland, orders that they should not be allowed to land. At the same time it bans the shipment of warlike materials to the same place.

31st   Sir John Hotham, at the head of the East Riding Trained Bands, occupies Hull for Parliament.

February

1st   Denzil Holles is sent by the Commons to request the Lords to support it in its endeavours to gain control of the militia.

2nd   More petitions flow in to the Commons, the most notable being from 15,000 porters and 'many thousands of poor people in London'.

A deputation from both Houses waits upon the King at Windsor pressing on him the Militia Bill.

3rd   Sir Edward Dering's published 'speeches' are debated by the Commons, declared a scandal and ordered to be burned by the common hangman, with the author to be confined in the Tower.

4th   A welcome diversion from the spectre of Civil War – a body of northern women demolish a fence round a new enclosure and celebrate with a feast of cakes and ale. Alas! They are all arrested.

5th   Rumours are rife of invasion by Charles I's uncle, Christian IV of Denmark.

6th   A gentleman writes to Lord Fairfax regarding the Irish/Popish massacres that 'it is up to us to prevent a like occurrence here'.

7th   The King announces his intention of sending his wife and daughter to Holland and agrees to pardon the Five Members.

8th   Upon a rumour that the Puritans intend to smash up the great organ in Norwich Cathedral the clergy set a guard over it. This provokes a riot, almost resulting in bloodshed.

9th   A group of would-be statue smashers are ejected from Kidderminster, and with their minister take refuge in Gloucester.

10th   Sir Edward Dering is released from the Tower and returns home to Kent.

11th   Sir John Byron is relieved of his post of Lieutenant of the Tower. He is replaced by Sir John Conyers.

12th   A maxim is established by Parliament that every member is protected by Parliamentary privilege, and may only be arrested by consent of the appropriate House.

13th   The King gives his assent to a bill to exclude bishops from the House of Lords.

14th   In thoughtful circles it is stated that the King is too confident of northern loyalty. It is apparent that in the north, as elsewhere, there are divisions both on the score of loyalty and local feuds and rivalries.

15th   The Central Committee of Kent complains about the cost of postage, i.e. 2*s* per packet, and states that at the present rate the annual expenditure will be £100.

16th   The King, Queen and Princess Mary arrive at Dover from Canterbury. The King returns a procrastinating reply to the Militia Bill.

17th   Prince Rupert arrives at Dover ostensibly to thank the King for his interest in securing his release from an Imperial prison, but in fact offers his services.

Henrietta Maria after
Van Dyck, c. 1635.

18th While Rupert is thus engaged his elder brother, the Elector Palatinate, is at Westminster assuring his friends there that he is neutral.

19th A Remonstrance is sent to the King by the Grocers' Hall Committee.

20th The King sends a message to both Houses designed to separate the members who favour peace from 'the ministers of confusion'.

21st The House of Lords receives the King's message with every sign of pleasure and returns a gracious answer.

22nd Stephen Marshall preaches his famous sermon 'Curse ye Meroz' before Parliament.

23rd The Queen and Princess Mary, accompanied by Rupert, set sail for Holland in the warship *Lion*, secretly taking the crown jewels with them to pledge as security for munitions.

24th   Parliament, hearing that the King has sent a summons to the Prince of Wales to attend him on his return to Greenwich, attempts to detain the Prince at Hampton Court.

25th   Sir Thomas Wroth presents a Somerset petition to the Commons expressing concern at the King's breach of Parliamentary privilege.

26th   The King's early arrival at Greenwich Palace thwarts Parliament's endeavour to keep father and son apart.

27th   The King and Edward Hyde draft a firm but courteous reply to the Militia Bill refusing to agree to its terms.

28th   Upon the assurance of a young Welshman, Griffith, Parliament enquires of the King if it is true he intends also to send the Prince of Wales to Holland. The King, presently at Theobalds, reassures Parliament in soothing terms.

Charles I by G. Honthorst, 1628.

March

1st   The Commons again waits upon the King, who is with the Prince of Wales at Theobalds, with regard to the Militia Bill and meets with a hostile reception.

2nd   Despite the protestation of Parliament the King departs for the north.

3rd   The King reaches Royston.

4th   Sir Ralph Hopton is confined in the Tower for sharply criticizing the committee which drew up the declaration.

5th   The Militia Ordinance is passed by Parliament, who, by converting it from a bill to an ordinance avoid the need for royal assent.

6th   The Queen of Bohemia writes to Sir Thomas Rowe, the King's Ambassador Extraordinary to the Emperor and Princes of Germany, telling him of the English Queen's reception in Holland and how disaster befell the baggage ship wherein were all the holy vessels for the Queen's chapel and all the clothes of the four ladies-in-waiting and their maids.

7th   The petition of Sir Balthazar Gerbier, Master of Ceremonies to the King, is presented in which he requests that he may be reimbersed with £1,300 spent on a diamond ring as a gift to the Count of Sols in Flanders by order of His Majesty.

8th   Receipt given by another petitioner, one Nicholas Goldisburgh, for £9 18s, being the balance due from an original total of £28 18s for 578 days' pay oustanding for his service as messenger to the army.

9th   The King is at Newmarket when the Lords Holland and Pembroke reach him with the text of Parliament's declaration which he rejects with passion.

10th   Ormonde enters Drogheda with 3,000 foot and 500 horse.

11th   The Queen and her party arrive at The Hague where they are cordially received by the Prince of Orange, his son and her sister-in-law, Queen Elizabeth of Bohemia, with her daughters, Henrietta and Sophia.

12th   Parliament orders the declaration to be printed and distributed to all parts of the kingdom.

13th   Sir William Bassett reports to Sir Thomas Rowe that although the Prince of Orange has welcomed his daughter-in-law Princess Mary cordially and abided by all the terms of the marriage contract, King Charles has not, as yet, lived up to the terms calling for a dowry and a setting up of his daughter in an establishment and provision for the maintenance thereof to the embarrassment of the English.

14th   It is the resolution of the Common Council of the City that as one Robert Alden has not taken the oath of allegiance he should be deprived of his membership of the said Council.

15th   The King sends a reproachful message to both Houses from Huntingdon.

Sir Ralph Hopton is released from the Tower after a period designed to teach him a lesson.

16th   Both Houses are infuriated by the tone of the King's message which makes members seem ruffians and the King the mildest and most generous of princes.

17th   The substantial citizens of the City, believing that Parliament is altering the constitution and privileges, prepare a petition to both Houses which so incenses the members that they propose to impeach the Recorder of London.

18th   Sir William Brereton informs the Commons that Lord Wharton wishes to be excused from his appointment as Lord Lieutenant of Lancashire. Lord Saye is appointed in his place.

19th   The King enters York.

20th   The two ancient towns of Rye and Winchelsea complain to the Commons via the Barons of the Cinque Ports that their trade and livelihood are being crippled because (a) they are restrained from free trading with the Low Countries and Germany, and (b) they are restrained from free buying and selling in London.

21st   The King issues a public declaration in answer to all that was published against him by Parliament.

22nd In a further move against the Papists the Commons sends for the Sheriffs of London to discover why seven priests lying condemned in Newgate have not been executed. When it is discovered that the said priests were reprieved by the King the Commons spreads it abroad as evidence of the monarch's pro-Papist leanings.

23rd   The King removes from office the Earl of Essex (Chamberlain) and the Earl of Holland (Groom of the Stole).

24th   Secretary Nicholas informs Rowe of how well the King and Prince Charles were received at Tadcaster on 18 March by Sir Thomas Gore, the High Sheriff and the mayor, aldermen and gentlemen of substance. He further reveals that the King passed an act requiring £400,000 to be raised.

25th   A committee formed by Kentish gentlemen, headed by Sir Edward Dering, proclaims the substance of a petition it has formulated to a gathering of 2,000 people.

26th   The King earnestly requests that the new Lord Lieutenant of Ireland should be permitted to leave the country to take up his duties.

27th   Sir Roger Twysden of Royden Hall rides out to solicit his neighbours to support the Kentish petition. Thomas Stanley does likewise in Maidstone, while Dering propounds the principles involved to the worshippers at Pluckley Church.

28th   Sir William Boswell writes to Rowe complaining of the further embarrassment caused by the non-arrival of the commission perfecting the Princess Mary's marriage treaty.

29th   A letter in cypher is sent to Rowe from Secretary Nicholas discussing the political situation in Europe and the official English attitude to it.

30th   Upon hearing of the Kentish petition the House of Lords commits Judge Malet to the Tower saying he advised and connived at it.

31st   Sir Roger Twysden and Sir Edward Dering, prime movers of the petition, are also arrested.

April

1st   Lord Cottington writes to Secretary Nicholas regarding the Pepper Debt owed to the East India Company, who intends to recover it by due process of law. The King's letter must be very promising, he urges, and the Treasury must be made to see the urgency of the matter.

2nd   A letter from a Roman Catholic prelate is sent to his agent. Among the instructions appears a very pregnant injunction 'to communicate with Father Hugh Sempil . . . to continue his good work for the conservation and augmentation of the Roman Catholic religion'. He also encloses two ciphers.

3rd   The foreign ambassadors are watching developments with a close interest. The Venetian ambassador reports to the Doge commenting on the King's arrival at York and his joyful reception, but adds shrewdly, 'It remains a question . . . whether such presentations of loyalty mean that they will undergo all the trials necessary.'

4th The Militia Committee appoints six colonels and thirty-four captains for the six extra regiments of London Trained Bands usually referred to as the Auxiliaries.

5th Receipts of three sums subscribed 'for the speedy reduction of the rebels in Ireland' from one John Perry, skinner, of London £50, £12 10*s*, and £37 10*s* are issued by Alderman Thomas Andrews.

6th An order in Parliament states that the Treasury should pay £1,000 to Mr Samuel Vassall to buy corn for the poor in Londonderry.

7th The Venetian Secretary at The Hague comments on the reaction of the Prince of Orange to Queen Henrietta's endeavours to raise money. 'Outwardly he shows every readiness to gratify the Queen but what is designed in secret is not easy to discover.'

8th The King sends a message to both Houses that he intends to go to Ireland 'to chastize those wicked and abominable rebels', since Parliament seems incapable of doing so.

9th Both Houses petition the King that the magazine should be removed from Hull to the Tower for safety. Despite the governor being their man it might seem that with the King in such close proximity they are apprehensive that the magazine might fall into his hands.

10th Charles Louis Elector Palatinate communicates to Sir Thomas Rowe, 'The King conceives the orders given you are sufficient to work on . . . . I would be satisfied with the Lower Palatinate . . . but do not engage the King for 10,000 men which will cost more than the Palatinate is worth at this time.'

11th The King writes to the Privy Council of Scotland from York assuring it that Sir Phillip Stapleton's allegation in the Commons that Charles intends to sever the union between the two countries is false.

12th The King writes to Ormonde thanking him for his services to date and hoping he will visit Ireland before long so that he can thank him personally.

The Tower of London. The Tower was held by Parliament throughout the war. It was used at various times as armoury, magazine, garrison, prison and place of execution.

13th   Both Houses are unanimous in requesting the King not to go to Ireland, and expose his royal person, the kingdom and Parliament to the greatest danger.

14th   Sir Henry Vane, the Younger, states his opinion that it is useless to enter into further negotiations with the King. 'Let us not trouble ourselves with further answers . . . as being unworthy of our further regard.'

15th   As in England the commonplace of life goes on, so in Scotland. This day a complaint is lodged by the Provost of Aberdeen and one Thomas Johnson, his bailiff, against the Laird of Caskieben for violently and illegally possessing himself of land which is the property of the Provost.

16th   A warrant of the Lord Mayor of London is issued to the master and wardens of the Company of Painter Stainers requiring to be informed what quantity of arms they have available for the City's defence.

17th   A certificate is supplied to James Cobbes of Aldington, Kent, to attest he has taken the oath of allegiance and supremacy before Sir James Wardour JP.

18th   The Venetian ambassador reports upon one of the numerous negotiations between King and Parliament: 'The replies have multiplied the mistrust and bitterness felt by the ill disposed . . . and have confirmed the disposition of the King's partisans to keep closely united.'

19th   Thomas Blount delivers a counterblast to the moderately Royalist Kentish petition but is attacked by an extremist Royalist element and his petition torn up.

20th   The King creates James, Duke of York, a Knight of the Garter and Prince Rupert also in his absence.

21st   Upon the return of Sir Phillip Carteret from his visit to King and Parliament with regard to the constitution and privileges of Jersey, he has to inform the Estates of Jersey that owing to the state of tension existing in England they must set their own house in order.

22nd   James, Duke of York, is sent with an entourage of lords and gentlemen to visit Hull and is received by the governor with the utmost courtesy.

23rd   When the King approaches this day the gates are closed in his face and he is refused admission.

24th   Royal heralds arrive at Hull's Beverley Gate and formally and futilely procaim Governor Hotham traitor.

25th   A message is sent from the King regarding his projected visit to Ireland, bewailing the fact that whatever he proposes will be misunderstood by the Houses and calling upon God to judge who is most sincere.

26th   The Earl of Warwick aboard his flagship *The James* sends a warrant to Sir John Minnes empowering him, 'to press as many officers, mariners and sailors as you possibly can . . . carefully observing the Act of Parliament 17 Car. for the better raising of mariners'.

27th   The life of the City flows on regardless. Mr Francis Walsall writes to the master, wardens and assistants of the Painter Stainers Company acknowledging the honour done him by the offer of the post of clerk to the company but regretting that his sense of his own unworthiness makes him unable to accept.

28th   Parliament publishes a declaration of several resolutions which include the jealousies of the Papists, the warlike movements of Newcastle, the intercepted letters of Digby, etc., that made it garrison Hull for its own security.

29th   Richard Lovelace and Sir William Boteler hold a meeting at Blackheath attended by a large multitude of people, 280 of whom are elected to convey the original Kentish petition to the Commons.

30th   A small party is allowed into the House, and Lovelace in person presents the petition. Both he and Boteler are imprisoned and the deputation dispersed.

May

1st   The young people of Ludlow set a representation of a head on a maypole and pelt it with stones in derision of Parliament.

2nd   The House divides on a motion to allow Sir William Waller to sit as second member for Andover. The result is 107 votes against, 102 votes for.

3rd   Parliament debates a declaration to clarify the situation regarding the Militia Ordinance, the King's refusal to assent to it and the consequences thereof.

4th   The King's reply to Parliament's declaration of 28 April is sharp, incisive and reasoned.

5th   Parliament appoints a committee to be its mouthpiece in future communications with the monarch. Committee members are Lord Howard of Escrick, Lord Fairfax, Sir Phillip Stapleton and Sir Hugh Cholmley.

6th   Secretary Nicholas writes to a Monsieur Briot, an engraver in London, notifying him that it is the King's command that he should present himself at the court of York without delay.

7th   Robert Dixon, JP for Westminster, issues a certificate to one Henry Woodhouse certifying that he had taken the oath of allegiance – this is an interesting sign of the times.

8th   Despite the tension of the times work must go on. The Earl of Holland instructs Sir William and John Whitton, Controllers of Works and Woodlands at Woodstock, that twenty-five trees 'not being worth more than 6s 8d per tree' should be felled and used to repair the High Lodge at Woodstock. He thriftily adds that the 'lops and tops' should be sold to pay the cost of the said repairs.

Major-General Phillip Skippon. The Parliamentarian commander led the troops at Turnham Green and was prominent in the relief of Gloucester and at both battles at Newbury.

9th The Committee presents its first full reply to the King's complaint regarding Hotham's conduct at Hull in a 'dialect higher and rougher than even themselves had yet used'.

10th London Trained Bands are reviewed by Skippon in Finsbury Gardens. Many Members of Parliament and gentry review the troops.

11th The Earl of Monmouth approaches the King with a unique financial proposal. The King owes him £1,550. One Thomas Wharton, lately the receiver of the Royal Revenues, owes the King £4,138. Monmouth suggests he should collect the money from Wharton, subtract his £1,550 from it, and treat the rest as a loan, repayable at a set sum per annum. There is no record of the monarch's reply to this ingenious suggestion.

12th The Bailiff of Andover is summoned to the Commons to show good reason why Sir William Waller should not be on record as second member for that town.

13th The King sends a summons to Skippon ordering him to report for duty at Royalist HQ at York, which the old soldier ignores.

14th The King issues a warrant summoning the horse of the county of York to attend him under arms.

15th The Elector Palatinate writes to the ubiquitous Sir Thomas Rowe thanking him for two previous dispatches relating to a proposed treaty, and in so many words, appreciates his efforts but implies that if this is the best he can do not to bother further.

16th Sir William Waller's name appears on the list of the Committee of Adventurers whose purpose it is to finance twelve ships to prevent supplies reaching the Irish rebels.

17th The King sends orders for the Law Courts to remove to York.
　　The Lord Keeper Sir Edward Littleton sends the Great Seal privily to the King, following shortly after in person.

18th Secretary Nicholas writes to Rowe telling him that in the opinion of the King's Council nothing more can be done for the King's nephew, the Elector Palatinate. 'We cannot approach the Emperor or Bavaria, indeed while our domestic diversions last we cannot help that Duke.'

19th Voluminous declaration of the Houses against the King's proceedings.

20th The King 'seeing the kingdom alight in so many places' at last acknowledges the necessity of a Lifeguard of Horse to protect his person, composed of gentlemen of whose allegiance he can be certain. The Prince of Wales is proclaimed their captain but the commander is Sir Thomas Byron.

21st John Symonds, an officer of the Court of Chancery for the Counties of Somerset and Lincoln, resigns his office to Lord Lyttelton.

22nd The Queen of Bohemia writes plainly to Sir Thomas Rowe: 'You need not be ashamed . . . for you have done what none of your predecessors have done, that is to make them pull off the mask and show they will not restore my son, although they admit he is restorable.'

23rd Parliament, on hearing of the formation of the King's Lifeguard, sends a hypocritically shocked message saying that the King should rely on the laws and affections of his people rather than on soldiers' swords.

24th Lord Fairfax, Sir Hugh Cholmley, Sir Phillip Stapleton and the others report to the Speaker, William Lenthall, that they have obeyed Parliament's orders and presented the King with the protestations of both Houses.

25th Secretary Nicholas again writes to Rowe with the official view of Continental affairs, with particular reference to the Portuguese treaty and his complaint to the French King.

26th The King replies to the criticism of his Lifeguard via the York Committee, stating that he 'could only wonder at the causeless jealousies raised and fomented by a malignant party in Parliament'.

27th Parliament declares that the King is intent on making war against it. Parliament enacts that, in future, the people should only obey its orders. The King forbids any obedience to be given to Parliament's Militia Ordinance under penalty of High Treason.

28th Parliament orders that all sheriffs of counties adjacent to Yorkshire should prevent, 'the coming together of any soldiers, horse or foot, by any warrant of His Majesty's without their advice or consent'.

29th Domestic matters still continue despite the crisis. Lord Saye and Sele sends a warrant to Sir Henry Croke, Clerk of the Pipe, for the grant of the office of bailiff to one George Middleton of Leighton.

30th A brief account of army arrears is rehearsed in Parliament: due to the officers of the Trayne of Artillery £11,035 1*s* 6*d* and due to the horse officers £2,756 3*s*. A total of £1,233 6*s* 6*d* is paid in part this day, leaving a balance of £12,557 18*s* undischarged.

31st A memorandum states that the homage fee for the consecration of Dr Ralph Brownrigg, Bishop of Exeter, due to the Lord Chamberlain is £10.

During June, July and August Royalist and Parliamentary supporters all over the country strive to obtain the adherence of their neighbours, to possess strong points and magazines, and most important of all to obtain financial aid.

June

1st   Both Houses approve of the Nineteen Propositions which propose radical changes that in fact would transfer supreme power from the King to Parliament.

2nd   The Propositions are sent to the King at York.

3rd   The King rides out to Heyworth Moor to receive a demonstration of Yorkshire loyalty arranged by Lord Savile. Sir Thomas Fairfax attempts to present a petition to the monarch who ignores him and almost rides him down.

4th   Parliament exhorts the deputy lieutenants of counties to be diligent in executing the conditions of the Militia Ordinance, and in mustering, training and exercising the inhabitants.

5th   Lord Paget, Lord Lieutenant of Buckinghamshire, goes north to join the King.

6th   The Earl of Lindsay and Lord Savile are declared enemies of the Kingdom by Parliament for their support of the King.

7th   John Hampden writes to Hotham concerning 'the great meeting at York', stating that Parliament is very sensible of the kingdom's danger, concluding that its wish is for peace 'which I assure you is our principle aim'.

8th   The King obtains a protestation signed by all the gentry present at Heyworth Moor testifying to his peaceful intentions.

9th   Parliament passes ordinance appealing for loans of plate, money and horses at 8 per cent.

10th   Parliament decrees that whosoever is resident in the counties of Leicester, Cheshire and Lincoln who fails to give obedience to the Militia Ordinance, or attempts to publish the Commission of Array shall be proclaimed a delinquent.

11th   Parliament orders the seizing of all munitions of war, horse, saddles, and so on that might be on all the roads to the north for Royalist use.

12th   The King resolves to put into execution the Commission of Array, a general call to arms and virtually a declaration of war.

13th   The King declares in full council that he would not demand obedience from any man that was not lawful but by the same token he does not expect any man to obey unlawful commands.

14th   The King writes to the mayor and aldermen of London, and to the masters and wardens of the Guilds, affirming that whosoever helps Parliament prosecute the war is a traitor whether he knows it or not.

15th   Parliament calls upon the distinguished lawyer John Selden to pronounce on the legality of the Commission of Array. When he states that it is illegal its members are jubilant but when he adds that neither is Parliament's Militia Ordinance legal they choose to ignore him.

16th   The two Houses declare nine peers who have gone over to the King 'enemies of the kingdom' and bar them from sitting in Parliament.

17th   The King replies in bitter tones to Parliament's complaints that had specifically mentioned his rebuff to Sir Thomas Fairfax on 3 June.

18th   The King replies in scathing manner to the Nineteen Propositions stating that in effect he would be deposing himself and his posterity if he agrees to it.

19th   The Commons enacts that not only shall a fine of £100 be imposed for absence from the House but the offender should satisfy a committee as to the validity of his excuse for being absent.

20th   The two Houses declare that, 'all those that are actors into putting into effect the Commission of Array are disturbers of the peace and be treated as such'.

21st   The Houses, becoming aware of the King's letter to the mayor, aldermen, etc., publish a declaration refuting his statements and warning the City of the sovereign's malicious intentions.

22nd   Parliament appoints thirty-two deputy lieutenants to be the Committee for Buckinghamshire. A quorum of at least five members is always to be resident at the George Inn, Aylesbury, to collect contributions, muster and pay the garrison.

23rd   Puritan clergy report to Parliament that they fear a Papist-inspired rising in Monmouth.

24th   Lord Chandos, attempting to read the Commission of Array in Cirencester, is driven out and his coach smashed to pieces.

25th   A continuance of the paper war when the King angrily replies to Parliament, saying that he will, 'have justice by God and the Law' for all the injuries done to him and his supporters.

26th   The Devonians become more divided in their opinions and declare that Parliament 'are all Puritans for the Protestants are all clean gone away to the King'.

27th   A petition is sent to the Commons signed by John James, Mayor of Nottingham, James Chadwick, Henry Ireton and others urging Parliament to give them instruction for the security of the town, castle and magazine.

28th   The King seeks to retain control of the Fleet and sends a letter to each ship's captain commanding them to ignore any future command of the High Admiral, Earl of Northumberland, and to put to sea individually, to make rendezvous at Burlington Bay, there to await further commands from the King.

29th   Henry Hastings endeavours to seize Leicester with a body of miners from his family estates but is repulsed.

Henry Ireton (1611–51), attributed to Robert Walker.

July

30th   The King revokes the Commission of Northumberland as High Admiral and sends Sir John Pennington to command the Fleet.

Henry Ireton is given command of a troop of horse at Nottingham.

1st   Parliament, hearing of Northumberland's dismissal, immediately commissions the Earl of Warwick as High Admiral.

2nd   The Fleet declares for Parliament and accepts Warwick as commander.

The Royalist warship *Providence* with a cargo of gunpowder is chased and captured by the Parliamentary *Mayflower* off Hull but slips away up a narrow creek where her adversary cannot follow. A small ketch captured at the time is brought into Hull where a supposedly French prisoner reveals himself to Governor Hotham as Lord Digby.

3rd   The King appoints his general officers:
      Earl of Lindsey, General of the Army
      Sir Jacob Astley, Major-General of the Foot
      Prince Rupert, General of the Horse
      Charles was, of course, his own Captain-General.

4th   Parliament appoints a Committee of Public Safety consisting of five peers and ten commoners to protect the kingdom and its defence.

5th   Digby, having lost no time in corrupting Hull's governor, enters into a conspiracy with him to yield up the town. His only condition is that a Royalist force should invest the town, giving the appearance of starting a siege by firing a few rounds so that he might appear to be rendering it up with honour.

6th   The Somerset Parliamentary faction issues a counter-blast to the Royalist petition issued in June, enquiring, 'If these few gentlemen have ambitions covetous or malicious ends of their own?'

7th   Lord Digby returns to Hull to discover Hotham in a less-confident frame of mind after oblique discussions with some of his officers.

8th   The King moves to Beverley, presumably to implement the Digby/Hotham plot.

Lord Digby (1611–76),
after H. Van der Borcht.

9th The County Committee of Devon prepares a petition to the King and also to the Commons explaining its dilemma: 'Unhappily we are made judges of contraries.'

10th Hull is besieged by the embryo Royalist army directed by the Early of Lindsey with the King in nominal command.

11th Sir Richard Gurney is committed to the Tower for causing the King's Commission of Array to be publicly proclaimed. The King sends a complaint to Parliament regarding the treasonable and rebellious behaviour of many of its supporters.

12th The King removes to Newark.

13th Oliver Cromwell, MP for Cambridge, moves that the town should be authorized to raise two volunteer regiments and forwards money to arm them.

14th–15th The King pays a short visit to Lincoln and returns to Beverley.

15th Parliament appoints the Earl of Essex as its Captain-General.

There is a skirmish at Manchester between Lord Strange and the citizens; this is possibly the first blood spilled in the Civil War.

At The Hague the Queen gives Rupert his commission as General of the Horse.

16th A great meeting of leading Kentish families is held at Dean Bargraves' house near Canterbury to discuss how they might implement the Commission of Array.

17th Captains Slingsby and Wake, the only ship commanders to refuse to join the Fleet, are arrested by their men and sent as prisoners to London.

18th In a letter to Sir John Hotham, Hampden, a member of the Committee of Public Safety, relates, 'how busy we are of affairs for the public weal' and of the munitions bound for Hull.

19th The Earl of Holland, leading a Parliamentary deputation with a proposal for a composition to avoid civil war, is answered by the King who asks as a token of good faith that they should render up Hull, which being refused he remarks that there is now no doubt who wants war and who peace.

20th The King enters Doncaster.

21st The King reaches Nottingham.

22nd The King is received at Leicester with great acclaim, and with a turn out of the Trained Bands.

23rd The Commons, apparently feeling that affairs in Kent are getting out of hand, sends a committee to sit on the bench at Maidstone to keep a watching brief. The committee members try to assert themselves and are received with such hostility that the assize breaks up in confusion.

24th A strange occurrence. The Earl of Stamford vacates Leicester a few hours before the King arrives but leaves a guard on the local magazine. The citizens fear Stamford so leave them unmolested. The King is so irritated by this occurrence that he refuses to leave the town while the guards are in charge of the magazine. A happy compromise is reached whereby the guard is evacuated and the King agrees to ignore the incident.

25th The Grand Jury of Somerset lodges with the County Assize a petition to the King protesting against the illegality of the Commission of Array and asking for its withdrawal.

The Right Worshipfull Sr Iohn Hotham Kt Gouernour of Kingston vpon HVLL

Sir John Hotham, Governor of Hull during the Royalist sieges of 1642.

26th   There are ten thousand volunteers for the Parliamentary parade in Moorfields.

27th   The King arrests his old opponent, Dr John Bastwick, whose ears were cropped five years previously. He would charge him with High Treason but is dissuaded by those about him.

28th   By now both sides seem to find the paper war tiresome and after a reply from Parliament which is published 'in all Churches and Chapels in England' both bend their efforts increasingly towards recruiting and arming.

29th   The newly formed Committee of Safety for Somerset issues its first directive. All the Parliamentary supporters in the county should meet at Shepton Mallet on 1 August.

30th   The Hotham/Digby plot against Hull fails because of an unforeseen circumstance. Reinforcements arrive by sea under Sir John Meldrum, a staunch Parliamentarian, who takes charge of the defence. Launching an attack, he drives the ill-trained, ill-armed Royalists pell-mell from their trenches. The King retires to York 'in much less credit than he came'.

August

1st   Parliament passes an ordinance requiring that customs dues should be paid as usual but to it and not the King.

2nd   Colonel George Goring, Governor of Portsmouth, declares for the King. King Charles commissions the Marquess of Hertford, Lieutenant-General of the West Country, with instructions to raise an army there. With him as potential senior officers go the Earl of Bath, Sir Ralph Hopton, Sir Hugh Pollard, Sir John Berkley and others.

3rd   As a result of the Shepton Mallet muster, Ashe, Popham and Horner order two regiments to assemble at Chewton Mendip.

4th   Action at Marshalls Elm, Somerset, where 80 Royalists under Sir John Stawell rout 600 Parliamentarians under John Pyne MP.

5th   The King calls together the 'people of honour and quality' of Yorkshire; he makes the Earl of Cumberland his Lord Lieutenant and begs the people to donate all the arms they can spare.

6th   Portsmouth is besieged by Waller. Hertford is not receiving the expected support for his proposed Western Army in Somerset and makes Sherborne Castle his headquarters.

7th The Earl of Portland, Governor of the Isle of Wight, is arrested and replaced by the Earl of Pembroke, a supporter of Parliament.

8th The King proclaims that the Earl of Essex and all those who serve under him are traitors and rebels.

9th Upon receipt of the King's declaration of war Oxford University, overseen by Dr Robert Pink, Vice Chancellor of New College, commences to parade and learn the rudiments of drill.

10th Oliver Cromwell defeats an attempt to donate the Cambridge College plate to the King's cause.

11th The King proclaims that he will raise his standard at Nottingham on 22 August and summons all well affected people north of the Trent to muster there.

12th Sir Richard Gurney is deprived of his office of Lord Mayor of London and ordered to be detained in the Tower pending the pleasure of Parliament. The Puritan merchant Isaac Pennington is appointed to succeed him.

13th The Earl of Bath, enraged at the slanders of the Parliamentary propagandists, publishes his commission which empowers him to take command of the Devon militia.

14th Colonel Edwin Sandys is dispatched to Sevenoaks to eliminate a Royalist group formed by Sir John Sackville, who is arrested as he leaves church, taken to London and incarcerated in the Fleet.

15th Cromwell seizes the magazine at Cambridge.

16th The King helps himself to the arms of the Lincoln Trained Bands.

17th Cornish Cavaliers muster on Bodmin Racecourse.

18th Parliamentary batteries are raised at Gosport to command Portsmouth Harbour and to bombard the town.

19th The King lodges at Stoneley, home of Sir Thomas Lee, and resolves to dislodge the Parliamentarians from Coventry.

20th The King attempts to take Coventry but is repulsed.

Prince Rupert and Prince Maurice, the King's nephews, arrive at Newcastle in a Dutch man-of-war and hasten to York only to find the King has left.

21st Rupert and Maurice catch up with the King at Leicester en route to Nottingham. Dover Castle is surprised and taken by Parliamentary forces.

22nd The King raises his standard at Nottingham Castle in an atmosphere of indifference, rather than acclaim or hostility.

23rd On another raid Sandys arrests and imprisons Lord Teynham and other gentlemen as they attempt to publish the Commission of Array in Rochester.

24th Sandys' men defile Rochester Cathedral and in a destructive raid throughout Kent effectively impose Parliamentary control in the county.

25th The King's standard, erected on three successive days, attracts few recruits. Sir Jacob Astley informs the King that in view of the enemy's successful recruiting there is nothing to stop his capture if the Parliamentarians attempt it.

26th Under pressure from his council the King sends a conciliatory message to the Lords. The Earl of Southampton bears the message to the Lords and is received with great insolence, being asked to leave the House.

  Sir John Culpeper, bearer of the same message to the Commons, is allowed only to deliver it at the Bar of the House.

27th Rupert is invested as Knight of the Garter.

28th Sir John Byron, ejected from Brackley by Lord Brooke's garrison, occupies Oxford with 200 men.

29th The King's two messengers return to Nottingham with Parliament's biting reply.

30th It is obvious that Parliament has a considerable lead over the Royalists in recruiting and equipping an army and both Houses feel the necessity to explain publicly the reason and need for forming an army.

31st Sir John Lucas, a gentleman of the privy chamber, dispossessed of his house and goods at Colchester, is delivered into the custody of the mayor pending Parliament's pleasure.

September

1st University troopers are sent to destroy Oxford's Osney Bridge with the intention of denying access to an enemy but are prevented from doing so by the town Trained Band.

2nd The Earl of Bedford besieges Sherborne Castle with 7,000 men.

3rd. Today they attempt to storm but are beaten back with loss.

  Southsea Castle is taken by Waller in a night attack.

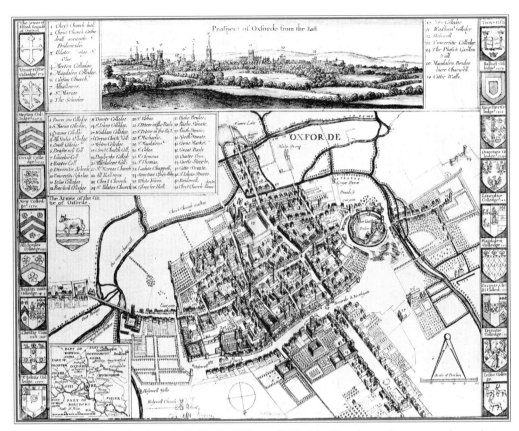

A contemporary Prospect of Oxforde from the East *and map of Oxford, by Wenceslaus Hollar. For several years during the war Oxford served as the King's capital, and was not seriously threatened until 1645.*

4th   Early in the day Goring summons a Council of War which decides to treat for terms with Waller for the surrender of Portsmouth.

5th   Rupert moves his HQ from Leicester to Queniborough and uses it as a centre to raise troops and funds.

6th   Rupert writes a threatening letter to the Mayor of Leicester in the Continental fashion, promising to devastate the town if a large sum of money is not forthcoming. Parliament seizes on this as excellent propaganda. The siege of Sherborne Castle is lifted and the besiegers retire to Yeovil.

7th   Goring surrenders Portsmouth to Waller. Hopton is sent to reconnoitre and clashes with Parliamentary forces at Babylon Hill near Yeovil.

8th The King reprimands Rupert for extorting money from Leicester and writes a letter of apology to the mayor but keeps the money.

9th Essex leaves London to take up his appointment as Commanding General of the Army of Parliament to the acclaim of the citizens.

10th Essex is at Northampton with 20,000 men.

11th Rupert attacks Caldecote House, home of a Colonel Purefoy. The Prince withdraws when he discovers that the spirited defence was made by six ladies and three men.

12th Parliamentary forces under Colonel Arthur Goodwin occupy Oxford after Sir John Byron prudently withdraws.

13th The King marches from Nottingham to Derby.

14th Essex reviews his men at Northampton.

15th Parliamentary troopers search Oxford colleges for plate and discover the Christ Church plate hidden behind wall panelling.

16th As the universities are for the King, Oxford town must of necessity be opposite. Oxford invites Lord Saye and Sele to view and inspect the town forces at Brokenhayes.

17th His lordship leaves Oxford and returns to Banbury.

18th The Earl of Hertford holds a Council of War and decides to retire on Bristol.

19th The King marches to Wellington. Byron arrives at Worcester with his regiment of horse and much of the plate from Oxford University.
Essex leaves Northampton for Worcester.
Hertford retires from Sherborne Castle.
Lord Saye and Sele, returning to Oxford, burns Popish books and manuscripts in front of the Star Inn.

20th The King reaches Shrewsbury. He is joined here by the Earl of Forth and the regiments of Rivers, Fitton and Thomas Aston.

21st Nathaniel and John Fiennes with Colonel John Brown's detachment leave the Parliamentary army at Allerton to join up with a group of Gloucester Parliamentarians advancing on Worcester.

22nd After a change of plan Hertford arrives at Minehead. He has been misinformed regarding the number of barges he would find there to transport his army to Wales via the Bristol Channel so he decides to split his command. Hopton marches into Cornwall while Hertford and the remainder are transported to Wales.

23rd   Rupert arrives at Worcester with forces designed to reinforce Byron. He withdraws finding the town indefensible. In order to cover this manoeuvre he rides to Powick Bridge 1½ miles south of Worcester. A force of Parliamentary dragoons, commanded by Colonel John Brown, blunders onto him and in a short engagement is routed. This skirmish assumes a disproportionate importance because it is the first serious clash between the two sides, and for the Royalists a great morale booster.

24th   Essex occupies Worcester and issues orders that the troops are to concentrate on the rudimentary drill only, ceremonious drill to be ignored.

25th   Sir Ralph Hopton leaves Chittleton and crosses the River Taw above Barnstaple.

26th   Essex sends Charles Fleetwood to Shrewsbury with a letter for the Earl of Dorset enquiring when the King will receive a further petition. On 29 August Charles replies that he would receive such a petition at any time provided it was not presented by a person he has not declared traitor.

27th   Lord Brooke brings about 3,000 men into Oxford to replace Saye and Sele's men who withdrew on 25 September.

28th   The Earl of Bath is arrested by Captain Dewett and his troop under a warrant from the House of Lords.

29th   Lord Grandison overawes the citizens of Nantwich, who take an oath of submission and obedience to the King.

30th   Sir Ralph Hopton and his men arrive at Sir Beville Grenville's estate at Stowe in north Cornwall.

October

1st   A Parliamentary writer records: 'Had not that town (Manchester) stood very firmly . . . in all probability the whole county had been delivered over . . . to the Cavaliers.'

2nd   At Worcester one of Parliament's soldiers, in training, discharges his musket loaded with two balls at random, killing a fellow soldier.

3rd With regard to the limitation placed on the receiving of petitions by the King on 29 September, Parliament publishes a declaration accusing him of yet another breach of privilege.

4th Hopton reviews his troops at Moilesbarrow Down and finds they number 3,000 well-armed men besides clubmen.

5th Manchester's garrison stand to their arms on an ill-founded rumour of the Royalists' return.

6th The Parliamentary soldiers in Manchester attend special services to give thanks for their deliverance from Earl Derby's Royalists who had besieged them for ten days.

7th The Houses order that the petition of 16 September should be presented once more and again the King refuses it.

8th The King's ships *Bonaventure* and *Swallow* are taken as they attempt to run the blockade at Tynemouth.

9th Earl Derby summons a meeting at Warrington to attempt to organize a coalition of the counties of Flint, Shropshire, Denbigh and Cumberland.

10th Local attempts at pacification occur. In Lancashire an attempt is made between both sides to bring about a peaceful county settlement.

11th The Committee of Public Safety orders the Deputy Lieutenant of Cornwall to raise 1,000 men and the Committee of Devon to provide 500 dragoons.

12th The King marches out from Shrewsbury, advances on London and stays overnight at Bridgnorth where the church bells ring and the citizens turn out to cheer.

13th The Royalist army grows in numbers so that the King is able to appoint tertia (brigade) commanders – Sir Nicholas Byron, Colonel Henry Wentworth, Colonel Richard Fielding.

14th The King is in such sore straits that he creates Sir Richard Newport a baron for a donation of £6,000.

15th The King is at Wolverhampton where he is joined by the last of the Welsh levies.

16th Hearing of the proposed peace meetings in Lancashire, Parliament sternly forbids them.

17th The King reaches Birmingham.

18th   The Militia Committee reports that the City is willing to send twelve companies of the London Trained Bands on detached service if required.

19th   Essex leaves Worcester.

20th   Parliament appoints the following colonels for every hundred in Lancashire: Assheton, Holland, Shuttleworth, Starkie, Rigby, Moore, Egerton and Dodding.

21st   A large supply of gunpowder reaches Manchester despite the vigilance of Royalist patrols.

22nd   The Royalist Army marches from Southam to Edgcote.

       In the late evening the Parliamentary army arrives at Kineton.

23rd   THE BATTLE OF EDGEHILL. *See separate account on pages 42–3.*

Reconstruction of Rupert's cavalry at Edgehill by The Sealed Knot Society.

The manor-house at Wormleighton; Royalist and Parliamentarian troops clashed over billets in the village prior to Edgehill. The house was held by the Royalists for many years until besieged and bombarded in the summer of 1644, whereupon the Royalist garrison quickly surrendered.

24th　The death of the Earl of Lindsey.

25th　Essex withdraws to Warwick. The King withdraws to Edgcote.

26th　The King makes the Earl Forth General in place of Lindsey.

27th　The King takes Banbury Castle and sends a proclamation of pardon to Westminster.

28th　Rupert takes Broughton Castle, home of Lord Saye and Sele and spoils it.

29th　The King occupies Oxford which becomes the Royal Capital. Peace negotiations are proposed in the House of Lords.

30th　There are Royalist troops to the number of 1,400 in six garrisons: Warrington, Preston, Wigan, Ormskirk, Eccleston and Prescot.

31st　Edmund Waller urges the Commons to open peace negotiations.

The Battle of Edgehill
23 October 1642

The aims of the opposing commanders were not in the least apocryphal. The King's intention was to march on London, therefore Essex had to stop him by interposing his army between the monarch and his objective. The intelligence service on each side was lamentable: both had only a very general idea where the other lay. On 22 October the Parliamentary army was at Kineton, some 18 miles south of Warwick, while the King was at Edgcote, 4 miles to the south-east.

Despite preliminary reconnaissance by the Royalist cavalry, the close proximity of the Parliamentary army was only discovered by accident when a party of quartermasters seeking billets at Wormleighton clashed with their opposite numbers who had arrived at the village on a similar mission.

At midnight the King ordered a concentration of his army the next morning on the commanding ridge of Edgehill with its 300 ft eminence rising from the plain with a 1 in 4 gradient. The ridge itself stretches for 3 miles and crosses the Kineton–Banbury road. Although a famous observation post it was totally unsuitable to the operation of cavalry, so that the deployment of Essex's army was accomplished without hindrance. It is judged that its position lay between the Kineton–Knowle End road and the Little Kineton–Radway road about 1½ miles from the centre of Kineton village. While Rupert was at the rendezvous at day-break, it took a lengthy period for the far-flung Royalist army to assemble, giving the King's high command time to decide that they would seize this opportunity which seemingly existed of bringing the war to a short sharp conclusion by annihilating the Parliamentary army. Therefore the orders went out to the troops to descend the hill and form line of battle at the foot.

It was about 2 p.m. before they were in position about 800 yards from the bottom of the hill with the village of Radway north-east of their centre, the enemy being only about half a mile distant. The opposing armies were fairly equal in strength, the Royalist numbering about 13,500 (all arms) and the Parliamentary some 14,500.

The battle consisted of four phases. The first was an hour-long cannonade, noisy but virtually harmless, followed by the cavalry phase, which commenced with the dragoons

November

1st   Princes Charles and James have the degree of Master of Arts bestowed on them. Essex marches from Northampton to Olney.

2nd   The Commons consents to peace negotiations.

3rd   The King leaves Oxford to advance on London.

4th   Royalists occupy Reading.
Essex is at Woburn.

of each side contesting for possession of the hedgerows. Wasting no further time Rupert, the right-wing cavalry leader, launched his men at the hostile cavalry under Sir James Ramsey. Disheartened by the defection of Fortescue's troops and the vehemence of Rupert's assault Ramsey's men broke and fled, hotly pursued, to Kineton.

A similar effort, although hardly so devastating, was achieved by Wilmott's men on the left flank followed by most of the cavalry reserves who joined in the joyous pursuit. Up to now fortune had favoured the King, for in a very short time the Parliamentary army had been reduced to two cavalry and seven foot regiments. Balfour, the sagacious experienced Parliamentary cavalry leader, initiated the third phase, and saved the day for his side. Seconded by Stapleton he not only badly cut up Fielding's brigade and mauled Sir Nicholas Byron's brigade, but also silenced the Royalist guns.

Essex followed this successful attack with a massive assault on Byron's brigade which contained the choicest Royalist regiments including the Lifeguard. There followed some of the bloodiest hand-to-hand fighting of the engagement during which the Knight Marshal, Sir Edmund Verney, was killed and the Banner Royal taken – to be recaptured later by Captain John Smith.

The Royalist brigade, harrassed flank and rear by the ubiquitous cavalry of Stapleton and Balfour, slowly gave ground and disintegrated. Now the fourth and last phase set in – what may be called the exhaustion phase. Brief though the engagement was (it lasted little more than two hours) the two sides had fought one another to a standstill.

By this time both armies were in a state of chaos, with units uncertain in the gathering darkness who were friend or foe, fighting with any who showed opposition and with various bodies of horse and foot returning to the field. Into this confusion the remanned Royalist guns were belching case shot. Eventually darkness fell and the two sides drew apart. Despite a night of intense cold and sharp frost they were still there next morning.

It was, to all intents and purposes, a drawn fight but history allows the King the best of it for Essex failed in his purpose of stopping the monarch's advance on London, withdrawing to Warwick leaving Oxford undefended to be the Royal Capital for the rest of the war.

For a very full account of the battle see *Edgehill* by Brigadier Peter Young (Roundwood Press, 1967) or *Edgehill and Beyond: The People's War in the South Midlands* by Philip Tennant (Alan Sutton, 1992).

5th   Essex reaches St Albans.

6th   The King disarms the citizens of Oxford, removing the muskets and powder from the Guildhall and storing them 'in the upper room of the Schools tower'.

7th   Essex and the Parliamentary army reach London and receive a hero's welcome.

The site of the Battle of Edgehill.

Meanwhile Rupert summons Windsor Castle but the Parliamentary commander John Venn MP vehemently refuses.

Parliament invites the Scots to enter England and eliminate the Newcastle army.

8th　The two Houses appeal to the Guildhall for aid.

9th　The King is at Colnbrook where he meets Parliamentary commissioners with a petition.

Parliament orders Essex to march out to face the King.

10th　Rupert rejoins the King at Egham.

Pym explains peace overtures at the Guildhall.

11th　Essex and Skippon move their forces out to Hammersmith.

12th　Rupert storms Brentford and decimates the garrison.

13th Essex's army is reinforced by the London Trained Bands under Skippon and bars the King's way at Turnham Green. Outfaced, the Royalist army retires to Kingston.

14th The King is at Hampton Court but removes to Oatlands the same day.

15th The City offers to maintain an additional 4,000 horse and dragoons.

16th Hopton continues to advance through Devon with little opposition. By 18 November he has reached Exeter which he besieges.

17th The Lord Mayor of London receives a communication from the Lord General Essex notifying him that he has appointed Skippon to be major-general.

18th The King sends to the Commons maintaining he meant no breach of faith in attacking Brentford while peace negotiations were proceeding.

19th The King withdraws to Reading where Prince Charles is found to be suffering from measles.

20th Strickland writes to Pym from The Hague that Lady Derby's letters to the States General show little love for Parliament.

21st Exeter's mayor leads an unexpected dawn attack on the besiegers, taking them in the rear. He is aided by the ardent citizens who pour from every gate and disperse them, so that they retreat on Tavistock.

22nd The Earl of Warwick resigns his commission as army commander, resolving that there should be only one general and that is Essex.

23rd Parliament votes that there is now only one proposition that could be made to the King, that is, that he should yield up his person having dismissed his evil counsellors.

24th The Danish ambassador comes to Oxford to seek an audience of the King. Discovering that Charles is at Reading he journeys thither.

25th Lord Derby is depressed by his failure at Manchester and declaims at Warrington that he 'was born under an unfortunate planet . . . with other words of passion and discontent'.

26th The Danish ambassador imparts to the King that the Danish king is not so willing to provide troops for England as was rumoured.

28th   Edward Hyde writes to Lord Falkland that as both Hampden and Goodwin are at home a visit by Royalist cavalry might be advantageous.

29th   The King retires from Reading to Oxford leaving Sir Arthur Aston to command the garrison.

30th   William Ruthin, hearing of the approach of the Royalists to Plymouth, sends out a detachment of 270 men to hold them at Plympton which proves impracticable.

December

1st   The Earl of Newcastle forces the crossing of the Tees at Piercebridge.

Waller takes Farnham Castle by storm from Sir John Denham.

2nd   The King writes privately that he would either be, 'a Glorious King or a Patient Martyr'.

3rd   Newcastle enters York.

4th   There is a proclamation in Oxford that all men not in the army must bring their horses to St Giles's Field to be viewed. Two hundred of them are requisitioned as dragooners.

5th   Willmott takes Marlborough.

The citizens of Oxford are compelled to dig the city fortifications.

6th   Today is the trial at Oxford of Lilburne, Vieurs and Catesby for High Treason.

7th   Newcastle routs a Parliamentary force under Lord Fairfax at Tadcaster and occupies Pontefract.

Rupert, having taken a large force to Aylesbury with the intent of storming the town, returns finding it is too strong.

8th   The King declares that the proclamation of Parliament (the Militia Ordinance) is a palpable and clear demonstration of the tyranny of Parliament.

9th   The Royalist army settles into winter quarters around Oxford.

Parliamentary prisoners of war are brought to Oxford to labour on the defences.

10th   Sir John Digby summons the justices of the county of Nottingham to discover how best they might secure the county for the King.

11th   A Royalist meeting is held in Preston where collectors are appointed in every hundred to raise money for the payment of troops.

12th   In retaliation for a foray by the Royalists of the Wigan garrison, a local company of Parliamentarians aided by others from Manchester attacks 'the House of a Roman Catholic Gentleman' but are surprised by a greater force of Royalists and flee.

13th   Waller takes Winchester, destroying two regiments.

14th   The King issues a proclamation establishing the Royal Mint at Oxford.

15th   An ordinance is passed by both Houses associating eight Midland counties for their mutual defence. Lord Grey of Groby is appointed major-general and commander-in-chief of the association.

16th   The King issues a proclamation stating that all persons paying poundage and tonnage to Parliament are without the law.

17th   The Commons resolves that Nottinghamshire should be asked to raise 150 horse and 400 foot for service in the north.

18th   In Nottingham itself an appeal is made to the gentry to join with the citizens to protect the town.

18th–23rd   Between these dates the Earl of Newcastle's 4,000 horse arrive at Newark to join the 400 men raised by the Sheriff of Nottingham. A further 400 men are brought in by one Robert Butler of Southwell.

19th   The City sends a proclamation to the King stating that it is distressed that the King seems to entertain doubts about its loyalty but . . .

20th   Sir Gilbert Houghton summons the Lancashire Royalists by beacon and occupies Blackburn with the forces so obtained.

21st   The King reviews the works at Oxford upon which 400 are employed.

22nd   Rupert, hearing of a projected attempt to recapture Banbury, sets out with a relief force.

23rd   Having battered Banbury all night, the Parliamentary force withdraws upon hearing of Rupert's approach.
          Skipton Castle is besieged by Colonel John Lambert.

24th Rupert returns to base around evening.

25th The King keeps Christmas at Christ Church College, Oxford, with splendour and ceremony.

26th Prince Rupert goes by coach to Abingdon and returns.

There is a skirmish at Chowbent between Lord Derby's troops and a hastily gathered force of 3,000 Parliamentarians. The latter are victors after a running fight.

27th The King and Rupert take their ease and play tennis on one Mr Edward's court.

28th A fast day at Oxford. A trumpeter comes from Essex with a message for the King. Charles is playing tennis and is not pleased to be disturbed.

29th Oxford. Anthony Wood records that as nothing is said about his wages, now owing for a full year, by the delegates at a meeting for the Vice Chancellors to consider accounts, he will appear before them on the morrow and demand payment.

30th Hopton summons Exeter. He is foiled by the nimble Parliamentary commander Colonel Ruthin who gets there before him.

31st The Spanish ambassador arrives at Oxford to complain about the seizure of the Spanish vessel *Santa Barbara* by the Earl of Warwick, the cargo of which was stated to consist of cochineal and silver among other things.

Summary of 1642

All through the year 1641 the long drawn out disputes between King and Parliament were steadily reaching a climax, stoked by the subtle double dealing of the monarch and the stubborn scheming of John Pym.

These two antagonists were evenly matched as their succession of chess-like moves and counter-moves prove. The event that transformed the war of words and paper into a shooting war was the King's ill-advised invasion of the House of Commons with armed men to arrest the Five Members. But finding his birds had flown he left the Chamber with chagrin, pursued by a long, low murmur of 'Privilege! Privilege!'

It seemed to Londoners, always touchy where their ancient rights and privileges were concerned, and to many waverers in the House, a vindication of all Pym's allegations against the King's rule of State and Church as set out in the Grand Remonstrance.

When the Royal Family left London, aghast at the Londoners' reaction, and the King eventually took refuge in the north it was obvious to all but the most optimistic that a conflict was inevitable. Moderate Royalist counsellors, like Edward Hyde, tried to prevail upon the King to act within the constitution, to concede where he might and be adamant only on basic principles, for thus he might discredit the more hot-headed Parliamentarians who might then be seen to have exceeded their privileges. What these honest advisers did not seem to realize was that by now both the King and the Parliamentary leaders were convinced that the most conclusive way to settle the dispute was by force of arms.

The King visualized that after his annihilation of Essex's army he would be restored to power as the undisputed master of the realm. Parliament's aim was equally simple. The destruction of the Royalist army would see the monarch's welcome return to his capital, his position ostensibly unchanged but in fact a pliant puppet in their hands.

Both sides were certain that a single battle would be sufficient to bring this desired result to pass. So it was that both hastily raised armies went seeking one another. This eagerly sought-after event occurred at Edgehill on 23 October where about 1,500 men were sacrificed to obtain a clear-cut result. But the result was anything but clear cut, for both armies were still in position the next morning.

History only allows the Crown a marginal victory because Essex retreated first, and it is also critical of the King's tactics when the path was thus left open to London. Rupert suggested a forced march on the capital, timed to appear outside the defences when the fugitives had spread the news of the field of slaughter. He was convinced that the authorities would be forced to sue for peace.

Other generals, perhaps more aware of the effect of the carnage on the morale of their amateur soldiers, felt that the risk was too great. Should the City not react as predicted the Royalist army might find itself crushed between the City forces and the returning Parliamentary army.

It is a fact that the King chose to close on his capital in easy stages, allowing Essex to reach London first. The City fathers, horrified by the tales of slaughter, prevailed on Parliament to seek terms from the King as he approached, and the negotiations were proceeding when the impetuous Rupert attacked and sacked Brentford, virtually destroying the two regiments that garrisoned it. This had the opposite effect from that anticipated, for it caused the City's attitude to harden and when the Royalist army advanced on 13 November it found its way blocked at Turnham Green by 24,000 men, the combined forces of City and Parliament under the command of the Earl of Essex and Major-General Phillip Skippon. Outnumbered and outfaced the King withdrew, and his armies were never to approach so close again.

The quick and easy solution to the Civil War was not to be. Each side had now to plan for a conflict that would drag on perhaps for years, becoming a war of attrition. Not only had they to raise money to keep their armies in the field but there was the complex task of keeping them supplied with munitions, clothes and food in a country where roads were mere muddy channels; the intricate business of foreign relations, two ambassadors to each country where formerly there was one; internal administration to prevent the upsurge of lawlessness, anarchy and chaos. In fact there were so many unexpected problems that one could be forgiven for thinking that many of the more sober-minded counsellors (on both sides) may have wished that the rush into war had not been precipitated.

1643

January

1st   Although General Ruthin was ordered to await the arrival of the Earl of Stamford with reinforcements, he marches from Plymouth regardless.

2nd   A Parliamentary committee arrives in Oxford with yet another petition for the King and is lodged at the Fleur de Luce Inn.

3rd   A convoy of twelve wagons reaches Oxford laden with the mint from Shrewsbury and sufficient silver ore for coining. The mint is set up in the New Inn.

4th   The Spanish ambassador, still at Oxford complaining about the seizure of the Spanish ship, has at last received a proclamation from the King forbidding the sale or purchase of this.

5th   Sir John Henderson, Royalist commander at Newark, reports to Newcastle that apart from a troop of dragoons Nottingham is empty of Parliamentary troops.

6th   John Hutchinson, commissioned lieutenant-colonel by Lord Grey of Groby, is to command the foot of Francis Pierrepoint's new regiment.

7th   The Earl of Stamford arrives in Exeter en route, as he supposes, to join Ruthin and to eliminate the Cornish army at Launceston.

8th   In a letter to the Speaker, read in the House this day, Waller explains that when Chichester surrendered on 5 January he forbore to plunder it because William Cawley MP gave every soldier and officer the equivalent of a month's pay.

9th   Essex sends a drummer to the King asking for an exchange of prisoners. He is led blindfold to his lodgings to await Charles's answer.

10th   The Lords and Commons vote to direct the Devon Committee

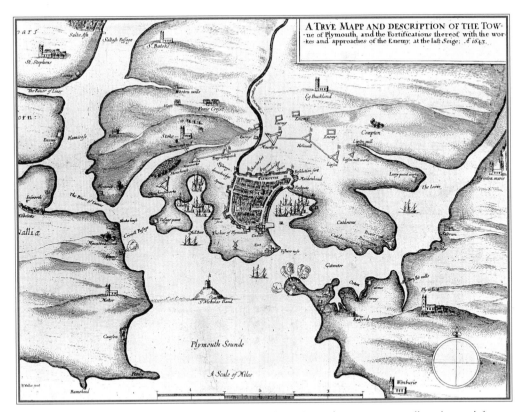

The town of Plymouth, showing the fortifications. Throughout the Civil War the town was repeatedly under attack from Royalist troops, but held out staunchly for Parliament.

to greater efforts to raising more money and troops to crush Hopton.

11th Chichester loses its store of cathedral plate when Hesilrige's troopers discover its hiding place behind the oak panels in the chapter house.

12th There is a review by the King and the Princes Charles and James of all the troops in Oxford at New Park. Forty-one colours and three thousand men are present.

13th Parliamentary county forces under Colonel William Strode gain control of New Bridge near Saltash with the intention of joining Ruthin's forces.

14th The King pardons a criminal brought to the place of execution in Oxford Market. Instead he is branded on the hand and shoulder.

15th Sir William Waller receives public thanks in the House of

Commons for his 'valour and fidelity' at Portsmouth, Chichester, Farnham and other places.

16th There is a meeting of the Royal Council at Christ Church, Oxford.

17th In a fierce gale, three Parliamentary warships, well laden with arms, supplies and money, are driven into Royalist Falmouth.

18th Hopton is invited to be commander-in-chief of the Western Army of the triumvirate appointed by the King.

19th THE BATTLE OF BRADDOCK DOWN. Hopton defeats Ruthin's army, resulting in Royalist control of Cornwall.

20th Stamford, who had dawdled at Plymouth, reaches Launceston before hearing of Ruthin's defeat, when he hastily falls back on Plymouth.

21st Prince Rupert issues out of the North Gate of Oxford 'with a greate army of horse and men', destination unknown.

22nd Hopton and Lord Mohun storm Saltash capturing 140 prisoners and a ship of 400 tons.

23rd Sir Thomas Fairfax takes Leeds and Wakefield from Lord Savile. Newcastle retreats from Pontefract when Fairfax's successes threaten his lines of communication.

24th At 1 p.m. a meeting of the Vice Chancellors' delegates is held at the New Schools, Oxford, to discuss accounts.

25th Hopton who has resumed the siege of Plymouth is reinforced by the troops of Berkeley and Ashburnham who occupy Plympton, Modbury and adjacent villages, thus sealing off the town by land.

26th Newcastle reaches York and recalls all his troops from Newark leaving Henderson with only the local volunteers to man the defences.

27th Parliament empowers the Somerset Committee to raise more troops and those who are unwilling to contribute voluntarily are to have goods seized to the value of the expected contribution.

28th Sir Peter Killigrew comes to Oxford with a message for Parliament with 'certain propositions for an accommodation with his Majesty'.

29th Lord Camden, Colonel Gervase Lucas and others take Belvoir Castle by stealth for the King.

The first steps towards a peace settlement at Plymouth occur when Hopton and Godolphin meet with the Parliamentary commissioners at Robert Trelawney's house. The talks break down and hostilities recommence.

30th A meeting of the Conventus Praefectorum (the Heads of Houses) at Oxford, as enjoined by the Laudian Statutes, ends in a very heated debate.

31st Edward, Lord Lyttleton and the judges then present in Oxford are made Doctors of Law at a convocation.

February

1st One William Lawson, gentleman, applies to Lord Brooke for the repayment of a £5 bond. Brooke replies that it will be repaid when the first of the levy money comes in.

2nd Rupert takes Cirencester and his secret destination is disclosed.

3rd The King appoints a solemn thanksgiving to be held at Christ Church, Oxford for the above victory, with everyone in full dress.

4th The Parliamentary committee dines together at the Star Inn and departs from Oxford with His Majesty's answer.

5th Northfield, Rolle and Bampfield raise the county militia of North Devon to relieve Plymouth.

The Queen sets sail from Holland with a nucleus of professional soldiers and munitions.

6th Sir John Seaton, hearing that the garrison of Preston is scanty, sets out with 1,600 men to assault that town.

7th Seaton's force arrives at Blackburn.

Rupert arrives back at Oxford, leaving Maurice governor at Cirencester.

8th A dawn raid on the Parliamentarians at Okehampton by Sir John Berkeley results in a confused skirmish and the death of the poet Sidney Godolphin.

9th Seaton's force, augmented by detachments from Blackburn and Bolton, takes Preston by storm. This is a great setback for the Lancashire Royalist faction.

10th Parliament agrees that should anyone wish to pay one-half of the money levied on him in kind he may do so, laying down a scale of payment, e.g. wheat 5*s*, barley 2*s* 6*d*, oats 1*s* 8*d*, malt 2*s*

10*d* per bushel. Beef 2¹/₂*d*, mutton 3¹/₂*d*, bacon 5*d*, butter 5*d*, cheese 2¹/₂*d* per pound.

11th The Western Association is formed consisting of Gloucester, Wiltshire, Worcester, Shropshire and Somerset. Sir William Waller is appointed to command.

12th Newcastle secures Bridlington in readiness for the Queen's landing there.

13th There is an ordinance in Parliament for levying money on Papists' delinquents, such as have been in the war or contributed money to the Royalist cause.

14th Hoghton Tower surrenders. A supposedly accidental explosion kills Parliament's Captain Starkie and sixty of his men.

15th A yearly account for beer and ale is delivered to Lord Francis Cottington at Bread Street by one Mr Waller, a brewer; it amounts to £26 9*s*.

16th The Royalist troops attack Bolton as retaliation for Preston but are forced to withdraw after heavy fighting.

17th The Scots Commissioners come to Oxford but on some pretext the King refuses to see them.

18th The King assures the University of Oxford that he will give no further honorary degrees so that the university's reputation and scholastic standards will not suffer.

19th An order is signed by Pym, Hampden and others to Sir Gilbert Gerard, Treasurer for the Army, authorizing the payment of £10,000 to Essex towards the troops' wages.

20th Digby with three troops of horse and likewise of dragoons sets out from Oxford bound apparently for Devizes.

21st Parliamentary forces fall upon the Royalist force of Slanning and Trevanion at Modbury. After a stubborn defence the latter fall back on Plympton.

22nd The Queen lands at Bridlington Bay, 'with a great supply of arms and power' and is bombarded by the Parliamentary ships.

23rd Prince Rupert sallies out from Oxford to intercept a munition convoy proceeding westward from Farnham, but Waller is warned by spies and Rupert arrives at Basing House empty handed.

24th Parliament, perchance realizing that the flow of voluntary subscriptions is not adequate to its needs, imposes a national weekly assessment on every citizen according to his needs.

25th   A body of 700 men set out from Nottingham to join Major-General Ballard and his Lincolnshire men in order to take Newark.

26th   The Duke of Vandome, who is in exile because of Cardinal Richelieu's displeasure, takes his leave of the King on hearing of the Cardinal's death.

27th   Ballard with his hastily raised force appears in front of Newark. The Royalist commander Sir John Henderson fights a delaying action and retires inside the town.

28th   Ruthin and Stamford agree with Hopton to a local cessation of hostilities which enables both sides to reorganize.

March

1st   The Assizes are held at Oxford by Lord Justice Hethe.

2nd   Sir Thomas Trenchard and John Browne, on behalf of Parliament (but without its knowledge) and the Royalist Commissioners of Array, agree to propound an accommodation to oppose any force whatsoever that endangers the county of Dorset.

3rd   Waller enters Winchester with a small force.

4th   Rupert and Maurice leave Oxford by the South Gate early in the morning with 'a great company of troopers and dragooners'.

5th   Waller reaches Romsey. The sectaries spoil the 'old monastery church' while a 'zealous brother in the ministry' preaches to them the while.

6th   Parliament declares that the proposed accommodation in Dorset is merely a Royalist ruse to gain time.

7th   The Queen arrives at York.

8th   The Mayor of Exeter writes to Parliament regarding 'the propositions for peace received by himself and those at Plymouth'.

9th   Waller reaches Salisbury and sends out warrants for money, arms and horses, acquiring many of the latter by a stratagem.

10th   Rupert and Maurice re-enter Oxford.

11th   A letter from citizens of Exeter is read in Parliament commending the care of the city to the Commons as 'Sir Ralph

Hopton and others are holding meetings about a proposed Association the nature of which we know not'.

12th The demands made on Waller for restitution of Salisbury's horses leads him to retort that the city has done little for Parliament at that time and they might well afford them the use of these mounts.

13th The Earl of Derby marches out of Wigan with 600 foot and 400 horse to assault Lancaster.

14th Ormonde, instructed by the King, opens up negotiations with the Confederate Irish for an armistice to enable the Royal troops engaged there to be employed on the mainland.

15th Waller secures Bristol with no more than 2,000 men.

16th Sir Arthur Aston, Royalist Governor of Reading, seizes a convoy of cloth and other items meant for the Somerset Parliamentarians.

17th A soldier is hung on the gibbet at Oxford's Carfax, for murdering a woman. In extenuation it is said that he was a Parliamentarian.

18th Having stayed at Lathom Hall to gather reinforcements the

An engraving of the north-east view of Lancaster.

Earl of Derby storms Lancaster. Although the castle holds out, the town is sacked and burned.

19th THE BATTLE OF HOPTON HEATH. Brereton and Gell unite to take Stafford but the Earl of Northampton moves out to engage them and after a hard struggle disperses them with heavy losses including his own life.

20th The Earl of Derby, avoiding the Parliamentary reinforcements sent to Lancaster, attacks Preston and takes it as the garrison has been denuded to swell the number of those going to Lancaster.

21st The Parliamentary committee appointed to treat for the cessation of hostilities arrives at Oxford and is graciously received by the King.

22nd Malmesbury is occupied by Rupert's troops.

23rd Charles Cavendish, son of the Earl of Devonshire, with Henderson takes Grantham in a surprise attack.

24th Massey defeats the Welshmen under Lord Herbert at Highnam.

25th The constables of Claverton and Bathampton are compelled to deliver to the Bath garrison three bushels of oats as a 'freewill contribution' and Camerton has seven horses requisitioned by Waller.

26th Malmesbury falls to Waller who leaves a garrison there under the command of Sir Edward Hungerford.

27th Parliament directs that the lands of bishops, deans and chapters are to be confiscated.

28th The Earl of Derby attempts to take Bolton for the second time but is again repulsed.

29th Rupert leaves Oxford bound for Birmingham. In Oxford some of the meat stalls and the Corn Market open in spite of the prescribed fast.

30th THE BATTLE OF SEACROFT MOOR. Lord Goring defeats Sir Thomas Fairfax.

   Parliamentary officials loot Somerset House and dismantle the Queen's private chapel.

April

1st Colonel Holland attacks the Royalist town of Wigan which is taken and sacked but not garrisoned.

2nd   Newcastle is on the offensive again and retakes Wakefield.

3rd   Rupert takes Birmingham.

4th   Waller marches on Monmouth whose garrison removes to Raglan Castle at his approach allowing him free access to the town.

5th   Parliamentary troops, under Sir William Brereton, Chief Commander in Cheshire, assault Warrington but are repulsed.

6th   The King appoints Lord Herbert as his Lieutenant-General in South Wales.

7th   All the householders in Oxford are called to a great meeting at Christ Church to debate the raising of a garrison from the town and university to release soldiers for active duty.

8th   The Earl of Denbigh dies from wounds received at the intaking of Birmingham.

9th   On or about this date, Sir William Pennyman deputizes for Sir Jacob Astley, who is sick, as Governor of Oxford. Some reports, however, suggest that Sir Lewis Kirke was the deputy at this time and Pennyman his eventual successor.

10th   An order in Parliament requires that whosoever comes into London or its vicinity from Oxford without a Parliamentary pass should be arrested as a spy.

11th   Troopers again assemble in New Park, Oxford for training under the eye of the King and Princes.

12th   Lieutenant-Colonel Edward Massey seizes Tewkesbury and is joined by Waller that evening.

13th   THE BATTLE OF RIPPLE FIELD. Waller meets with a sharp reverse from Maurice.

14th   The Commons orders its committee at Oxford to discontinue negotiations with the King and to return to Westminster.

15th   Essex besieges Reading with 1,600 foot and over 3,000 horse.

16th   Alexander Popham takes two troops of horse to investigate the fluctuating position of Sherborne, and sends a trumpeter to request quarters in the town for himself and his men. But the citizens have planned to ambush Popham and open fire on the Parliamentary soldiers as they ride in. Popham's brother is killed and many more but Popham himself escapes. Later he returns and takes his revenge on the perfidious townsfolk

Dauentry

Brimidgham

The moſt Illuſtrious and High borne PRINCE RUPERT, PRINCE ELECTOR, Second Son to FREDERICK KING of BOHEMIA, GENERALL of the HORSE of H's MAJESTIES ARMY, KNIGHT of the Noble Order of the   GARTER.

Prince Rupert with Birmingham in flames behind.

'wasting and spoiling the towne . . . to the value of many thousands of pounds'.

17th   Sir Samuel Luke records that Parliament is working day and night on the siege works around Reading.

18th   Lieutenant-General Wilmot sends 500 troops and a supply of powder by river from Sonning to Reading.

19th   The King, having also enacted the Triennial Act for Scotland, refuses to call the Scottish Parliament before the appropriate date in June 1644.

20th   A small force of Parliamentary troops under Colonel Shuttleworth makes a surprise attack on the Earl of Derby's men near Whalley and destroys them. This is said to have been the decisive encounter of the war in Lancashire.

21st   Rupert takes Lichfield after a ten-day siege. He mines the Close walls; this is the first time that gunpowder is used for such a purpose in England.

22nd   Prince Maurice returns to Oxford victorious from Ripple.

The Scottish commissioners leave Oxford.

23rd   A body of foot leaves Oxford for Dorchester.

24th   Today they rendezvous with the King for the attempt on Reading. The King and Rupert, with a hastily gathered force of horse, are to relieve Reading.

25th   The Royalist forces are thrown back at Caversham Bridge and the deputy governor refuses to issue out of the town as there is a truce in force.

Waller takes Hereford without a shot fired.

THE BATTLE OF SOURTON DOWN. After the expiration of the Cornish truce Major-General James Chudleigh launches his Parliamentary army at Launceston. Countered by Hopton, the struggle continues all day, until dark when Chudleigh retires. Hopton follows him up and a night engagement takes place where the Royalists are discomfited and retire in disorder on Bridestowe.

26th   John Hutchinson is sent to London to acquaint Parliament with the affairs at Nottingham where the garrison is in 'a weak and languishing condition', and to ask for aid.

27th   The governor, Sir Arthur Aston, being injured, his deputy, Colonel Richard Fielding, surrenders Reading to Essex.

Oliver Cromwell (1599–1658), by an unknown artist.

28th   Oliver Cromwell's first siege ends successfully when, with Sir Miles Hobart and Sir Anthony Irby, he besieges his cousin, a Captain Cromwell who commanded at Crowland.

29th   Following Hutchinson's appeal to Parliament the two Houses direct Lord Fairfax to aid Nottingham. This order is fruitless as Fairfax himself is on the defensive.

30th   The King, with Rupert and Maurice, returns to Oxford with their troops and the Reading garrison.

May

1st   Sir Edward Hungerford arrives in the vicinity of Wardour Castle near Tisbury with 1,300 horse and foot.

2nd   Hungerford sends a surrender demand to Lady Arundel, wife of the owner, who is on active service with Hopton.

3rd   'A great number of foote men' are seen by Wood going from Oxford allegedly to siege Abingdon.

4th   The Duke of Richmond returns to Court at Oxford from Holland.

5th   Colonel Richard Fielding, who surrendered Reading, is put on trial for alleged criminal conspiracy with the enemy. He is condemned to death but later reprieved.

6th   Henry Moggridge, 'one of the King's footmen' who has served him for thirty-six years, asks that his post of Keeper of the Mews at Greenwich, for which he is paid 8*d* per day, may now be enjoyed by his son 'drum major in the Reading garrison'.

7th   Major Hercule Langrish writes to Colonel Nathaniel Fiennes from Weymouth saying that he hopes to be back in Bristol in three days' time.

8th   Lady Arundel surrenders Wardour Castle after the besiegers have planted and exploded a mine in the drainage system.

9th   Sir William Waller is troubled by lack of money to pay his men. In a letter to the Speaker he states: 'Pay is the poor man's *aqua vita*, but lack of it is the *aqua fortis* as eats through the iron doors of discipline.'

10th A petition of one Robert Bennett, wagoner, is presented to Lord General Essex. It states that seven horses pressed by the army in the train of artillery were lost at Kineton Field (Edgehill). As they are all his living he asks if he can be compensated £82. The petition is ordered and granted on 26 May.

11th The Lords and Council in Ireland send a rather desperate note to the King stating that the English cause is 'suffering exceedingly for want of provisions, money, and ammunition' and as none are forthcoming from Parliament what can His Majesty do?

12th A letter from Sir Thomas Dacre of Cheshunt to Speaker Lenthall complains of the difficulties he and his colleagues have experienced in collecting the weekly assessment in his area.

13th SKIRMISH AT GRANTHAM. A Royalist force under General Charles Cavendish is driven from the field by the headlong charge of Colonel Oliver Cromwell's horse.

14th In France the Queen Mother is made Regent as Cardinal

Richelieu and the King are dead. She professes great good will to Henrietta Maria and King Charles' cause.

15th   A complaint is presented to the Committee of Customs by a merchant named William Garway. He states that out of 40 tons of currants imported the previous year, of which 1 ton was detained as port tax, a large number were found to be damaged. He is claiming the 1 ton back as compensation.

16th   THE BATTLE AT STRATTON. The Royalists under Hopton attack a Parliamentary force on Stamford Hill at 5 a.m. After a fierce and bloody struggle the Royalists are victorious by 4 p.m.

17th   The Blandford Committee writes to Speaker Lenthall to assure him that 'thankes be to God the business of settling the afayres of the County go cheerfully on'.

18th   Hungerford marches out of Wardour leaving Captain Edward Ludlow in command of the tiny garrison.

19th   The King approaches both Houses in an endeavour to negotiate a settled peace.

20th   The garrison of Manchester marches out against Warrington and is later joined by Brereton with a great force of Cheshire men. They commence the siege.

21st   Sir Thomas Fairfax storms and takes Wakefield. Lord George Goring is captured.

22nd   Alexander Popham writes to Nathaniel Fiennes requesting the release of the remaining companies of Popham's regiment from garrison duty for service with Sir William Waller.

23rd   The Commons impeach the Queen of High Treason for the prosecution of the war against Parliament and bringing into the country arms and ammunition for that purpose.

24th   Sir John Hotham writes to the Constable of Bainton in Yorkshire that 'tithes must not be paid to the Church as heretofore but must be retained until Parliament's pleasure is known'.

25th   *Mercurius Aulicus* tells how the Mayor of Swansea is summoned to deliver the town by Robert Moulton on board the Parliamentary warship *Lion*. The citizens send back a sharp reply.

26th   Sir William Waller sends 'five trunkes of Plate taken at the gaining of Hereford' to London 'to be coyned there and returned to pay his soldiers'.

27th The joint force of Parliamentary troops under Brereton besieging Warrington are called to parley by Colonel Norris the Royalist commander, who surrenders on terms.

28th Sir George Booth, Lord of the Manor of Warrington, is installed as governor by Brereton.

29th Sir William Waller organizes a rendezvous at Bath of all Royalist commanders of the Western Association.

30th Edmund Waller's pro-Royalist plot is discovered in London.

31st Edmund Waller is arrested with his fellow conspirators.

Hopton advances out of Cornwall to check Sir William Waller's victorious campaign. This day he reaches Honiton.

June

1st John Ashe, one of the treasurers for the Somerset Parliamentary faction, writes to Nathaniel Fiennes, Governor of Bristol, complaining that if citizens are expected to give troops free quarter they can hardly be expected to pay assessments.

2nd The sporadic work on the defences of Dorchester, instigated in 1642, now reaches new heights with work proceeding night and day.

3rd Hopton arrives at Chard.

4th Hopton is joined by the Marquess of Hertford and Prince Maurice who have been dispatched from Oxford by the King with a substantial force.

The Queen leaves York with a force of 4,500 men, which Newcastle has raised and she has armed.

5th About this date the Luttrells render up Dunster Castle, and Taunton and Bridgwater surrender without a blow being struck.

6th The full details of Edmund Waller's plot are disclosed to the House of Commons which formulates an oath of loyalty to be taken by members of both Houses.

7th Fiennes refuses to weaken his garrison further when Anthony Nichole and William Gould request the return of 500 men to Bath.

8th Wood states how, 'the Parliament forces advanced from Reddinge and came stealynge along . . . the woodes to

Nettlebed . . . to Stoken Church and so to Thame where they quartered'.

9th   About this date Naval Captains Swanley and Smith report to Parliament in person regarding their successful operations based on Milford Haven. Parliament bestows on them valuable gold chains and the thanks of the House.

10th   Lieutenant Lee garrisons Bridport for Parliament.

11th   The Marquess of Hertford appoints Sir John Stawel, Colonel Edward Wyndham and Mr Francis Wyndham Governors of Taunton, Bridgwater and Dunster respectively.

12th   Parliament passes an ordinance appointing Sir Thomas Middleton (MP for Denbigh) major-general for the six counties of North Wales.

13th   The Commons votes to make a new Great Seal to replace the one that was carried away to the King, but the Lords refuse to agree.

14th   Bury's accounts show preparation being made to siege Corfe Castle, 'this day paid for unloading great guns brought in from Portsmouth to Corfe'.

15th   Twenty-four gunners arrive at Dorchester from Weymouth 'with four pieces of ordnance'.

16th   The Queen arrives safely at Newark.

     Waller writes his famous letter to his friend Hopton telling him of his detestation of 'this war without an enemy'.

17th   Essex sends a substantial detachment to hold the passage over the River Cherwell at Oxford.

18th   ACTION AT CHALGROVE FIELD. John Hampden is wounded and the Parliamentary force discomfited when it intercepts Rupert's raiding party, who had endeavoured to capture a pay convoy for Essex's army.

19th   Lord Grey of Groby is superseded by Sir John Meldrum as commander-in-chief of the Association forces.

20th   The minute books of Dorchester show how great the town's efforts to prepare for an emergency really are. The mercer, Matthew Harvey, has supplied goods to various commanders, George Bartlett is owed for iron fitments for the fortifications, Richard Williams requires payment for candles as does John Roberts for the supply of some arms and the repair of others.

21st The Queen launches some of her troops in a raid on Nottingham.

22nd The Earl of Newcastle takes the Parliamentary strong point of Howley House, home of Lord Savile, situated between Leeds and Wakefield.

23rd Sir William Waller is still worried by a shortage of infantry. In a letter to Parliament he boasts of his vast superiority in cavalry but adds ruefully, 'this part of the countrie is altogether unfitte for Horse'.

24th John Hampden dies from wounds received at Chalgrove Field.
    Colonel Edward Cooke writes yet again to Fiennes for the return of 500 men requested on 7 June.

25th Wood notes 'Elegies on the death of Colonel John Hampden' by J.S. London and also that the deceased was a 'grand rebell of Bucks'.

26th John Fiennes writes from Bath to his brother Nathaniel, Governor of Bristol, concerning 'the motion of Colonel Popham, Sir William Waller and Sir Edward Hungerford'.

27th The Royalists announce that the Oxford troops are to be paid by taxing the scholars; there is great outcry among the scholars.

28th John Hotham junior is arrested for High Treason against Parliament on 18 June. He escapes from Nottingham Castle but is re-arrested at Hull.

29th Colonel John Hutchinson is appointed Governor of Nottingham when Meldrum is ordered to join Cromwell.

30th THE BATTLE OF ADWALTON MOOR. Newcastle defeats the Fairfaxes.

July

1st Sir William Waller and Haselrig send an urgent request to Fiennes to spare them more garrison regiments, asking, 'What good will these regiments do Bristol if we perish?'

2nd The combined Royalist army with Hopton acting as a sort of chief-of-staff arrive at Bradford-on-Avon.

3rd The Queen leaves Newark.
    Sir William Waller makes dispositions to meet Hopton upon Claverton Down near Bath, with a large detachment at

Monkton Farleigh Hill. When contact is made, the Cornishmen drive the latter position back as far as Batheaston.

4th   Compelled to retreat back on Bath, Sir William Waller takes up his position on Lansdown Hill.

Mr Tomkins, Edmund Waller's brother-in-law, and Mr Chaloner, 'a citizen of wealth and credit' implicated in the Royalist plot, are hanged outside their own houses.

5th   THE BATTLE OF LANSDOWN. Sir William Waller crowns the steep crest of Lansdown Hill which Hopton feels bound to assault, incurring heavy casualties. When the Royalists gain a toe-hold on the summit, Waller falls back and after the onset of darkness retreats on Bath to refresh his men. The Royalist victory was dearly bought for among the dead and wounded were Sir Beville Grenville, Lord Arundel of Wardour, Sir George Vaughan and the Earl of Carnarvon.

Edmund Waller, brought to the Bar of the House of Commons, pleads his case with such flights of oratory 'that he exceedingly captivated the goodwill and benevolence of his hearers' and eventually he is allowed his liberty for the sum of £10,000, which will be very useful to the Parliamentary war chest.

6th   Early in the morning a cart containing gunpowder suddenly explodes, temporarily blinding and paralysing Hopton and mortally wounding Major Thomas Sheldon. The dispirited Royalists, more demoralized by victory than their opponents by defeat, and deserted by two-thirds of their horse, fall back on Marshfields.

7th   Sir William Waller again occupies Lansdown from where he harries the Royalist retreat, which retires on Chippenham.

8th   Emboldened by Waller's victory out of defeat, the countrymen enlist in the Parliamentary army. Waller sets out with these and reinforcements from Bristol in pursuit of the Royalists.

9th   Hearing of Waller's approach the Royalists march from Chippenham and reach Devizes by nightfall, only a short distance ahead of the enemy.

10th Waller confidently invests Devizes.

11th Hertford and Maurice, having broken out of Devizes, make a dramatic dash for Oxford to get help.

12th Waller offers Hopton surrender terms, which the latter, to gain time, affects to consider.

13th THE BATTLE OF ROUNDWAY DOWN. The Royalists are reinforced by Wilmot, with nearly 2,000 fresh horse which the King sent as soon as Hertford and Maurice arrived at Oxford. The Royalists engage Waller and inflict such a crushing defeat on him that his army virtually ceases to exist.

14th The King and Queen enter Oxford having been reunited on the battlefield site at Edgehill.

15th Rupert marches out from Oxford with a substantial force to join the Western Army, in order to subdue the entire West Country which the defeat of Waller makes possible.

16th An allegedly Royalist rising in Kent in the tradition of Cade and Tyler threatens London and the Thames Estuary. Tonbridge and Sevenoaks are plundered indiscriminately.

17th Sir John Conyers, Royalist Lieutenant of the Tower, finding his position more impossible each day, requests permission from both Houses to retire to his estates in Holland.

18th Sir William Brereton makes a probing attack against the defences of Royalist Chester, but retires, achieving little.

19th Parliament orders the Earl of Rutland, Sir Henry Vane the younger and three other members of the Commons to treat with the Scots at Edinburgh and to make an arrangement that will bring them into the war on Parliament's side.

20th Lord Willoughby, a Parliamentary commander, surprises and takes Gainsborough. Its defender, the Earl of Kingston, is accidently killed by his own side while in transit to prison.

21st Halton Castle surrenders to Parliamentary forces after siege.

22nd Both Houses grant Sir John Conyers permission to withdraw from the Tower and appoint the Lord Mayor, Isaac Pennington, to be lieutenant in his place.

23rd Parliament introduces the Excise Ordinance, increasing the excise duties to increase their war potential.

24th Prince Rupert summons Bristol, the natural outcome of Waller's defeat at Roundway Down. Despite drastically impoverishing the garrison to accommodate Waller, Colonel Nathaniel Fiennes declines.

Sir Henry Vane (1613–62),
by Robert Walker.

25th   Waller rides into London accompanied by a great number of officers. The City gives him a hero's welcome with cannon roaring and bells pealing.

Willoughby is soon cornered at Gainsborough by a strong force of Newcastle's army under General Cavendish. Cromwell and Meldrum are ordered to assist Willoughby.

26th   Rupert storms Bristol at daybreak. The casualties on the Royalist side are very heavy as they come under the fire of the well-sited defences. After a fierce struggle until darkness Fiennes is compelled by circumstances to ask for terms.

27th   The Parliamentary garrison marches out with the honours of war. Meldrum and Cromwell join forces at North Scarle, 10 miles from Gainsborough.

Waller addresses the thronged congregation in the Merchant Taylor's Hall and tells them he would, 'spend his blood in the Defence of their Religion, Lawes, and Liberties'.

28th   Skirmish at Gainsborough. Cromwell defeats Cavendish who is killed in action.

29th   The Earl of Essex retaliates in the face of the almost universal criticism of his administration. Why, he asks, was he blamed for other men's mistakes? Why did the Queen pass safely to Oxford in the face of Fairfax and Cromwell? How was it that Waller's great army was annihilated by a handful of Royalist horse?

30th   The King issues a Declaration of Policy stating that his position is the same as it was at the start of the war and laying the blame for all the carnage on Parliament. He promises rewards to his supporters and disaster to his enemies.

       Newcastle, appearing before Gainsborough in overwhelming strength, retakes the town.

       Waller is voted as general of the New Army which is 10,000 strong and is to be largely raised in London by the Common Council. This outrages the Lord General Essex.

31st   A raid against Basing House by Colonel Richard Norton is beaten off by the fortuitous arrival of part of Rawdon's regiment which had force marched from Oxford.

August

1st   Gainsborough is surrendered by Willoughby after three days, Newcastle having conducted a full-scale siege.

2nd   The King enters Bristol to the acclaim of the citizens.

       Dorchester, despite all the costly preparations to defend the town, surrenders without a blow struck to the Royalists.

3rd   The Commons considers the Lord General's request for an official enquiry into the reasons and responsibility for the loss of the West, but decides no useful purpose would be served by doing so by 51 votes to 30.

4th   Colonel Henry Marten, leader of the army committee for recruitment, reports that recruitment for Waller's New Army is not proceeding at a sufficiently desirable rate and attributes this to the fact that Essex has not yet commissioned Waller to command.

5th   A discussion in the Commons by the peace party who wish to reach an accommodation with the King results in a near riot being stirred up in the City.

6th   The City is again incensed by pamphleteers stating that the 'well affected party' has been outvoted and the King is bringing 20,000 Irish soldiers into the country.

7th   A proposal for peace is voted against by a narrow margin.

Sir Richard Byron, who superseded Henderson as Governor of Newark, sends a request to Hutchinson for a safe conduct for his representative.

8th   On or about this date, Byron's representative reaches Nottingham with a surrender demand from Newcastle. Hutchinson sternly replies, 'If his Lordship would have this poor castle he must wade in blood to it.'

9th   Nottingham is saved by the clamourings of the Yorkshire gentry requiring protection from the Hull raiding parties.

10th   The King commences to besiege Gloucester, as Lieutenant-Colonel Edward Massey, the governor, refuses to yield, contrary to expectation.

11th   By this date Erle assures Speaker Lenthall that Royalists have taken Weymouth, Melcombe Regis and the 'Island and Castle of Portland', the latter by a ruse.

Colonel Edward Massey, Governor of Gloucester.

12th   The Chamberlain of Bath has to find money to 'remove the greate guns from the Mounte' and for 'making clene the hall'.

13th   The authorities at Poole write to those at Portsmouth asking for the promised reinforcements.

14th   Gabriel Smith's certificate to the Earl of Warwick states that Captain John Holman and Aaron Williams have saved for the service of Parliament 12 demi-culverins, 2 culverins and 30 sakers.

15th   The Commons sends John Pym, John Glynn and the elder Vane to Essex's headquarters at Kingston, ostensibly to advise him about the enemy's movements but in fact to urge him to grant Waller's commission.

17th   Colonel Richard Whitehead writes from Portsmouth regarding Poole's appeal for reinforcements and states that the garrison is

Digging the defences in Gloucester, 1643.

too weak to lend any, but he has passed the request on to Essex.

18th An ordinance is made by the Commons for 'a speedy supply of money within the City for the relief and maintenance of the forces raised for the defence of the City'.

19th The citizens of Pembroke and Haverfordwest pledge the Earl of Carbery to provide the sum of £2,000 within ten days of this date as an earnest of their loyalty to the King.

20th The Militia Committee in London commands, 'that by virtue of an ordinance of both Houses . . . [they] have the power to shut up all shops within the lines of communication to the end that all citizens may be better fitted to defend the city' – a reflection of the gravity with which the seige of Gloucester was viewed.

21st The end of the Poole affair seems to have been satisfactory, for this day the committee writes to Speaker Lenthall thanking him for the £300 sent to it, but urging the appointment of a competent commander to order the defences.

22nd Sir William Pennyman dies of *Morbis Epidemis* at Oxford and is buried in Christ Church. Sir Arthur Aston, the unpopular governor, is assaulted while doing his rounds in Oxford City.

23rd A pamphlet printed at Temple Bar this day tells of the 'goodly success lately achieved against the Fellowship of Bristow by Captain William Smith, etc.'

24th At Hounslow Heath, Essex reviews his army for the relief of Gloucester, which includes five regiments of the Trained Bands of London.

25th Anthony Nichols reports that Essex is now willing to grant Waller's commission but wishes to know the names of the proposed colonels as 'he had exception to take to some of them'.

26th Pym presents a blank signed commission to the House with a covering letter from Essex stating that members might fill in whose name they cared to. In a unique ceremony the assembled MPs vote unanimously for Waller.

27th *Mercurius Aulicus* records: 'We hear from Dorchester how miserably the inhabitants have been cozened by their Patriarch Mr White and his sub Levites' – with Parliament propaganda.

28th Henry Percy, General of Ordnance, issues a warrant to one Daniel von Hecke that upon receiving said warrant he should deliver to the bearer Mr Marsh all the arms and ammunition brought from Dunkirk. Percy lists the going rate of the following commodities: Match 30s per cwt, backs and breasts 15s each, iron shot £15 per ton.

29th Cromwell writes his famous letter telling how he selected his officers: 'I would rather have a plain russet coated captain . . . .' Waller issues his commissions for the New Army.

30th Sir Andrew Carew plans to surrender 'that island with a fort on it with a good command of Plymouth Sound' (Drake's Island), but is apprehended and sent off by sea to London to await trial.

31st A complaint from John Van Haesdonck to Newcastle states that one Captain Antonio Vernatts, his agents and soldiers have, in the absence of the complainant, plundered and terrorized his tenants and taken their goods and harvest, saying that as he is a King's man he is above the law. The complainant says that at the time he was absent on the King's business.

September

1st Essex's relief force reaches Brackley Heath where he is further reinforced, bringing his army to a total of 15,000 men.

2nd Newcastle, with 15,000 men, lays siege to Hull.
Barnstaple falls to Maurice.

3rd William Constantine MP is charged with conspiracy to render up the town of Poole to the enemy. He is discharged from sitting in the House and on 28 September has his estate sequestrated.

4th Maurice takes Exeter city largely because Warwick is unable to supply it by sea. Sir Ralph Hopton is elevated to the peerage.

5th Essex's relief force halts on Prestbury Hill only 10 miles distant from Gloucester.

6th The King, not wishing to be trapped between the town and Essex, lifts the siege and withdraws to Sudeley Castle.

7th Parliament, realizing the strategic value of Lyme Regis, puts twenty barrels of powder, a ton of match and a ton of shot into the town.

8th Essex's relief force enters Gloucester to the great joy and thanksgiving of the citizens, who were short of almost every necessity and down to the last three barrels of gunpowder.

9th The cost of conveying letters to Sir Thomas Rowe in Portugal is

Summoning Hull.

shown to be £25 19*s* by an anonymous person 'laying in the college'.

10th   Since the King's object is to cut Essex off on his way back to London, an elaborate game of cat and mouse begins when the Parliamentary army leaves Gloucester this day.

11th   A letter from Colonel Edward Massey, Governor of Gloucester, is read in the House this day, relating to the condition of the army and of the city of Gloucester.

12th   Justice Berkeley, who had been arrested on 13 February 1641, is now brought to judgment by the Lords and fined £20,000 to line Parliament's impoverished war chest.

13th   The Committee for Preventing the Misapplication of Money, sitting at Saddler's Hall, directs that Sir George Sandys should pay £2,500 to the Clothworkers' Guild, being a legacy from the late Ralph Treeman, merchant.

14th   As part of the cat and mouse game Essex throws a bridge of boats over the River Severn and makes a feint towards Worcester.

15th   After several days of move and countermove Essex plunges south towards Cirencester during the night. On entering the town he captures a much-needed convoy of provisions meant for the Royalist army, and gains a 24-hour lead in the race for London.

16th   As a countermeasure to the enlistment of the Scots by Parliament, Ormonde, by the King's order, concludes a truce called the Cessation with the Confederate Irish, thus freeing the Royalist troops in Ireland for service in England.

17th   Essex spends the night at Swindon; the King is at Alvescot, 10 miles to the north-east. The Parliamentary army is 8 miles closer to Newbury than the Royalists.

18th   SKIRMISH AT ALDBOURNE. Rupert attempts delaying tactics against Essex to allow the Royalist army to catch up.

19th   Essex's pace is slow owing to heavy rain which makes the roads a morass. The advance guard of the King's army surges into Newbury just as the Parliamentary quartermasters are allocating billets. By this narrow margin Essex has lost the race.

20th   THE FIRST BATTLE OF NEWBURY. This is a marginal Parliamentary victory. *See separate account on pages 78–9.*

21st   *Mercurius Civicus* notes that, due to the occupation of Bristol and the subsequent unattended garbage in the street, 'the new disease is very hot in that city for which cause the King has diverted his attention of going thither'.

22nd   On or about this date, Colonel Nathaniel Fiennes, who yielded up Bristol and feels his honour and good name have been besmirched by Essex's success at Gloucester, demands a public enquiry into the circumstances of Bristol to restore his reputation.

23rd   In response to a call for help from Colonel John Hutchinson, the Governor of the City of Nottingham, under attack from Royalist troops, Captain Charles White sets out with a small relief force from Leicester. As they approach, the garrison sallies forth and helps the defeated Royalists on their way.

24th   A warrant is issued from the King to the Lord Carbery for £240 to repay a part of his disbursements.

25th   A Solemn League and Covenant is signed between the Scots Commissioners and those of Parliament.

26th   *Mecurius Aulicus* reports: 'His Majesty's subjects go a better way of work especially those in the county of Pembroke for the famous port of Milford Haven, Tenby, and Haverfordwest being reduced by the Earl of Carbery . . . .'

27th   An attempt to take Poole by a strategem on the night of 27/28 rebounds when Royalist troops charge triumphantly through

The First Battle of Newbury
20 September 1643

It would seem to a casual observer that the odds were heavily in favour of a decisive, if not crushing, Royalist victory, when the dawn of 20 September broke over the damp, chilly, autumnal landscape.

The King's men had slept snug and warm in bed around Newbury town, their bellies full of the food intended for their opponents who were encamped at Crockham Heath in the pouring rain, footsore, weary and short of food. The Parliamentary army was astir early, taking up its positions along the edges of the plateau that rises steeply in parts from the plain of Wash Common. Two short spurs project to the north towards the River Kennet; one of these was to be a key point known to history as the Round Hill. Before this position on the far side of the common blocking their way home to London was the Royalist army. The left and centre way encroached upon by the expanding town, while the present-day Falkland Memorial is considered to be approximately at the Royalist centre.

While the exact numbers of the opposing armies cannot be known with any certainty, the Royalist force can be computed as at least 14,000 men, probably 6,000 horse and 8,000 foot. This figure may err on the low side, and the actual number could have been considerably more. Essex started out from London with 15,000 men and, allowing for the casualties resulting from Rupert's attacks at Stow-on-the-Wold and Aldbourne Down, sickness and desertion, the wastage could well have reduced the Parliamentary army's strength to a similar number to the King's (14,000 men), certainly not more. This would have comprised of about 4,000 horse and 10,000 foot, half of which were from the often derided London Trained Bands. The battle commenced at 7 a.m., the King's priorities being to dislodge the enemy from Wash Common and from the Round Hill. The first was soon achieved by Rupert, but at the second, Sir George Lisle and Colonel Henry Wentworth, supported by Sir John Byron's horse and strengthened by Sir Thomas Aston's regiment, were repulsed by a hail of musketry and case shot. After the initial phases the battle seems to have had little direction because, according to Clarendon, 'By the precipitate courage of some

the main gate. As their plot was known they are met by a devastating storm of case and musket shot at close range.

28th Essex and the victorious Gloucester relief forces reach London to receive a hero's welcome. The streets are lined with cheering crowds and they are welcomed by civic dignitaries. Deputations from both Houses, the City, the Lord Mayor and the Speaker wait upon Essex at his great house in the Strand.

of the young officers who had good commands and who unhappily undervalued the courage of the enemy strong parties became so successively engaged that the King was obliged to hazard the whole.' In other words the gallants had no mind for strategic planning but only to attack the despised enemy with loose rein and bloody spur.

It can be seen that the Royalist offensive consisted of no more than two major attacks and two minor ones. On the Parliamentary right where the terrain favoured cavalry action, Rupert, after successive charges, had driven the stubborn Stapleton almost off the field. Minor attacks were made by, among others, Vavasour's Welshmen on the extreme Parliamentary left but these were repelled without difficulty.

Essex now threw his reserve in, save one regiment, and stabilized his centre which was hard pressed. At this time the London Trained Bands, particularly the Red Regiment, proved their worth and covered themselves with glory. Their resolution under cannon fire and in repelling Rupert's choicest horse caused Clarendon's grudging admiration: 'They were even the saviours of their side.' Fighting went on for twelve hours until darkness shrouded the field. Even then there was sporadic fire until 10 p.m. when the final shots rang out from the Royalist artillery. By this time a Royalist Council of War had been held, the King giving the order for a night retreat on Oxford. Officially he was influenced by the fact that his army was down to the last ten barrels of powder, but it may have been his casualties which may have amounted to twenty-five officers, including the Secretary of State, Lord Falkland, whose death struck a severe blow to the Royalist cause as did John Hampden's to the Parliamentary, and also Lord Carnarvon and Lord Sunderland.

When 21 September dawned the Parliamentary army was still in its position and rank, and resolved to cut its way through to London. It was, however, no doubt relieved it did not need to.

First Newbury is considered to be a Parliamentary victory for the same reason that Edgehill was awarded to the King – that is, that the agressor left the field with his purpose unfulfilled.

The standard work for this battle is Walter Money's *The First and Second Battles of Newbury and the Siege of Donnington Castle* (1881).

29th A Royal Council of War is held at Oriel College, Oxford, where the grand strategy designed to finish the war is re-examined. Lord Hopton of Stratton is to command a new army designed to 'cleer Dorset, Wiltshire and Hampshire and point toward London'.

30th Colonel James Wardlaw, a professional soldier, arrives with 500 men to take command at Plymouth for Parliament.

The coat of arms of Gloucester. The lion, sword in hand, is a reminder of the valiant defence of the city in 1643.

October

1st Prince Maurice arrives to commence the siege of Plymouth. The Parliamentary commander in Lancashire, Colonel Alexander Rigby, learning that a relief force has been formed by Colonel Huddleston of Millom, marches to meet him and after a short engagement disperses the Royalists at Lindale.

2nd Hearing of Rigby's victory, Sir Phillip Musgrave commanding at Thurland Castle asks for terms.

3rd Essex, basking in the glory of his Newbury victory, gains a further victory in the House, where it is agreed that Waller should be subordinated to him and that Essex alone should grant commissions.

4th A warrant is issued under the Privy Seal to pay Andrew Grove, 'a native of Denmark', £50 for the making of fireworks for the Lord Hopton.

5th Reinforcements are sent by Manchester from Lynn to reinforce Hull this day.

6th Maurice takes Dartmouth. Sir Lewis Dyve takes Newport Pagnell.

7th   Essex's proposal regarding his seniority having been passed by the Lords is submitted to the Commons. Essex threatens that he will resign if it is not carried.

8th   The Commons agrees to Essex's proposal. Waller who is present at the debate expresses that, 'he would be ever ready to receive his Excellency's commands'.

9th   Newcastle launches a two-pronged attack on Hull. After an initial success the attackers are vehemently repulsed.

10th   The advanced guard of Manchester's foot march from Boston and lay siege to Bolingbroke Castle.

11th   THE BATTLE OF WINCEBY. Manchester, Cromwell and Sir Thomas Fairfax trounce Sir William Widrington and Sir John Henderson.

12th   The meeting of deputy lieutenants at Preston decides that Hornby Castle should be slighted and that the garrisons of Warrington and Liverpool should be maintained.

13th   An ordinance of the Commons is issued for upholding the government of the Merchant Adventurers Fellowship for 'the

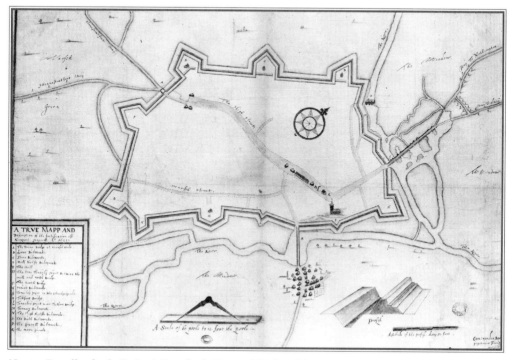

Newport Pagnell, taken by Sir Lewis Dyve for the King on 6 October 1643.

better maintenance of the clothing trade and woollen manufacture'.

14th As an example of the burdens placed on even a small township, note the following items: 'For his Majesty's service £1.'

15th And on this day 'for provisions of oates butter and cheese £2' (both Hatherton).

16th The Chevalier Harcourt, Prince of Lorraine, who was received with great ceremony on his arrival on 7 October, is searched and his entourage likewise on leaving for Oxford, despite his safe conduct pass.

17th Maurice is stricken with the 'ordinary raging disease of the army, a slow fever', according to Dr William Harvey in his report to Rupert.

18th Sir William Brereton overtakes a force of Lord Capel's which has been repulsed at Wem and is retreating on Shrewsbury. Brereton inflicts a crushing defeat on the Royalists at Lee Bridge.

19th A letter is sent from one 'WB' to his 'loving master' giving an eyewitness account of the above fight. It is later printed as a pamphlet.

20th The Earl of Manchester re-occupies Lincoln.

21st An interesting letter is sent from the Privy Seal to the Treasurer, stating that the upkeep of the royal children, Prince Charles and Prince James, is estimated to be £653 17s per month.

22nd The Treasurer is empowered to pay Sir George Strode and John Wandesford from time to time such sums as may be required for armaments of war, not exceeding £2,000.

23rd Another ordinance is issued from the Lords and Commons who are still wrestling with the thorny problem of how to raise money speedily.

24th Parliament passes an ordinance for the Impressment of troops and votes £200 for the use of Poole's garrison.

25th Strode and Wandesford soon make use of the Privy Seal mentioned previously as they draw £100 this day.

26th A letter sent from Ormonde to the Archbishop of York concerns 'the Consignment of Arms for the defence of Anglesey and the probable transportation of the soldiers in Ireland to North Wales'.

27th By error Sir Lewis Dyve evacuates Newport Pagnell, leaving a valuable base open to the enemy.

Newcastle is created Marquess for services rendered.

28th Abraham Shipman, on behalf of the Lancashire Royalists, writes to Ormonde requesting that the troops coming back from Ireland should be used to secure the north for the King.

29th Sir Robert Pye is removed from his office of Writer of the Tallies as he has gone to Oxford to the King. His office is given by Parliament to one Robert Long.

30th Three regiments of the London Trained Bands are sent to serve with Waller. Lieutenant Elias Archer records they marched to a green outside Windsor and thence to Farnham.

31st The Trained Bands reach Farnham very fatigued and fall out to rest until the rendezvous next day.

November

1st Newcastle marches south to Chesterfield. His intention is the reduction of all Parliamentary garrisons in the area.

Waller receives his regiments at Farnham Castle.

2nd The Bath Royalists utilize the local Trained Bands to establish regular courts of guard. It is noted that the local authorities make use of 'wood, cole and candells' and the officers 'wine at the Newe Taverne'.

3rd Waller's army, perhaps 8,000 strong, camps at Alton this night.

4th Parliament appoints Waller to command the new South-eastern Association consisting of Hampshire, Kent, Surrey and Sussex. Sleet and snow delay the march of Waller's men.

5th Waller's army reaches Alresford but learning of the approach of a strong body from Oxford he abandons his march on Winchester and strikes out for his secondary target, that of Basing House.

6th Waller arrives at Basing House in a thick fog and deploys his forces.

7th Basing House refuses to yield, and is heavily bombarded after which it is heavily assaulted. Stormy weather causes the besiegers' withdrawal.

In order for soldiers to recognize each other more easily in battle they adopted different insignia, such as oak leaves worn in the helmet, or different coloured sashes.

8th Thirty-two pairs of pistols, which have been seized and forfeited, are delivered to Erle for the use of the garrison at Poole.

9th In the evening Sir William Brereton enters Wrexham en route to besiege Chester.

10th Rumours are rife in London that the King's Attorney General, Sir Richard Lloyd, sent his commission to Middleton offering to bring 1,500 men 'if they would only forgive him'.

11th Brereton and Sir Thomas Middleton march on Hawarden Castle which surrenders tamely.

12th Waller returns to the offensive at Basing House where another full-scale assault, continuing until dark, is barely repulsed.

13th   At Basing, the weather again turns to sleet and snow. Again the attackers retire to dry out.

14th   Hearing that Hopton is advancing from Andover with a superior force Waller retires on Farnham Castle 'having bruised and dishonoured his army'.

15th   The Parliamentary troops reach Farnham and are set to work constructing earthworks which greatly annoys the London regiments.

16th   Maurice heavily assaults the northern defences of Plymouth but is repulsed. His offer of a full pardon for surrender is ignored.

17th   Five thousand Irish troops land at Mostyn and Anglesey and form such a threat to Brereton's rear that he retreats to Nantwich.

18th   Alexander Rigby's letter concerning his victories is read in Parliament. He is accorded a vote of thanks and his proposed destruction of Thurland Castle approved.

19th   Middleton writes in friendship to Colonel Salesbury desiring, 'a prudent and friendly negotiation to avoid the shedding of Christian blood', to which the old churchman replies very definitely, 'In the name of Christ – No!'

20th   Lincoln falls to Sir John Gell.

21st   Sir John Byron (lately created a baron) leaves Oxford with 1,000 horse and 300 foot to assist Lord Capel in his endeavours to facilitate the passage of the 'Irish' troops.

22nd   The horses lost by the Royalists at Poole are ordered to London to be sold, the proceeds to be divided among the Poole garrison.

23rd   Captain Lay (or Lea) mounts an amphibious operation from Poole against Wareham with 200 musketeers. After a brisk engagement the Royalist garrison flees.

24th   Poole harbour is occupied by the Earl of Warwick, the Lord Admiral, whose ships proceed up the channel to Wareham.

25th   The Royalist endeavours to fortify Bath are best seen in the entries in the minute books. This day 'payments made for the walling up of gates and doors about the cittie wall' and other similar arrangements made on 20 November.

26th   The execution takes place at Old Exchange of David Knyveton, a King's messenger, who was apprehended by Parliament as a spy. Another messenger is more fortunate, being reprieved and sent to Bridewell.

27th　Hopton's force advancing on Farnham Castle is joined by a deatchment from Reading.

28th　At Farnham, Hopton attempts to lure Waller out of the strongly fortified castle. When the Royalists come too close Waller disperses them with cannon fire.

29th　Chatsworth falls to the Marquess of Newcastle.

Orlando Bridgeman writes to 'Ormond from Beaumaris telling of the military situation in North Wales and of the strenuous efforts made to outfit the "Irish troops"'.

30th　Despite its previous objections, the House of Lords, 'being less scrupulous', agrees that Parliament should have its own Great Seal. This was introduced into the Commons this day with great ceremony.

A ·treaty is signed in Edinburgh today between the Commissioners of Parliament and those of the Convention of the Estates of Scotland 'concerning the enforcement of the Solemn League and Covenant'.

December

1st　Ormond writes from Dublin to the Mayor of Chester notifying him of the departure of more 'Irish' troops under Colonel Robert Byron and of their intention to land at Chester.

2nd　Waller is at this time in London representing the condition of his army to Parliament.

3rd　Parliament confirms the appointment of the Earl of Warwick to the possession of the Inland Letter Office and to such deputies as he might care to appoint, to whom all postmasters are directed to carry the mail.

4th　The Chevalier Harcourt, having complained to both Houses via of his ill treatment on his return from Oxford via the Earl of Northumberland, receives a very tart reply in which his status of ambassador extraordinary is not recognized.

5th　Colonel James Wemyss, who introduced the light field piece known as the 'leather gun' into this country, leaves London to join Waller at Farnham with a convoy of leather guns and ammunition.

THE SOUTH VIEW OF BEESTON CASTLE NEAR CHESTER.

Beeston Castle, Chester. The castle was left in ruins after surrendering to the Parliamentarians in November 1645.

6th   On or about this date Byron reaches Chester.

        The new Great Seal is used for the first time to seal the patent of the Earl of Warwick as Lord High Admiral of England.

7th   The small garrison left by Brereton at Hawarden Castle surrenders on honourable terms.

8th   John Pym dies from cancer this day.

9th   Hopton takes Arundel Castle with Sir Edward Ford, High Sheriff of Sussex, and Colonel Joseph Bamfield. Ford is appointed to command the garrison.

10th   An aside on ecclesiastical matters: about this date Benjamin Holford, Clerk of the Faculties to the Archbishop of Canterbury, receives £5 8s 9³/₄d for dispensations for the quarter.

11th   The troops from Ireland, having thus far carried all before them, proceed to Northwich to cut the line of communication between Manchester and Nantwich.

12th   Waller parades his command in Farnham Park, persuades the London Trained Bands to stay with him a week longer and sets off in the direction of Basing once more.

13th   In the early hours the Parliamentary forces change direction and storm Alton, inflicting heavy losses on the garrison. Lord Crawford gallops to Winchester with his cavalry, leaving the

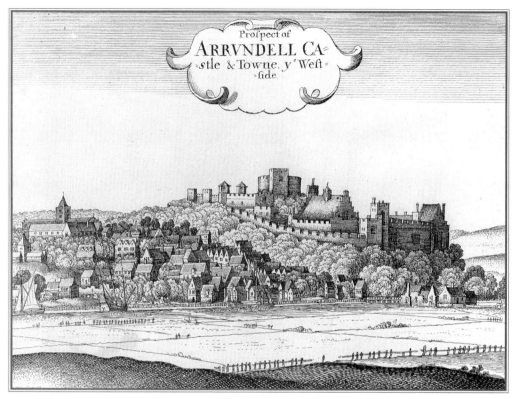

Arundel by Wenceslaus Hollar, 1644.

foot under Colonel Bolles to fall back on the church, the final strong point, where he is killed. Hopton is greatly distressed at this disaster. The Trained Bands return home in triumph.

14th A warrant is issued to Richard Fanshawe, Remembrancer of York, from Sir John Culpeper, Chancellor of the Exchequer, requiring 'a perfect particular of the lands and tenements of one William Garbutt' outlawed on 17 June 1642.

15th Anthony Cole, a collector of the King's forced loans, is summoned by the Sheriff of Worcester to explain why this has not been carried out.

16th Hopton writes Waller the famous letter in which he states: 'This is the first evident ill success I have had . . . .' Clarendon comments that the loss of Bolles' regiment galled Hopton 'as a wound that will not heal'.

17th Waller leaves Farnham Castle bound for Arundel with 5,000 horse and foot.

18th   Maurice concentrates a heavy bombardment on Maudlyn Fort, key to the northern defences of Plymouth, to no avail.

        Waller reaches Haslemere.

19th   In the late evening, Waller arrives at Arundel where his men prepare to sleep 'under the best spred trees in the park'.

20th   Gainsborough falls to Sir John Meldrum. Waller blockades Arundel Castle.

21st   A number of Royalist warships come up the Mersey river and it is speculated that they are there to transport troops for a waterborne-attack on Liverpool.

22nd   The Royalists lift the siege of Plymouth and start to withdraw.

23rd   Many Royalist prisoners taken at Dorchester are allowed to compound with Governor Bingham of Poole and the money so gained is spent on the defences.

24th   Rigby, hearing of the ships in the Mersey, calls upon Captain Pateson of *The Fylde* to raise volunteers to oppose the expected landing. Despite the proximity of Christmas a large body of men leaves Preston and marches as far as Prescot before they find the ships gone and their journey wasted.

25th   The defenders of Arundel Castle sally forth from the castle gate but when it is seen that the besiegers have prepared a warm welcome for them despite it being Christmas Day, they 'presently took to their heels as the best remedy to prevent danger'.

26th   Lord Byron issues forth from Chester with 1,000 horse and 300 foot with the intention of besieging Nantwich. Brereton confronts him between Northwich and Middlewich. After a brisk engagement Brereton is driven from the field and the bulk of the survivors retreat on Nantwich.

27th   Waller takes Chichester after a ten-day siege.

28th   The troops from Ireland take Crew House.

        Nathaniel Fienne's efforts to clear his name fail and result in the death penalty for dereliction of duty, but he is later pardoned by Essex.

29th   Parliament orders Sir Thomas Fairfax to relieve Nantwich.

30th   A certificate is made to affirm that one Peter Newton has sworn in Thomas Parnell 'His Majesty's servant to be Prince Charles's post and letter carrier'.

31st An order is issued from the Lords that Peter Burlamachi should present himself within eight days to John Worfield the City Auditor, to account on oath for all the moneys derived from the Inland Letter Office 'and how same have been disposed of'.

Summary of 1643

Counties and even communities were fragmented into small warring factions as the conflict spread like the plague. Local magnates formed and armed detachments the size of which varied according to their wealth and influence, rampaging up and down their own sectors, seizing towns, villages and strong points, burning, looting and raping.

For the sake of an ideal or just plain greed they were prepared to strike hard even against life-long friends if they held contrary views to themselves. Lancaster, Chinnor and a score of other places were given to the flames, while at numerous hedge fights, no less bitter for their small scale, men fought to the death for their convictions and felt they were privileged to do so. At one of these skirmishes the great John Hampden received his death wound, which grieved a large proportion of the country, Royalist and Parliamentarian alike. Noblemen, commoners, merchants, farmers, apprentices in their hundreds were all stricken with the common malady.

While these belligerent county leaders were acting with little regard for the conduct of the war outside their own areas, the armies recruited for use on a national scale by leaders like Hopton, Waller, Manchester and King Charles were intent on their own strategic conception of how to end the war.

Charles I was no great strategist, indeed he had no battle experience prior to the Civil War, but on his day he was capable of a certain clarity of vision and determination to see things through. No doubt aided and guided by his advisers he conceived a plan in which London must fall by a trident attack. Hopton should come straight through from the west, himself from Oxford and Newcastle from the north, all converging on the heart of the Parliamentary faction, crack it like a nut and bring all to a successful conclusion.

It looked well on the planning board and indeed right into midsummer looked well in reality, with Newcastle defeating the Fairfaxes at Adwalton Moor, Gell and Brereton badly mauled at Hopton Heath, a trio of successful engagements in the west by Hopton, Maurice sharply handling Waller at Ripple, and the intaking of Bristol, second city in the kingdom. But the imponderables inherent in such a campaign, particularly of that period, brought the grand plan to nought. Hopton's reinforcements would not venture beyond their county boundaries, and concerned themselves with parochial issues. Newcastle became absorbed with the beguiling prospect of the capture of Hull and sat down around

Sir William Waller, 1643.

it, to the detriment of the grand stategy, leaving the King to carry on single-handed which he was not equipped to do.

In view of the collapse of the grand plan the monarch decided that his best objective was the city of Gloucester, the gateway to southern Wales, and the key to the River Severn. Believing that the governor Edward Massey was prepared to turn his coat, he laid siege to the city but made little progress due to the citizens' determined and unexpected opposition.

Hearing the thunder of Glevum's guns, metaphorically, Parliament sent a relief force from London under Essex which compelled the Royalists to withdraw the siege, only just in time. The King's resolution to force a battle onto Essex on his return to London materialized at Newbury. Certain of a decisive victory, Charles discovered with chagrin that cornered Englishmen, though they are weary, footsore and hungry, react like wolves not lambs, and his mounting casualty list and dwindling powder supplies compelled him to withdraw to Oxford and allow the triumphant Parliamentary army to continue home.

It became apparent, however, to Parliament's guiding genius, John Pym, that he could not win without outside help. The military events of the year had caused the growth of a sizeable peace party in the Commons and even the most partisan of his supporters in the City were groaning under the burden of enforced loans and taxes. It was enough to daunt anyone. Not only was Pym dying of cancer but his right-hand man, John Hampden, was killed at Chalgrove Field, and stretching before him now was the spectre of the destruction of all he had worked for and the ruin of his cause.

Undaunted Pym performed his final service for Parliament, a gesture of defiance to the grim reaper treading on his heels. He negotiated with the Scots to throw the not inconsiderable weight of their army in on the side of Parliament. This military alliance between two races, enemies for centuries, was not brought about wholly by money or political promises. In the Scots' eyes at least the religious aspect was most important and Parliament entered into a Solemn League and Covenant with them to reform the English church. Pym, having performed his last miracle and thereby, as time was to show, ensured victory for his faction, died on 8 December.

Yet in spite of the result of the Battle of Newbury and the collapse of the grand plan it was the King's year. He had regained much of the ground he had lost earlier, half of England at least was Royalist, beside almost the entirety of Wales. Rupert's cavalry was markedly superior to any that had been raised by Parliament. Not only the 'fence-sitters' but many of those not totally committed were wavering in their allegiance and commencing to drift into the Royalist camp.

1644

January

1st   In Arundel Castle the garrison is in a 'necessitous condition'. It is so low on fodder for the horses that the men tear down ivy from the castle walls. The men's rations are cut down to 'two sodden spoonfuls' of wheat a day.

2nd   A petition is sent to Parliament from the Parliamentary Mayor of Lyme Regis advising of Lords Hopton and Paulet's approach and stating the danger in which the town stands.

3rd   An interesting item appears in the Stafford accounts, 'for making the Church clean and perfuming it after the souldiers lying in it. 4/10.'

4th   A body of 500 well-armed soldiers mutiny while marching from the west to join Hopton. Marching to Poole and Lyme they offer their services to Parliament.

5th   Two regiments of London foot set out to replace Harrington's brigade with Waller.

6th   Arundel's governor, Sir Edward Ford, is forced by shortages to accept Waller's surrender terms.

7th   About this date the King's ship *Mayflower* (450 tons) is taken by the Parliament's warship *The Eighth Whelp* (162 tons) and held at Portsmouth.

8th   Three Dutch privateers drive aground a Dunkirk vessel laden with a rich cargo. Rather than surrender to the Dutch the master yields to Waller who personally inspects vessel and cargo.

9th   As soon as Newcastle has withdrawn, 500–600 horse are sent to Nottingham to gather money and provisions. Next day Lord Byron's house at Newstead is looted.

10th   Waller's army is confined to quarters because heavy snowfall makes roads impassable. Byron summons Nantwich.

11th   John Ashburnham writes to the Marquess of Winchester at Basing. He relates that a poor widow whose husband had been a Royalist colonel is now required to contribute to the upkeep of Basing House. He requests that she be excused.

12th   Colonel Thomas Mytton meets a Royalist detachment proceeding to Shrewsbury from Chester. At Ellesmere he totally routs them and captures two high Royalist officers, Sir Nicholas Byron and Sir Richard Willis.

13th   A warrant is issued under the Privy Seal to the Treasurer of the Exchequer to pay £2,000 on account to Thomas Bushell who 'disbursed great sums of money for the clothing of soldiers and other acceptable services'.

14th   Depositions are made by John Stephens and Thomas Pury concerning abuses by Archbishop Laud in the High

Archbishop William Laud,
after Van Dyck, c. 1636.

Commission Court and also by Sir Thomas Trevor concerning the interference of said Archbishop in the Court of Exchequer.

15th   Edmund Cooper is re-elected Mayor of York for the third time, apparently at Newcastle's wish.

16th   Laud answers the first and further articles of impeachment brought by the Commons against him.

17th   The death of Sir William Savile, Governor of York.

18th   Byron vigorously assaults the mud walls of Nantwich and is equally vigorously repelled.

19th   The Scots army under the Earl of Leven crosses the River Tweed.

20th   Examinations take place of several depositions made against Laud concerning illegal proceedings in the High Commission Court.

21st   Fairfax arrives at Manchester where he has arranged a rendezvous with Captain Hodgson with the object of relieving Nantwich.

22nd   On the same day that the Royalist Parliament assembles at Christ Church Hall, Oxford, the Westminster Parliament formally expels forty of their number who were absent with the King.

23rd   Brereton joins Fairfax with a small detachment.

24th   Fairfax moves on Nantwich from the north-west. A detachment of Royalists endeavours to bar his advance in Delamere Forest but is swept aside.

25th   Waller reaches London.

26th   THE BATTLE OF NANTWICH. Hampered by a sudden thaw that makes the fields a mud bath, Fairfax none the less achieves a resounding victory, utterly dispersing Byron's army.

27th   Colonel James Wardlaw is surprisingly replaced by Colonel Gould at Plymouth, causing great controversy until Gould's death the following March.

28th   The Lords at Oxford write in a reproachful letter to Essex that he should have espoused the cause of Parliament instead of answering the King's summons to attend him.

29th   The London regiments, which have been noted as leaving home on 5 January and making a very slow passage because of the inclement weather, reach Petworth this day.

30th   The York Year Book notes that it was ordained that whatsoever money was disbursed in 'making provision for 200 soldiers in [Clifford's] Tower it should be paid for by this chamber' and adds 'provided it could not be obtained anywhere else'.

31st   Reference the previous entry, 'It was ordered that £100 be borrowed for the use of necessary occasions for the Towre.'

February

1st   Sir Edward Dering of Kent, distressed by the Royalists' 'reckless and immoral' politics, resigns his commission and takes advantage of Parliament's offer of pardon, one of a stream of exiles from the county to do so.

2nd   Newcastle's army enters Newcastle upon Tyne and takes command the day before the Scots appear before the town.

3rd   A letter from one John Jones of St John's College, Oxford, to Lord Hopton reminds him that his Lordship has promised exemption of his 'little estate in Cardiganshire' from taxes for the public service.

4th   Certificate from one Joseph Wanscott tells 'all that I can tell about the Bishop [Laud]'.

5th   ACTION AT CORBRIDGE. Langdale beats the Scots away.

6th   A warrant of the King is issued under the Privy Seal to pay £883 12*s* to 'our surgeon in ordinary' Anthony Choqueux for 'his pay in our service in the Army, 8 August 1642–1 February 1644'.

7th   It is ordered by the Council of York that the city plate be pawned to meet £100 of a £500 debt and that the plate should be redeemed as soon as possible.

8th   The Earl of Dover contributes £100 to the King's war chest. A receipt is signed by the Earl of Bath, John Ashburnham the King's Treasurer at Warre, and two others.

9th   The Committee of Sequestering the Estates of Delinquents and Papists meets in London to consider several cases.

10th   The Lord High Admiral writes to both Houses commenting on the insufficiency of the Navy and on the slowness of Parliament's preparations.

11th A letter is sent from Sir William Boswell to Phillip Burlamachi in London, stating that the States of Holland gave audience to Parliament's agent Walter Strickland while their ambassadors were mediating with the King, which he thought in bad taste.

12th The council in Bath agrees to provide 'tenne barrels of powder at their owne cost and chardges for his Maiesties service' at a cost of £50.

13th General muster of the Oxford garrison comprising six regiments in the New Parks.

14th An interesting sidelight is thrown on methods of raising forced loans. The Privy Seal under the Sign Manual to William Wyatt, merchant of Bristol, states that the King has decreed that a loan of £100,000 must be raised by his loving subjects to prosecute the war thrust on him by Parliament. Wyatt's personal contribution is assessed at £20. He is asked to let the High Sheriff have it as soon as possible.

15th The testimony of one Richard Culmer gives him as being 'heretofore minister of Goodnestone, Kent, relative to Archbishop Laud's suspension of him'.

16th A letter is sent from Sir Gilbert Talbot to his brother at Court complaining that his design of raising levies is all laid aside because of the lack of a grant promised by Secretary Nicholas. He asks his brother to look into this matter.

17th Lord Jermyn reports to Rupert from Oxford on the arrival of munitions at Weymouth from France: 190 barrels of powder, 500 muskets, 300 pairs of pistols.

18th The King writes to Rupert drawing his attention to the exposed position of Newark and recommending 'the succouring of the city'.

19th The Committee of Both Kingdoms sits at York House this day for a lengthy and weighty session.

20th The Parliamentarians keep a sharp look out for the Weymouth gun runner for they apprehend him near Dorchester and take £3,000 in gold from him.

21st Were returns to Lyme from London with 200 men.

22nd An ordinance of Parliament appoints a committee to oversee the accounts of all the kingdoms, and stipulates that every member of it must take an oath before the Speaker.

23rd With a force of 300 men, Were marches out of Lyme with the intent of falling on Colyton but after reaching Stidcombe House he is recalled.

24th The Committee writes to Lord Ferdinando Fairfax that it shall in future send despatches by road as the 'seas are inclement and the winds contrary'. It asks if he will also forward the letters intended for the Scots. The Committee also encloses a cypher he might use.

25th A warrant is sent to the Exchequer commanding that William Legge 'master of our armouries', having erected a mill to grind swords at Wolvercot and forges at Gloucester Hall, should be paid on account 'a sum not more than £2,000' for the provision of swords and belts, 'the same to be made to the usual price and agreed pattern' as required.

26th Jermyn again writes: 'We have news of three more ships coming to Weymouth with armes. I hear that in one there is 15,000 arms but I know not the kinds or proportions in the other.'

27th A skirmish occurs this day between a party of the Wareham garrison commanded by Captain Francis Sydenham and a small body of Lord Inchiquin's regiment at Holmebridge.

28th Latham House is besieged by Sir Thomas Fairfax.

29th Newark is besieged by Sir John Meldrum.

March

1st The Committee is in session at Derby House this day where it debates ten items of moment.

2nd The same body writes to the Earl of Denbigh and assures him that there is no need to be anxious for the safety of Gloucester. The Commissary General Behre knows their thoughts on the matter and will diligently carry out his instructions.

3rd An order of the House of Lords is issued that Archbishop Laud should appear before it on Tuesday 12 March 'when the House will proceed on the matter of the first articles of his impeachment'.

4th A party of Parliamentary supporters approaches Colonel Were, who is acting for Waller in the matter of recruiting in Devon, saying that the whole county being in arms they desire the protection of the Lyme Council of War.

5th In consequence of the above it is agreed that Major William Butler should go to Hemyock Castle near Wellington and fetch all those there to Were.

6th Apparently the Royalist gentry learn of this expedition. Scraping up a scratch force they descend on Hemyock and Butler, who has lingered too long, is trapped.

7th Meldrum storms Muskham Bridge, Newark, in a new attempt to take the vital fortress town.

8th Meldrum, whose force numbers 5,000 foot and 13 pieces of ordnance, attempts to carry the city by storm but is repulsed.

9th Were, who has marched on Colyton to divert the Royalists from Hemyock, retires on Stidcombe House upon learning of Butler's ill fortune.

10th The Committee writes to Sir John Gell regarding his request for extra troops for garrison duty. Before the members reach a decision, they ask where it is that he wants to garrison.

11th The Essex Committee of Public Safety writes to Mr Leigh, vicar of Walthamstow, appointing him to preach the sermon at Romford when the high officials gather there to take the Solemn League and Covenant.

12th Messages have passed to and from Lathom House as Lady Derby plays for time. Fairfax at length calls a halt. In the meantime the besiegers have encircled the house with earthworks.

13th The Committee writes to Waller urging him to join Balfour at Petersfield.

14th A petition from Michael Moleyn is sent to the King in which he claims damage to his house and lands at Clapcot to a total of £3,000 due to the depredations of the Wallingford garrison. Although the King promises satisfaction Moleyn is still petitioning in 1661.

15th Colonel Tillier descends the Severn with 1,120 men to Bridgnorth where he joins Rupert with 800 horse.

16th Rupert and his men then march to Wolverhampton where they are joined by 300 more men under Colonel Thomas Leveson.

17th Sir William Waller's Horse moves from Arundel to Chichester.

18th Colonel Assheton reports to Colonel Moore that 'We heard the Prince's forces are joined and fear their objective may be Lancashire by way of Haleford or Liverpool.'

19th Waller, having rejoined his army, sets out for Petersfield to join with Balfour. His three horse regiments proceed from Chichester to Havant.

20th Losing patience the besiegers open fire on Lathom House. Their ordnance includes a 24 pounder, a 15 pounder, three 3 pounders and a mortar.

21st Rupert relieves Newark and after bitter fighting forces Meldrum to surrender with the honours of war. The spoil is 3,000 muskets, 11 brass guns and 2 mortars.

The London Brigade under Major-General Browne sets out from Midhurst to Treyford.

22nd Sir Thomas Aston, with a party of horse, falls on a body of 120 enemy horse and chases them almost back to Poole before a blast of musketry makes him retire.

23rd A commission granted by Lord Denbigh describes him as 'Lord Lieutenant of Warwick, Denbigh, Flint, and Salop, General of all the forces in Warwick, Worcester, Stafford, and Salop'.

24th John Ashburnham has £100 repaid that he had loaned the King.

25th The London Trained Band brigade march forward to meet with Waller's main body at West Meon.

26th At East Meon, 3 miles from the rendezvous, Waller holds a muster for his horse to be followed by a general muster of the army.

27th Royalist Colonel Walter Slingsby attempts to surprise the Londoners encamped around Warnford but is too late.

Waller sets out from Westbury Forest for Alresford. Hopton, knowing his methods well, suspects this move and, once it is confirmed, a headlong race develops which Hopton wins narrowly. Waller's army lies in Lamborough Fields this night.

28th In the afternoon the Parliamentary Council of War meets in Hinton Ampner manor-house and after discussion decides to stand and fight.

29th THE BATTLE OF CHERITON. Decisive Parliament victory. *See separate account on pages 102–3.*

30th Waller declines to pursue the beaten Royalists and moves on Winchester. The town soon surrenders but the castle does not.

31st Forth and Hopton leave Basing House upon which they had retreated after Cheriton and march on Oxford to report to the King.

April

1st Sir Thomas Fairfax is ordered to take as many horse and musketeers as he can mount to join his father's forces and proceed to the Tees, 'there to make the best advantage as you can of all occasions that might present themselves'.

2nd Warrant under the Privy Seal to pay £1,000 on account to Leonard Pinkney, Commissary General, for the victualling of 'our foote army'.

3rd The Committee sends out to various other commanders letters with instructions to give Sir William Waller and Sir William Balfour all available strength to enable them 'to prosecute the victory that God has been pleased to give you'.

4th An interesting warrant is issued to 'pay George Kirke, Gentleman of our Robes, £250 on account for provision of apparel for our royal person'.

5th An order of the Navy Committee that the sum of £3,292 7*s* 8$\frac{1}{2}$*d* should be paid to Sir Walter Erle and the officers of the Ordnance for the first prize brought into Portsmouth.

6th The Committee orders Essex and Manchester to rendezvous at Aylesbury on 19 April.

7th Prince Rupert is at Shrewsbury.

8th Essex writes a complaining note to the House of Lords regarding the comparative treatment meted out to himself and Manchester and their armies.

9th The bombardment against Lathom House is intensified, with chain shot being used.

10th The King reviews his army at Aldbourne and returns to Oxford next day to recess Parliament.

The Battle of Cheriton
29 March 1644

A Royalist officer rode up to the crest of the ridge and checked the lay of the land, no doubt with an impatient oath. The far reaching view that he had hoped for was obscured by rolling banks of fog.

The officer was Lord Hopton of Stratton, commander of the Royalist Army of the West. His professional pride had been shattered by the decimation of his garrison at Alton and he yearned to get even with his friendly enemy Sir William Waller, whose army was all that lay between him and London. Let a victorious Royalist army appear before the capital and there was every reason that the peace party within the government would force the others to sue for terms, so great issues hung on the result of that day's work.

Waller had advanced up the Meon Valley which had given Hopton the opportunity he desired. He advanced to contact from Winchester in an endeavour to bring about a battle he felt sure to win, for had he not beaten Waller twice before? It had been like a game of chess with move and counter-move ending in a race which the Royalists had won.

It was reasonably certain that the battle was inevitable but it was also possible that the Parliamentarians, taking advantage of the fog, might have retired on the capital to fight on more favourable terms, which was why Hopton gazed so earnestly into the thick fog. But when the sun gained strength and caused the fog to rise like a theatrical curtain it revealed that Waller was still there and that he had every intention of fighting.

The corresponding ridge across the valley was bright with the Parliamentary banners; the sun struck gleams of light from the helmets, breast plates and weapons of the lines of armed men. So far, so good, but which valley and which ridges? There is some doubt as to the precise site of the Battle of Cheriton. Gardiner, visiting the site at the beginning of the nineteenth century, discerned a semi-elliptical ridge enclosing a shallow valley, one side resting on Tichborne Down, the other on the hinge of Cheriton Wood. This is now termed the traditional site. But others believe in the site suggested by John Adair, which due to his interpretation of various contemporary accounts places

11th The storming of Selby. Sir John Bellasis, Governor of York, is captured by Lord Fairfax.

12th Unable to follow up his victory at Cheriton, Waller is back at Farnham by this date.

13th A party from the garrison of Lathom House under Lieutenant

it in the large valley to the south. The Royalists he places on Cheriton Wood ridge while Waller's men he sites on the 300-foot contour opposite.

Whatever the reader's opinion may be the account of the battle is as follows. Waller occupied the 'high woody ground', that is to say Cheriton Wood, the ridge of which Hopton in consultation with Lord Forth decided to occupy. At first all went well with the Royalists. A thousand musketeers under Lieutenant-Colonel Appleyard drove the Parliamentary musketeers from the wood and the Royalists lined the ridge. Their scheme was to stand in their positions daring Waller's men to attack. But it did not work out that way. Several young Royalist officers impatient to engage – Slingsby nominates Colonel Sir Henry Bard – charged down into the arena and were cut to pieces by the Parliamentary cavalry.

Encouraged by this success, the Parliamentarians went straight on into the Royalist line. Lord John Stewart's Royalist horse retired after 'only one unhandsome charge'. On the right 1,000 picked horse were sent down by Forth to challenge Haselrig's famous 'Lobsters'. Emerging from a lane in column they had difficulty in forming, and after half an hour's hard fight they were driven off. Almost frantically Forth poured in nearly all the remaining cavalry.

The foot at this point joined in and the arena became a hell's kitchen of powder smoke lit by musket flashes where swords gleamed and fell, men shouted and died, horses neighed and kicked. Within two hours the Royalist cavalry almost ceased to exist. Many of its best officers were dead including Lord John Stewart, the King's nephew and Major-General Sir John Smith, the hero of Edgehill. The Royalist foot on either flank was being gradually pressed inward, and the whole of Hopton's army seemed on the verge of total collapse. By virtue of leadership they fell back in some semblance of order to Tichborne Down. Had Waller continued to advance he would have obliterated them but content with his victory he allowed Hopton and Forth to withdraw on Basing House.

Edward Walker, the King's secretary, in an oft-quoted report said, 'Cheriton was a very doleful beginning into the year 1644 and broke all the measures, and altered the whole scheme of the King's Counsels . . . .'

For a full account of the battle and arguments regarding the site see *Cheriton: The Campaign and the Battle* by John Adair (Roundwood Press, 1973).

Farmer storm the gun emplacements of the besiegers and nail several of the cannon.

14th   Beaminster is accidentally burned by the negligent firing of a musket which set alight the thatch of one John Sargent's house. Some 140 houses are destroyed.

Up to 1,000 Royalist musketeers, under Lieutenant-Colonel Appleyard, routed their Parliamentarian counterparts during the Battle of Cheriton.

The well-equipped pikeman.

15th   The damage to the besiegers' cannon must have only been minor for this day several test shots are fired against Lathom House, as well as a number of discharges from a borrowed mortar.

16th   Newcastle's army enters York.

17th   The Queen's time being nigh, the King, fearing for her safety, sends her to Exeter to give birth.

Essex's army is at Henley.

18th   Sir Thomas Soame and nine others named, who have offered £50 each so that the artillery train might march the next day, are requested to pay the money to Sir Walter Erle, Lieutenant of the Ordnance.

19th   The Committee advises Manchester to make haste to York to 'do what he might for the best of the Service' because Rupert's army is larger than anticipated.

20th   Were's regiment holds Stedcombe House as an advanced post. Later they evacuate it with speed but retreat on Lyme with small loss.

21st   Leven and Fairfax's armies take up their siege positions around York which takes three days.

22nd   Newcastle gets the bulk of his horse out of York, retaining only about 300 to supplement the garrison of 4,500 foot.

23rd   The Countess of Derby is summoned to surrender Lathom House, but with a theatrical gesture she refuses.

24th   Sir Edward Nicholas sends the following intelligence to Forth: 'Some of Manchester's men are drawing into Lincolnshire and others are at Cambridge. Cromwell's forces are at Bedford and Newport Pagnell. I have heard nothing of Waller and no further levies are yet come to Aylesbury.'

25th   Rupert is summoned to attend the King until 5 May.

26th   The Committee writes to Waller informing him that Browne is to command the London Brigade which is to rendezvous with him at Aylesbury.

27th   The committee writes to the Earl of Warwick, acknowledging the value of Lyme as a base and its appreciation of the straits the town is in. The members are informed that the Governor of Poole has sent three ships to relieve it. If they are not dispatched Warwick is to expedite them.

28th   A proclamation is issued for the raising of Dover's and Littleton's auxiliaries.

29th   York Council orders that, 'there shall be 4,000 soldiers that shall have 4*d* a day paid for their diete' and that the money should be delivered to the various housekeepers where the men are billeted.

30th   On or about this day three appointments are made to the College of Heralds: Sir Henry St George to be Garter, Sir Edward Walker to be Norroy, William Dugdale to be Chester Herald.

May

1st   The Queen reaches Exeter where she intends to stay until she has given birth.

At Lyme, Rushworth relates, 'The enemy gave us a thundering alarum and commences to make their Fort Royal against Captain Davey's Fort.'

2nd   The York Siege states that seven windmills on Heweth Moor were burned by the Royalists. Robert Douglas, Leven's pastor, comments from Psalm 83, 'Fill their faces with shame, O Lord.'

3rd   Drake's Siege Diary of Lyme notes: 'All this day the enemy laid quiet – the weather being turbulent.'

4th   The two Houses write a congratulatory letter to the Earl of Leven, the Scots' commander, on his 'diligent pursuit' of Newcastle.

5th   The strong fort of Buttercram (Buttercoms, Buttercrambe) is taken by the Parliament forces before York.

6th   Royalists storm Lyme Regis defences in several places with vigour but are repulsed with equal vigour. Among the notable Royalist dead are Captain Paulet, kin to the Marquess of Winchester, and Captain Francis Blewett.

7th   Maurice asks for a truce to bury the dead and in particular the corpse of Blewett which is handed over 'encoffined and enshrouded'.

8th   Newcastle writes a stinging letter to Leven pointing out the breach of military etiquette involved when an army surrounds a city and raises batteries without a formal invitation to surrender.

9th   The Lords and Commons announce their plan of campaign.

Some 4,200 men are to join Waller to capture Reading. A similar number is to join Essex to take Oxford.

10th   In Lyme the ship *Mayflower*, which arrived two days previously, offloads as much powder and provisions as she can safely spare.

11th   A squadron of ships under the joint command of Captains Jordan and Mann arrives at Lyme carrying supplies and 240 men commanded by a Major Catoforch.

12th   Captain Jones (sometimes Joyce), master of the *Ann and Joyce*, disembarks a personal representative of Waller to observe at first hand the conditions in Lyme. The enemy launches fire balls into the town.

13th   A demi-cannon is unloaded from the *Mayflower* to allow the garrison to reply better to the enemy's bombardment.

14th   In Lyme all is quiet. So the suspicious garrison sends out a raiding party to probe the quarter where they have deduced the enemy is weakest. They discover their mistake and retire in haste.
    The Earl of Essex marches from Beaconsfield launching the 'Oxford Campaign'.

15th   Yet another Parliamentary ship arrives at Lyme. It is commanded by Captain Milne and has come from Portsmouth with army Captain Chase and '400 foote of Sir Arthur Hesilriges'.

16th   In response to the Parliamentary leaders' heart cry to stop Rupert at either Stockport or Warrington the Lancashire Committee replies, 'We profess willingness to send troops but if the older soldiers are withdrawn for this service, the new recruits are not to be trusted.'

17th   The besiegers of Lyme concentrate their fire on the Cobb, an artificial harbour, causing damage to the shipping therein.

18th   Reading is abandoned by the Royalists to swell the ranks of the Oxford army.

19th   Reading is occupied by the Parliamentarians. Essex and Waller meet there for a personal consultation.

20th   Drake's Siege Diary notes: 'The enemy busy at the building of their West Fort and breastworks round and about.'

21st   Drake again: 'The enemy raise a new battery with cannon baskets (gabions) at the very edge of the cliff next the Cobb.'

22nd A surprise attack on the Cobb with incendiaries almost destroys the ability of Lyme to resist.

23rd The Countess of Derby is summoned again to surrender Lathom House and surrender to the mercy of Parliament. She replies, 'The mercies of the wicked are cruel.'

24th Lieutenant-Colonel Robert Blake (later Admiral) with other Lyme leaders row out to the flagship *James* for a conference with Lord High Admiral Warwick, who arrived the day before with eight ships.

25th Lyme is further heartened by an announcement that the seamen of the fleet have declared their willingness to go on short rations to enable the town to be provisioned.

    Rupert storms Stockport. Abingdon is abandoned by Royalists.

26th Essex occupies Abingdon. The King, fearful for the safety of Bristol, sends Hopton to secure it.

27th Rupert storms Bolton and massacres the defenders.

28th Essex crosses the Thames at Sandford and camps at Islip.

29th Sir Richard Crane, commander of Prince Rupert's Lifeguard, enters Lathom House in triumph, the besiegers having withdrawn on 25 May.

30th Rupert, reinforced by Goring and Lucas with 5,000 horse and 800 foot, now commands a sizeable army of 7,000 horse and almost as many foot.

31st Eight Parliamentary ships appear off Portland Point. Lyme is agog with anticipation hoping they bring news of the expected relief.

June

1st Waller secures the passage of the Thames at Newbridge.

2nd The Dutch ambassadors wait upon Essex, urging him to open direct negotiations with the King. Essex refuses brusquely and intimates they should apply to Parliament not himself.

3rd The Earl of Manchester's army arrives to take up its siege position around York and in doing so complete the encirclement. In order to avoid being trapped by the forces of Essex and Waller the King leaves Oxford.

4th The King reaches Bourton-on-the-Water.

5th   Fairfax raises a battery on Lamel Hill, the hill near the Walmgate Bar in York.

6th–12th   The King is in quarters at Worcester.

6th   Essex and Waller, in pursuit of the King, confer at Chipping Norton.

7th   Essex departs for the West Country and Waller continues to shadow the King.

     Rupert attacks Liverpool. The garrison under Colonel Moore resists strongly.

     Leven attacks three Royalist gun emplacements south-west of York and succeeds in capturing two of them.

8th   The Earl of Warwick's letter setting forth the condition of Lyme is received in London. It is voted that he should have a letter of thanks and that £1,000 should be given to the town from Lord Paulet's estates.

9th   Sudeley Castle, seat of Lord Chandos, surrenders to Waller.

     Parley negotiations continuing until 15 June commence at York.

10th   Parliament receives a letter from Edward and Thomas Ceeley (the latter the mayor) stating that unless Lyme is speedily relieved it will be lost.

11th   The Commons writes to Essex: 'It is most convenient for Sir W. Waller to go into the West to relieve Lyme.' Essex ignores this letter and marches on.

12th   Warwick again writes to Parliament regarding the state of Lyme. 'The enemy continues his siege bringing his approaches daily nearer the town.' Essex meanwhile reaches Blandford with the relief. This makes Maurice's position untenable and he commences to withdraw by degrees.

13th   The King is in quarters at Tickenhill until 15 June. At this time he writes his famous apocryphal letter to Rupert: 'If York be lost I shall esteem by crown little less . . . .'

14th–17th   Waller is in quarters at Stourbridge.

15th   Maurice is totally withdrawn from Lyme Regis by this date.

16th   The Parlimentary forces fire a mine under St Mary's Tower, York. A premature attack by Manchester's men on King's Manor is repulsed with loss.

The ruins of Sudeley Castle, Gloucestershire. After surrendering the castle was slighted by the Parliamentarians.

At Exeter the Queen gives birth to a daughter, Princess Henrietta.

17th   Four burgesses come to Essex to treat for terms of surrender for Weymouth and Melcombe Regis but their terms are too exacting and after negotiations they agree to more acceptable conditions.

18th   The Royalist foot from Oxford join the King at Witney.

The Royalist garrisons at Weymouth and Melcombe march out.

19th   Warwick writes to Parliament with the suggestion that several committees might be set up in Dorset to promote tighter control of the county.

20th   Waller, having lost contact with the King, arrives at Gloucester.

.21st   The Royalist army rendezvous near Woodstock.

22nd–26th   The King is in quarters at Buckingham.

23rd   All Devon is apprehensive of a Parliamentary attack. On 19 June Maurice writes to Dartmouth warning it to be on the alert. Sir John Berkeley reinforces this warning this day and exhorts Colonel Seymour to reinforce the garrison.

24th   Major-General Browne leaves London this day with 4,500 men.

25th   By order of the Grand Committee of the Association Counties the monies raised from eleven hundreds of south Devon were to be used by the armies besieging Devon. There was therefore little left for financing garrisons.

26th   Rupert and his relief force reach Skipton Castle.

27th   Waller, having force marched from Gloucester, quarters at Hanwell near Banbury.

28th   The King at Brackley hears of this and turns back to Banbury.

29th   THE BATTLE OF CROPREDY BRIDGE. The King brushes Waller aside. *See separate acount on pages 114–15.*

30th   The Royalist relief force under Rupert reaches the vicinity of Knaresborough. The Parliamentary and Scots armies raise the siege of York and offer battle at Marston Moor.

July

1st   Rupert's forces reach York but do not enter the city. They camp in the Skelton/Clifton area.

2nd   THE BATTLE OF MARSTON MOOR. Fairfax and Cromwell decisively defeat Rupert and the north is lost to the King. *See separate account on pages 118–19.*

3rd   Royalist leaders flee from the scene of carnage, Newcastle to Scarborough and Rupert to Richmond. York is left to its fate under the command of Sir Thomas Glemham.

        The King quarters at Evesham en route to Exeter.

4th   The Navy Committee orders that the ketch *Charles* commanded by one John Seignoir should take on a specified quantity of match, shot and powder to be delivered to the Earl of Warwick at Weymouth, for the use of Essex's army.

5th   After consultation with the governor and engineers at Weymouth Warwick forwards his recommendation for making the town defensible.

6th   A procrastinating letter is sent from The Committee to Waller saying it has taken note of his numerous letters requesting arms and saddles. The letter also states rather mysteriously that The Committee will look into the matter of the £5,000 and Mr Trenchard.

7th   Waller writes his famous letter to The Committee regarding the mutinous nature of Browne's troops: 'Such men are fit only for a gallows now and a hell hereafter.'

8th   Blake takes Taunton, which in his hands 'became a sharp thorn in the side of that populous countryside'.

        Rupert reaches Hornby Castle with the remnants of his army.

9th   An erroneous report reaches Oxford that Rupert is the victor of Marston Moor, that Manchester has been slain, and that both Leslie and Sir Thomas Fairfax are captives. A day of rejoicing is proclaimed, bonfires blaze and ale flows.

10th   Essex informs Parliament that Lord Robartes is still at Barnstaple with three foot regiments and two of horse.

11th   Colonel Richard Norton invests Basing House with a force of 2,000 men with the intention of starving them out as Waller's storming attempts failed so dismally.

12th   The Royal army continues its march westward. This night the King receives Rupert's dispatch regarding Marston Moor.

The Battle of Cropredy Bridge
29 June 1644

After a fruitless march to Gloucester in search of the elusive King, Waller turned about and by 28 June was at Hanwell near Banbury. The King, evidently tired of manoeuvring, upon hearing of this retraced his tracks from Brackley and was in the vicinity of Banbury by the same date.

Waller was drawn up at the foot of Crouch Hill so the King took up his position at Grimsbury Hill. It might seem that the monarch did not care to assault the very strong position Waller had found for himself so that at about 8 a.m. on the 29th he removed himself and marched northward for Daventry. Waller saw him depart and took up the chase again, moving north on a parallel course. The Parliamentary army had a numerical supriority, for while both sides had approximately 5,000 horse, Waller had over 4,000 foot to the King's 3,500. At the village of Cropredy a bridge spans the River Cherwell. Further north the river bends to the right and is crossed again by Hays Bridge. In addition a mile south of Cropredy is a ford at Slat Mill. In order to attack the King it was necessary for Waller to cross the Cherwell. The King, therefore, sent a party to block the bridge at Cropredy. Once this had been achieved an alarm was raised that 300 Parliamentary horse had appeared from the north en route to join Waller.

The King ordered his advanced guard forward to seize Hays Bridge before the newcomers could seal his advance route off, requiring him to stand at bay. This unit accelerated away from the main body, which made as much haste as possible. As no one had bothered to notify the rear guard of these circumstances a gap of about $1^1/_2$ miles was opened up. Thus the Royalist army was sundered into three parts, each vulnerable to attack. This did not escape the notice of the vigilant Waller. His first move was to cross the Cherwell at Cropredy and cut off the rear guard. Lieutenant-General John Middleton moved against the bridge with two regiments of horse and nine companies of foot while Waller himself with about 1,000 men crossed the Cherwell at Slat Mill.

13th *Mercurius Civicus* provides a curious sidelight (perhaps slanderous) on the type of officer most successful as a tax gatherer, describing the Governor of Bath as 'one Ridgely that had escaped from Newgate Prison'.

14th Essex writes to Sydenham from Taunton praising him for his good works in forestalling Lieutenant-Colonel O'Brien's attempt in Dorchester.

15th Essex writes this day thanking The Committee for the £20,000

Middleton crossed the bridge without trouble and harried the rear of the main body as far as Hays Bridge. Northampton, reacting quickly, swung his brigade about and faced Waller whom he drove helter-skelter back again over the ford.

Cleveland, equally quick-witted, charged and drove part of Middleton's horse and his foot into disorder. He then formed his men up to make a stand by the 'Wardington Ash' where the King had dined shortly before.

By this time Charles, with the main body, had realized what was afoot and detached Sir Bernard Stuart and the Lifeguard to succour Cleveland. Accordingly he charged and drove off those of Middleton's horse threatening the earl, who fell back on the disordered and milling remains of the Parliamentary force that had issued across the bridge.

They were charged again by Cleveland and Willmott and were thrown back to the bridge, while the artillery situated in the fields east of the bridge was captured by the Royalists along with Colonel Wemyss, its commander. Waller left his dragoons and foot to hold the ford and the bridge while he retired to Bourton Hill. The King had by now marched the main body back and took up a position at Williamscote facing the Parliamentarians. It was now about 3 p.m. with plenty of daylight left to reach a definite conclusion. As Waller made no move Charles launched an attack on both bridge and ford. At the former a stout defence by the Tower Hamlets and Kentish regiments probably saved the day for Waller.

The King sent his usual offer of grace and pardon which Waller declined, saying he had no authority to treat. There was no further action although the two armies faced each other for the whole of the following day. Then the Royalists, learning that Waller's reinforcements under Major-General Browne were at Buckingham and fearing a juncture between the two, marched off westward to Evesham. Waller's men 'being in no very good temper' at the repulse and subsequent inaction were in a very mutinous condition and drifted off regiment by regiment until Waller abandoned the remainder at Abingdon and reached London on 26 July. Clarendon, the historian, commented 'that his defeat at Cropredy was much greater than it appeared to be . . . it even broke the heart of his army'.

it has sent him and assures its members that his army will give a good account of itself.

16th   York surrenders inevitably. Parliamentary forces march in and hold a thanksgiving service in the Minster. The Fairfaxes hold the men on a tight rein.

17th   Woodhouse surrenders to Sir Francis Doddington.

18th   The Parliamentary army marches out of York leaving a garrison commanded by Lord Fairfax.

Prince Rupert by G. Honthorst, c. 1641.

The Battle of Marston Moor, *July 1644, by James Ward.*

19th   The Committee writes to Colonel Stapeley thanking him for his offer of assistance for the forces before Basing House which was conveyed to them by the Hampshire Committee. It gratefully accepts his offer.

20th   The Bath Committee provides 'straw for sick and maymed soldiers' and 'milk and earthenware pans for Prince Rupert's soldiers' according to the minute books.

21st   The Princess Henrietta is baptized in Exeter Cathedral with great state and ceremony.

22nd   Norton returns from Cropredy Bridge to resume command at Basing House from Colonel Herbert Morley.

23rd   Essex reaches Tavistock after relieving Lyme Regis.

24th   A butt of sack and a tunn of French wine is presented by the City of York to Lord Fairfax in appreciation of the great love and affection he has shown the city.

25th   Rupert reaches Chester and makes Byron governor.
        Essex enters Cornwall intent on relieving Plymouth. The King, who is giving chase, reaches Exeter.

The Battle of Marston Moor
2 July 1644

On 1 July 1644, hearing of the approach of Prince Rupert's relief force, the triumvirate of lords, Leven, Fairfax and Manchester, withdrew their hosts from around York and drew them up in battle array to bar Rupert's approach. But the Prince was not to be drawn in this manner; he sent a diversionary force to show itself and lull the enemy into believing it was his advance guard. Meanwhile, he took his army north, crossed the enemy's bridge of boats at Poppleton and approached the city from this direction. He did not enter it but sent a letter to Newcastle ordering him to parade his troops for battle next day.

Newcastle, while professing himself 'made of nothing but thankfulness and obedience to your Highness's commands', was horrified, as was his chief-of-staff, Lord Eythin. All they wanted was to rest their garrison and citizens after a harrowing siege and wait for the enemy to disperse.

This placid attitude was not Rupert's way at all and next day his men assembled themselves on Marston Moor. The allied armies of Leven, Fairfax and Manchester were in full retreat for Tadcaster at that time but learning that Rupert wanted to fight they returned with all speed. The day was spent in marshalling the armies on both sides. Newcastle at last, bowing to the inevitable, brought out his troops and appeared very late. The Royalist strength is calculated to have been 17,500 men while the allies might have had 27,000. It was the greatest battle ever fought on British soil. The Royalists having arrived first had the pick of the ground and were drawn up on moorland. The allies on the other hand were standing in rye fields. Between them was a deep ditch, which would be bound to cause havoc among the cavalry which would charge first.

At 4 p.m. neither side had made a move. The allies with all their units now assembled began contemplating an attack themselves instead of waiting for Rupert. At 7 p.m. the Royalist commanders decided that there would be no action that day and had gone to the rear. While their army stood in their ranks the smoke of cooking fires rose as they cooked their evening meal. Cavalrymen dismounted and loosened their girths. This was the moment the Parliamentary commanders had awaited. A cannon barked; it was the signal for the advance. The surprise gave the horse the chance to cross the ditch without encountering a blast of musketry. Everywhere the Royalists were dressing their ranks, their supper forgotten. Sir Thomas Fairfax operating on the right wing could not develop the full momentum of his charge by reason of 'the whins [furze] and ditches which we had to cross over to reach the enemy'. He was opposed to George Goring 'who perceiving the disorder they were in, charged and routed them'. Colonel John Lambert who might have seconded him could not get to him 'but charged somewhere else'.

Meanwhile on the left wing Cromwell had charged down on Byron and dispersed him as thoroughly as Goring had Fairfax. Rupert coming up saw the flying ranks and swore roundly at them. More afraid of the Prince than Cromwell they reformed and charged again.

The Ironsides and Rupert's men were so evenly matched that they hacked at each other until they barely had strength enough to lift their swords. At this critical moment the Scots cavalry with their lances and light horses under the command of David Leslie charged home on the flank. They went through the wearied Cavaliers like a knife through butter. Thus both wings of horse were temporarily absent. Meanwhile both infantry centres were at push of pike and many soldiers decided it was time to leave the field.

Meanwhile two Scottish regiments, the Earl of Lindsay's and Lord Maitland's, stood like stone walls and repelled all comers, gaining much honour. Sir Thomas Fairfax having removed his sash and field sign rode through the Royalist army unobserved and, meeting up with Cromwell, supplied him with accurate information on the situation. With his disciplined regiments well in hand, Cromwell rode round Wilstrop Wood and mopped up Goring's cavalry which, being less well-disciplined, were looting Fairfax's baggage train, while others had taken themselves off.

Newcastle's White Coats, which they had sworn to dye red with the enemy's blood, were still there, and still fighting. With their right flank in the air they had fallen back to White Sike Close where they were assaulted on all sides and are by legend credited with dying to a man.

It was the most devastating defeat of the Civil War for, with one stroke, the rash, overrated Rupert had lost the north permanently for his uncle. Next day the captured Sir Charles Lucas could only weep as he went about the field viewing the 4,150 Royalist dead. 'Alas for King Charles', he cried, 'Unhappy King Charles.' Unhappy indeed for in his famous letter to Rupert the monarch had written: 'If York be lost, I shall esteem my crown little less.'

For a full account of the battle see *Marston Moor 1644. The Campaign and the Battle* by Brigadier Peter Young. For an account of the siege of York see *The Great and Close Siege of York 1644* by Peter Wenham. Both published by the Roundwood Press.

26th Waller reaches London after Cropredy Bridge.

27th The King travels 7 miles from Exeter to Crediton to review the Royal army.

28th Essex reaches Bodmin.

29th The Committee writes to the Essex Committee to thank its members for their forwardness in furnishing their proportion of men on the new ordinance and states that other counties would be advised that their backwardness would not be excused.

30th Vicars relates that a report of Essex's progress towards Plymouth has been received and that Grenville's force numbered 3,000.

August

1st Sir Thomas Fairfax is requested to return the fifty barrels of gunpowder he borrowed from Hull.

2nd Essex receives the unwelcome news that the Royalist army has reached Launceston, less than 20 miles distant.

3rd Essex writes to The Committee that three armies, those of the King, Hopton and Maurice, are approaching from the east with another (Grenville's) coming from the west.

4th Colonel Edward Massey averts an uproar between city and garrison when Major Hammond of Massey's horse and Major Grey of Stamford's regiment quarrel and come to blows, resulting in the death of the former. With consummate diplomacy he prevents the men of both sides taking the quarrel upon themselves.

5th Gage's attempt on Abingdon.

6th Manchester is diverted from his march on Lincoln by the prospect of taking both Sheffield and Welbeck.

7th Welbeck House surrenders to Manchester. He takes 350 muskets, 11 pieces of ordnance and 20 barrels of powder from the garrison.

8th Lord Willmott, Lieutenant-General of Horse, 'at this time the second officer of the Army', is arrested on a charge of treason and sent to Exeter under guard.

9th The Committee informs Essex that a party of 2,000 horse will be sent to his aid but that is the full extent of its ability to help.

10th   Sir John Meldrum is ordered to clear Yorkshire of any remnants
of Rupert's army.

Wareham surrenders on terms to Sir Anthony Ashley Cooper
and Sir John Middleton.

11th   The King waits for Grenville's force to come up before
proceeding against Essex. This day Grenville with 2,400 men
drives the Parliamentary horse out of Bodmin and takes
Respryn Bridge, thus keeping open his lines of communication
with the King.

12th   The Committee sends letters to the Parliamentary commanders
of Weymouth, Lyme and Dorchester requesting that any men
they can spare should be sent to Essex's aid.

13th   Goring and Astley reconnoitre the east bank of the River Fowey.

14th   As a result of the previous day's reconnaisance the Royalists
post 200 men and a number of guns in Polruan Fort at the
mouth of the Fowey.

15th   Some of the fugitive northern Royalists attempt to reach
Lathom House but encounter the Parliamentarian Colonel
Dodding who disperses them and captures Lord Ogleby and
Colonel Huddlestone near Walton.

16th   Sir John Meldrum, reinforced by Dodding, reaches Preston.

17th   The King from his headquarters at Boconnoc personally
reconnoitres the southern end of Essex's line.

18th   Goring and the other Royalists, numbering about 2,700,
plunder the vicinity of Lytham and Kirkham. Meldrum draws
up his forces on Penwortham Moor intending to give battle.

19th   Failing to contact the Royalists, Meldrum marches south-west
and intercepts them at Ormskirk. A brisk charge disperses
them and they are 'quite scattered'.

20th   The Committee for Huntingdon is praised by The Committee
that its forces are armed, equipped and ready to move out
before anyone else. It is instructed to contact Manchester for
orders.

21st   THE BATTLE OF BEACON HILL. This commenced at 7 a.m. on
a foggy morning. The precipitate fall of Restormel Castle
outflanks the Parliamentary lines resulting in the taking of the
strong points on Druids and Beacon hills.

22nd   Cambridge is required to pay the forces at Aylesbury which are to march on Abingdon under Lieutenant-Colonel Sadler.

23rd   The Committee writes to Middleton thanking him for the good services he has rendered at Wareham against Sir Francis Doddington and others.

24th   The Committee for Kent is chided for being so tardy in sending men to reinforce Waller in his march to the west.

25th   The commanders of all the Warwickshire troops are instructed to join the Parliamentary troops besieging Banbury.

26th   Goring, with 2,000 horse, and Sir Thomas Bassett, with 1,000 foot, march to St Blazey to prevent supplies reaching the Parliamentary army which is by now short of provisions and ammunition.

27th   This day Rupert is at Bristol.

28th   Major-General Browne notifies The Committee that his commanders have been to him this day requiring match and bullet as they have none. He begs that a supply will be sent speedily.

29th   General Middleton, with reinforcements for Essex, has progressed no further than Tiverton owing to Royalist attacks, virtually sealing the fate of Essex's army.

30th   Two Parliamentary deserters are captured. They state that their cavalry is planning to cut its way out of the closing trap, while the foot are falling back on Fowey.

31st   About 3 a.m. this day the Parliamentary cavalry is led by the indomitable Balfour out of Lostwithiel, through the fog up the Liskeard road, in an attempt to escape the Royalist encirclement. The musketeer outpost designed to give warning of such an attempt fails and the 2,000-strong force makes good its escape to Plymouth.

   THE BATTLE OF CASTLE DORE, 31 August/1 September. The Royalist army advances at 8 a.m. and marching westward finds everywhere signs of a hasty and disorderly retreat. The horse attacks driving all before it but eventually has to await the foot which arrives at 2 p.m. At 4 p.m. the Parliamentarians counter-attack and are successful, initially. Two hours later they attack again in strength to gain the ramparts of Castle Dore, an Iron Age fort, which they succeed in doing.

September

1st   The messengers find Essex and Robartes about to desert the army and leave it to its fate. After they have embarked in a fishing boat Skippon calls a Council of War determined to cut his way out, but the other officers believe that morale has deteriorated so far that this is impracticable and they call a parley.

     THE BATTLE OF TIPPERMUIR, SCOTLAND. Lord Elgin is defeated by Montrose.

2nd   The Parliamentary foot, numbering 6,000, is surrendered on terms. The regiment keeps its colours and the officers their swords but despite the Royalist escort, it is stripped and looted by the Cornish in contravention of the terms, which at this time of the year and with the bad weather virtually signs the death warrant of 4,000 men.

3rd   Lord Mayor Edmund Cooper of York is deposed and Thomas Hoyle established in his place. (In January 1650 this same Hoyle was to commit suicide at his Westminster home.)

4th   Upon the arrival of the 36-pound mortars and their use at Basing House, Colonel Richard Norton sends in a demand for surrender which is met with a defiant reply.

5th   This day the retreating Parliamentary horse which escaped from Lostwithiel leave Crediton hotly pursued.

6th   Waller informs The Committee that he has ordered 400 men from the Isle of Wight and the Sussex forces to rendezvous with him at Salisbury.

7th   The 500 Irish from Wareham are to be billeted by Colonel William Jephson at Hayling Island. Ships are to be chartered to convey them back to Ireland, and they are to receive one month's pay according to the terms of surrender.

8th   Manchester moves south on hearing of the disaster of Lostwithiel and arrives at Huntingdon this day.

9th   In response to a desperate message from Basing House, Colonel Henry Gage forms a scratch relief force and taking twelve barrels of powder on pack animals sets out from Oxford on his hazardous venture.

10th   Colonel Were, one of the gallant heroes of the siege of Lyme, is accused by Essex of dereliction of duty: he 'is in good part responsible for Lostwithiel'. Essex is seeking a scapegoat having already endeavoured to implicate Middleton.

11th   The King moves tardily towards London. He summons Plymouth this day, perhaps believing the disaster of Lostwithiel will have demoralized the garrison. It has not and the Royalists move on, leaving Sir Richard Grenville to conduct the siege.

    Gage, by strategem, reaches Basing House and attacking across Chineham Down on a foggy morning cuts his way through the besiegers and succours the house.

12th   Under cover of darkness and fog Gage withdraws silently from Basing.

13th   THE BATTLE OF ABERDEEN. Balfour of Burleigh is defeated by Montrose.

14th   Gage and his men arrive safely at Oxford having swum their horses across the Kennet and Thames to avoid the waiting Parliamentary detachments.

Restormel Castle at Lostwithiel. The surrender of the castle by the Parliamentarian Colonel Were was a key element in the Royalist success which forced the surrender of 6,000 Parliamentarian troops in Cornwall in September 1644.

15th   Waller informs The Committee that he has thrown his train of artillery into Poole.

16th   Essex again storms against Were; 'He played the Judas and is revolted', and again refers to the 'Renegade Were'. But it might appear that the colonel was not without influence in high places as no one seemed eager to proceed against him.

17th   The Governors of Poole, Wareham and Weymouth are ordered to prepare themselves to stand at instant readiness and to state their shortages.

18th   Waller and Haselrig inform The Committee that Colonel John Birch has been sent to Plymouth with instructions to raise the siege and to return to Weymouth when this is done.

19th   Major-General Sir Arthur Aston, Governor of Oxford, is thrown from his horse while showing off its paces to the ladies at Bullington Green. He badly crushes his leg.

20th   Weymouth's fortifications are reported to be progressing and the citadel is almost complete.

21st   Waller, having pushed foot into Weymouth, Lyme and Poole, this day stations his horse at Shaftesbury.

22nd   Waller complains to the House that he has no money. 'One of my majors has been fain to borrow sixpence for the shoeing of his horse', and ends on a sarcastic note, 'Indeed we are a gallant forlorn hope.'

23rd   The King is at Chard where he stays a week to rest his men and recruit more.

24th   Dalbier writes to Essex that the enemy at Chard has twenty pieces of ordnance but few carts and carriages. They give out that they mean to siege Lyme but having sent 300 men to plunder Axminster it does not seem likely this is their intention.

25th   A report comes in from country sources averring that the King intends to march over Blackdown. The observers point out that it is the quickest route to Taunton or Bridgwater.

26th   The Committee writes: 'We have once before written by order of the House of Commons requiring Colonel Were to be sent up.' Such is the reluctance to proceed against this officer, that a year later he is still under arrest without action taken.

27th A tragedy occurs at Oxford: a Hampshire man, Lieutenant-Colonel Arthur Swayne, is killed 'while teaching his boye the use of armes'. Not knowing the musket was loaded he told the lad to aim at him with fatal results.

28th A party of Sydenham's horse intercepts Sir Edward Waldegrave's regiment en route to Bridport and after a brisk skirmish take forty horses.

29th An order is made for the delivery to Poole and Brownsea Castle of four pieces of ordnance each, in case the King should attempt something against these places when he does decide to move.

30th The King sets out from Chard with an army said to number about 5,500 foot and 4,000 horse. He dines with Lord Paulet at Hinton St George and quarters at South Perrot.

October

1st The King quarters at Maiden Newton, staying at the house of the Reverend Matthew Newton.

2nd The Royalist army reaches Sherborne. By this date Manchester has reached Reading.

3rd *Mercurius Aulicus* states that the troops in Shaftesbury under Middleton and Balfour 'much oppress the country' levying maintenance money.

4th In a report to The Committee Essex names Were's regiment as one of those whose cowardice contributed to the catastrophe of Lostwithiel – 'His men (or rather sheep) flung away their armes and ran away'.

5th At a Royalist Council of War the King makes it obvious that his plans for the immediate future do not involve an attack on London, but merely involve the relief of several beleaguered garrisons. It is agreed that in the face of the three Parliamentary armies now gathering another battle will have to be risked. Rupert and Hopton leave for Bristol to attempt diversionary tactics.

6th Sir Richard Grenville is granted £1,100 by the Devon Commissioners and the right to collect a further £6,000 in arrears to promote the siege of Plymouth.

7th The King is at Sherborne staying at Lord Bristol's residence.

8th The Royalist army moves out and the King lodges that night at Lord Cork's house at Stalbridge.

9th   Maurice's army is at Sturminster Newton and the King's horse at Durweston.

10th   The Royalist army rendezvous at Durweston Down and the Court at Bryanston, the house of Mrs Rogers, widow of Richard Rogers MP.

11th   Intelligence reaches the King that Waller with only 1,500 men is quartered near Amesbury.

12th   Lord Cleveland and Sir Bernard Astley advance from Blandford to Dorchester.

13th   Cleveland and Astley reach the Isle of Portland and prepare to put provision in Portland Castle.

14th   Cleveland and Astley leave the island, where Sir William Hasting is now governor, having done all things necessary to prolong occupation of the place.

15th   At last the King advances to Salisbury, occupying it on a 'wet, cold and windy day'.
         Waller is at Andover.

16th   The Governor of Poole advertises that he has attacked a detachment of the Queen's horse near Blandford, killing 16 and taking 40.

17th   Manchester, with 4,000 foot and 3,500 horse, reaches Basingstoke.

18th   Waller stands near Andover in an attempt to delay the Royalists reaching Basing House before Manchester and Essex's reorganized army can rendezvous. In the afternoon Goring, with the Royalist advance force, drives him back.

19th   About this date Cooper, with a force of 1,500 horse and foot, takes the field to prevent Dyve from fortifying certain strategic points in the neighbourhood.

20th   Essex's force consisting of 3,000 foot commanded by Skippon reaches Alton.
         The King arrives at Whitchurch.
         Newcastle upon Tyne falls to the Scots.

21st   The King reaches Kingsclere.

22nd   Thwarted in his intent to relieve Basing House the King strikes north to relieve another of his objectives – Donnington Castle. He reaches Red Heath near Newbury and establishes his

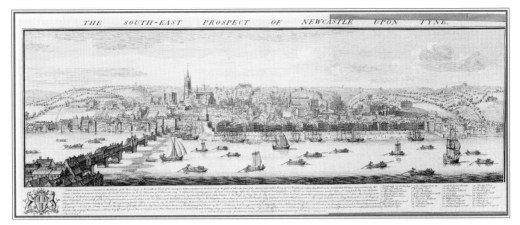

Newcastle upon Tyne fell to the Scots on 20 October 1644. The Scottish Parliamentarians are said to have used mines to break down the city walls.

headquarters in the town. He sends the Earl of Northampton with 800 horse to relieve Banbury Castle.

23rd   Sir Hugh Cholmley 'hovering about Colyton, Beaminster and Axminster drives off a multitude of cattle' but is intercepted by Colonel Seeley of Lyme who in a running fight drives off the raiders, wounds Cholmley and recaptures the cattle.

24th   The Dorset Committee complains about the outrages committed in the county by the 'French Papists of the Queen's Regiment'.

25th   The united Parliamentary armies of Essex, Waller and Manchester reach Thatcham.

 The Earl of Northampton relieves Banbury Castle where his brother commands.

26th   The opposing armies face each other just north of Newbury.

27th   THE SECOND BATTLE OF NEWBURY. Although the Parliamentary forces under Cromwell, Manchester and Waller (Essex has been taken ill and left at Reading) possess the field, they do not achieve their object of crushing the King who withdraws under cover of darkness. *See separate account on pages 130–1.*

28th   The Royalist troops who have slipped away make for Oxford. The King with an escort of 500 horse makes for Bath and Rupert.

29th   The Governor of Weymouth is ordered to exchange one John

Donnington Castle, Berkshire. Secured by the Royalists in 1642, the castle came under repeated attack and siege. However, it was held for the King throughout the war by Colonel John Boys.

Dan for one Mr Giles Stoodley of Broadwinsor taken in Melbury by Colonel Strangeways. Dyve agrees to this deal.

30th The King leaves Bath with Rupert and some 3,000 horse and foot.

31st The garrison of Weymouth is reported to have had further skirmishes with the Queen's regiment and professes to have taken a large number prisoners.

November

1st The King enters Oxford. Colonel Henry Gage is knighted.
      After a ten-week siege, Liverpool surrenders to Meldrum.

The Second Battle of Newbury
27 October 1644

In the First Battle of Newbury the odds were heavily weighted in favour of a Royalist victory, while in the Second the odds were equally in favour of a disastrous Royalist defeat. In the event it was only the jealousies and professional rivalries of the Parliamentary commanders that prevented the capture or death of the King and a sudden termination of the Civil War.

The eve of the battle found the King in a defensive triangular position whose points rested on Shaw House, Donnington Castle and Speen village. His army was only about 9,000 strong, for on his march from the West Country he had left garrisons at various places and had furthered weakened his strength by sending 800 horse under Northampton to relieve Banbury Castle.

On the other hand the three Parliamentary armies of Essex, Manchester and Waller were 19,000 strong, which included about 8,000 horse. Essex had been left behind, allegedly sick, at Reading so that the command was divided between the other two generals. The battle commenced at dawn on 27 October, when a tertia (brigade) a thousand strong descended Clay Hill in two units and forced the 'guard of the pass' next to Shaw House, causing the Royalists to fall back. Sir Bernard Astley counter-attacked with his musketeers and broke the assault which retreated in some disorder. It has been suggested that this was in reality a feint to disguise the Parliamentary commanders' true intentions, for there were no further attacks, Symonds noting 'they lay quiet until three in the afternoon only our cannon and their playing.'

When the attack came it was from an entirely different quarter than had been anticipated. Waller and Skippon with a large command had set out during the hours of darkness and marched round the Royalist position. By approximately 3 p.m. they appeared on the ridge west of Speen and deployed for the attack. In the centre were the foot under Skippon, with Cromwell on the left and Balfour on the right. The plan was to take the Royalists' front and rear simultaneously, the firing of the cannon by Waller being the signal for Manchester to attack. It was rather late in the day for a major attack, for sunset was at 4.26 p.m. with the moon in its first quarter. Nevertheless Waller's men went in and, while the Parliamentary soldiers must have been fatigued by their long march, the sight of the hated Cornish colours among Maurice's army which was defending Speen village was enough to lead them on. Advancing steadily through a hail of case shot that tore gaping holes in their ranks, the psalm tune never faltering, they came up to the guns and past them. Those who had lost those guns at Lostwithiel embraced the brass barrels with tears in their eyes and the others, as the running Cornishmen shrieked, gave no quarter as they remembered the treatment meted out to their defeated comrades in the West Country. Waller's command moved forward steadily, expecting at any moment to link up with Manchester advancing from Shaw House, but Manchester in his normal dilatory fashion did not attack until about 4 p.m., which ruined the strategic plan.

At one time the King was in some danger as the fight swirled around his position in a vicious mêlée. The danger was averted when Lord Bernard Stuart and Sir John Campsfield with their horse surrounded him.

The lateness of Manchester's attack enabled the Royalists to stabilize their front aided by the falling darkness. When Manchester did at last launch a two-pronged attack it was thrown back vehemently, the valiant Sir George Lisle throwing off his buff coat and fighting in his shirt so that his men could identify him. The darkness was now intense and it is true to say that its onset saved the Royalists, otherwise renewed attacks by an enemy which outnumbered them two-to-one could not have had any other result than a crushing defeat. This was patent even to a man so everlastingly optimistic as the King so he gave the order to retreat. There was a 1,500 yard gap between Shaw House and Donnington Castle, and it was through this that the Royalist force silently slipped away into the night, the bulk making straight for Wallingford while the King made for Bath, there to rendezvous with Rupert. Whether the enemy was pleased to see them go, as Clarendon suggests, or whether the sporadic firing of muskets which still aimlessly continued, combined with the dark night, masked the retreat is a matter of conjecture. But what is fact is that the senior officers quarrelled so much among themselves that there was no one single officer with sufficient authority to initiate the Third Battle of Newbury. This should have followed when the King returned reinforced by Rupert to withdraw the cannon which he left with Sir John Boys at Donnington.

The only benefit the Parliamentarians gained from Second Newbury was the realization that a unified command was essential. This led in part to the creation of the New Model Army.

2nd   Essex writes to The Committee from Reading; 'I thank you for your great favour in enquiring after my recovery, which I thank God begins, though it makes small progress. I can now sit up an hour a day without pain.'

3rd   The Committee orders that 150 barrels of gunpowder and 'three battering pieces be sent to Donnington Castle from Reading for use in the reduction thereof'.

4th   A service of thanksgiving is held for the 'mercy of the surrender of Liverpool'.

5th   Sir Anthony Ashley Cooper takes Abbotsbury – Sir John Strangeway's house – by storm after a six-hour engagement.

6th   Rupert is appointed Lieutenant-General of the Royalist Armies in place of the Earl of Forth who is thought to be too old and infirm for further service – an appointment that pleases few.

7th   Cooper marches to Sturminster intent on sieging the castle but the Royalist garrison under Colonel Radford marches out at his approach.

8th   The King marches south and reaches Blewbury this day.

9th   The relief of Donnington Castle by the arrival of the Royalist Army – the purpose of the mission being to 'fetch away those things. . . . as were most material'.

10th   The Parliamentary army draws up on Speenham land in battle array very much on the defensive but the King declines combat and goes his way.

11th   The King reaches Lambourn and decides to attempt the relief of Basing House.

12th   Concluding that the business can be achieved best by a mobile force the King sends Sir Henry Gage with 1,000 horse, each with a bag of corn at his saddle bow.

13th   Manchester is advised that at Windsor there is a munition barge laden with 5 ton of bullet and 5 ton of match and 'if he saw fit to send a convoy to bring it to Reading then the army would be supplied'.

14th   Sir William Waller writes to The Committee asking for a fortnight's pay 'for those poor foot I left in Dorset which will be a great encouragement'.

15th   The Lyme garrison attacks the Royalists who are fortifying

Axminster. At the second charge they enter into the town slaying Sir Richard Cholmley, brother of Sir Hugh, and taking four pieces of ordnance.

16th   Prince Rupert 'gave the passe to the Trumpetter for the Parliament Treaters'.

17th   The Committee orders the Committee of Militia 'to send one of your number to Windsor with instructions which will be ready for him by 2 p.m'.

18th   The Committee writes to Colonel Venn, Governor of Windsor Castle, saying it is sending him thirty more men after hearing of the mutiny in his garrison. The seven mutineers whom he apprehended must be sent to London to be dealt with.

19th   Gage arrives at Basing House only to discover that Norton, hearing of the inconclusive result of Second Newbury, has lifted the siege before his arrival.

20th   The Committee sends word to Waller that £800 is available for his Dorset forces and it hopes to raise money speedily for the remainder of his men.

21st   Sir Lewis Dyve arrives back at Sherborne after a raiding mission to dislodge an enemy detachment in the neighbourhood.

22nd   The Committee writes to the Committees for Kent, Surrey, Sussex and Middlesex, thanking them for their willingness to send troops to Farnham but asking them to cancel the request as the King is reported to be going into winter quarters.

23rd   The information is correct; the Royalist army quarters around Oxford.

24th   The Commons orders The Committee 'to consider of a frame or model of the whole militia', that is the formation of the New Model Army.

25th   Colonel Sydenham, enraged by Dyve's insolent raiding, draws out a party of '50 or 60 horse double pistolled' to Dorchester and surprising the Royalists in their beds harries them out of the town, slaying one Major Williams who was supposed to be responsible for the death of Sydenham's mother.

26th   An ordinance of Parliament decrees that all goods imported from or exported to New England should be free of tax.

27th   Sir James Harrington is ordered to report to Essex at Abingdon with his brigade.

28th   Major-General Crawford is required to carry a ton of match to Abingdon strapped in small parcels to his horsemen's saddles.

29th   Parliament decrees that it is the duty of the constituent counties of the Eastern Association to pay the forces of Colonels Raineborough and Lillburne while they are undertaking the safety of the Isle of Ely.

30th   A collection of papers relating to the accusation against Henry Broad, auditor to Essex's army, is to be made available, as it is wished to proceed against him for falsification.

December

1st   An ordinance is passed for the raising of a loan for £66,666 13*s* 4*d* 'for the better enabling of our brethren in Scotland to assist us in this war'.

2nd   Lord Fairfax writes rather petulantly that, although The Committee continually urges him to put pressure on Newark, it occupies all his resources to contain the garrisons of Pontefract and Knaresborough.

3rd   Captain James Haynes, long-time prisoner in Portland Castle, escapes and arrives in London with useful information for Parliament.

4th   George Vane complains to his father that although he has tried to remove the soldiers billeted on his father's tenants whose officers are agreeable, 'the truth is that the soldiers are our masters and do as they list'.

5th   The King sends to Essex asking for a safe conduct for the Duke of Richmond and Earl of Southampton that they might take peace proposals to Parliament.

6th   The Committee recommends the foundation of an army of 22,000 men under a central commander, comprising 11 regiments of horse, each 600 strong, one regiment of dragoons 1,000 strong, and 12 regiments of foot 1,200 strong. This is to be the New Model Army.

7th   Unfortunately for Sir Arthur Aston, the leg broken on 19 September has to be amputated. Five years later in 1649 the Parliamentary soldiers dash out his brains with his own wooden leg at Drogheda.

8th   Sir Thomas Middleton writes to The Committee: 'I assume the boldness to acquaint you with my present state and the conditin of these remote parts' and relates that, using Montgomery Castle as a base, he has reduced an enemy garrison, 'anciently an abbey called Abbey-cum-hir' which he burned.

9th   In the Commons Cromwell argues that apportioning the blame for the lost opportunities of Second Newbury is pointless. A progressive viewpoint would be to learn from the mistakes and seek a remedy. Zouch Tate, MP for Northampton, proposes the Self-Denying Ordinance which would bar all members of both Houses from holding military command. The Commons agrees.

10th   After much debate a safe conduct pass is issued to the King's messengers.

11th   The Committee directs that the frigate *Griffin* be desired to entertain and set out to carry intelligence between England and Ireland.

12th   The Independents in the Commons propose a fast day 'to seek truth of the Lord'.

13th   The Lords rejects the Self-Denying Ordinance.

14th   When the relief force marches to Taunton it is composed of the troops of Holborn, Cooper and Ludlow which joined to succour that place so long and gallantly defended by Blake.

15th   Cooper, who by strength of character seems to have overborn Holborn, the senior officer, reports to Essex on the relief of Taunton.

16th   After lengthy debate it is agreed to hold a conference in the Pointed Chamber, between the two Houses and the King's commissioners, with the Scots being present.

17th   The fast day is held on or about this day, for eight or ten hours. The preachers pray that Parliament might be inspired by honourable thoughts.

18th   Colonel Robert Butler, Governor of Wareham, writes to Cooper at Wimborne desiring money: '. . . a little now will be worth a great deal later. It is only money that will take Corfe Castle.'

19th   The Self-Denying Ordinance is passed by the Commons. A revised version is passed by the Lords on 3 April 1645.

20th   Knaresborough Castle surrenders to Lord Fairfax. Among the useful booty are 'some hundreds of pounds in ready money and about £1,500 of plate and silver'.

21st   When the House assembles this day Sir Henry Vane tells it that if ever the Lord appears to its members it is when they appeal to him with fasting and prayer.

22nd   Major-General Browne writes complainingly to The Committee that Colonels Fiennes, Martin and Washbourne's troops have arrived at Abingdon but do not total more than 300 horse, so that instead of having a sufficiency of horse he still lacks numbers.

23rd   The Committee writes to Major-General Holborn thanking him for his good services at Taunton and informs him that it is sending him reinforcements (1,200 horse and 600 foot) which he may use as he sees fit, although the members suggest he might garrison Ilminster.

24th   The House resolves that after reading Cooper's letter to Essex The Committee should be urged to reinforce Taunton.

25th   William Vavasour writes from Leyden to his cousin Sir William Vavasour lengthily explaining why he left the King's service after the York defeat.

26th   The Committee of Militia is instructed that as the three militia regiments at Abingdon are so weak they must be telescoped into one as an economy.

27th   The Treasury is instructed this day to pay Colonel Fiennes at Abingdon a fortnight's remuneration.

28th   Sir John Bankes, Chief Justice of the Common Pleas, dies in Oxford and is buried at Christ Church.

29th   John Alwyn of Lewes writes to Mr Tomeson at the Rose in Paul's Churchyard, London, with prices of wheat and other grain with the quantity available in his locality. He comments, 'if it be for Ireland the merchants must send their own shipping for our men will not undertake it.'

30th   Major-General Browne has more trouble with Fiennes' men and bitterly complains, 'Their own officers reviewed the town, desiring to quarter them therein but declared the accommodation unfit . . . that they quartered outside the town, that is about 1½ miles away'.

31st The Committee writes a stiff letter to Colonels FitzJames and Ludlow 'and the officer in charge of the Plymouth horse' who want to split up, positively forbidding them to do so.

Summary of 1644

The year 1644 saw the war getting ever more bitter. Neither side had derived a marked advantage over the other. There had been a victory here and a victory there, with one very often cancelling out the benefits of the other.

In both camps lukewarm supporters threw up their hands in horror at the outpouring of money and materials and even more at the ever-lengthening casualty figures. The really committed soldier or politician had found his temper growing ever sharper, honed on the whetstone of frustration and disappointment. The noticeable desire of both parties to reach conciliation at the beginning was now hardening into a harshness amounting almost to a demand for unconditional surrender. Even so the King made two unacceptable attempts to reach a settlement, but the Parliamentary terms presented late in the year amounted almost to a demand for abdication.

John Pym's last work, the entry of the Scots, was gradually tipping the scales in his party's favour, while the entry of the Irish/English regiments had little benefit for the King. The affect of the Scots was felt almost immediately at bloody Marston Moor where the flank attack of David Leslie's light horse turned the tide by deafeating Rupert's hitherto matchless cavalry.

Both in the north and the Midlands Parliament was successful after the Battle of Marston Moor. Montgomery Castle fell to Sir Thomas Middleton, Liverpool to Sir John Meldrum, while Lord Byron's attempt to recapture the former ended in disaster when he encountered Brereton.

In the south honours were even, with perhaps a slight bias towards the King, who had relieved Basing House, Donnington and Banbury Castles. He had luckily escaped annihilation at Second Newbury and had contemptuously brushed Waller aside at Cropredy. Christmas found him still serenely wintering at Oxford.

Meanwhile Hopton had lost at Cheriton and Alton. In order to make up a good-sized field army the King had to absorb the remnants of Hopton's army and to strip the garrisons of some of the fortified towns that protected Oxford. Of course, he had won handsomely at Lostwithiel but had gained little but prestige from it.

The Westminster Parliament spent much of the winter of 1644/5 debating the reason for the failure of Second Newbury to crush the King. It commenced with a furious Cromwell accusing a haughty Manchester of 'backwardness', or perhaps as we might call it at the least 'unprofessional conduct'. The debate ended in a serious discussion of the need for a single, unified army under one commander. This resulted in an order being sent to the Committee of Both Kingdoms 'to consider of a frame or model of the whole militia' or in other words a recommendation as to the formation of the New Model Army.

On 9 December Cromwell urged that it was pointless to argue over blame for something that was past, declaring it was now up to the Commons to decide the remedy to prevent a recurrence. Zouch Tate, MP for Northampton, proposed a Self-Denying Ordinance which excluded members of either House from holding military command. This motion was passed by the Commons. It was these two measures which perhaps more than anything else, even the entry of the Scots, were to lead to the defeat of the King's cause.

1645

January

1st   Captain John Hotham is executed on Tower Hill for conspiring to deliver Hull to the Royalists.

2nd   Sir John Hotham, late Governor of Hull, father of the above, is executed for same reason. The long existing doubts regarding their guilt are finally resolved by the capture of Newcastle's correspondence after the Battle of Marston Moor.

3rd   The Committee directs that a clause be added to the contract for the employment of Lord Broghill's 'Green Frigate' to pay for the victualling for three months.

4th   Parliament abolishes the Prayer Book and authorizes the new Directory of Worship.

5th   In a letter to Giles Greene MP, George Alleyn states that all the great houses around Lyme are burned by the enemy 'or ourselves, save only Chidiock House and the governor will attend to that shortly'.

6th   An interesting financial note. This day it is announced that the monthly wage bill of 14,000 foot in 12 regiments with 6,000 horse in 10 regiments plus 1,000 dragoons amounts to £17,860 5*s* 4*d*.

7th   Fairfax is ordered to send 1,000 horse to Newark, Warwick 300 horse and foot, Northampton 200 and Colonel Fox 100 horse.

8th   An order is sent to Colonel Anthony Weldon from The Committee: 'not doubting your continued zeal . . . and assuring you that we have set a just value on your merits we desire you to continue your stay at Weymouth.'

9th   Goring, who had been commissioned Lieutenant-General of Hampshire, Sussex, Surrey and Kent, executes a lightning push through to Farnham this day.

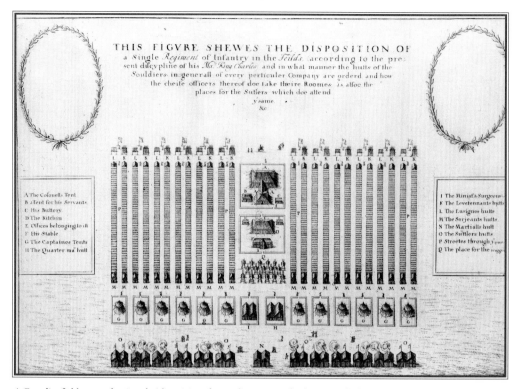

A Royalist field camp, showing the 'disposition of a single regiment of infantry in the field'; an etching by Wenceslaus Hollar.

10th   The Committee writes to Colonel Jephson at Portsmouth thanking him for the care taken to ensure the safety of the port, and stating that steps are being taken for the payment of £1,000 from The Committee at Haberdashers Hall.

11th   Rupert makes a surprise attack on Abingdon. After an initial success the Royalists are driven back by a vehement counter-attack by the garrison under Major-General Browne, with heavy losses. Among the casualties is Sir Henry Gage, the hero of the relief of Basing House, who is mortally wounded.

12th   A letter to Colonel Venn at Windsor states that The Committee considered 200 men too small for the garrison and that it would be reinforced shortly by another 400 men. In the meantime Venn should 'look diligently to his charge'.

13th   Gage is buried in the north transept of Christ Church Cathedral, Oxford.

14th   Colonel Massey is instructed to command a body to go against

Campden House to prevent the enemy fortifying there. The force is to be augmented by 500 horse and foot from Gloucester and 200 horse from Worcester.

15th Goring makes an attempt on Christchurch after falling back from Farnham, 'a little unfortified fisher town from whence he was beaten off with loss'.

The Commons vote Waller to command a force of 6,000 horse and dragoons to serve in the west.

16th A press of 3,000 men ordered in the Eastern Association and recruits so obtained are to be sent to Henley for Sir Miles Hobart's and Colonel Monagu's regiments.

17th Sir Walter Erle is ordered to supply Reading garrison with 300 barrels of powder and 2 tons of match this day.

18th Sir William Brereton is ordered to assist the Committee of Salop to reduce Tong Castle, Lindsill Abbey and Shrawardine House.

19th £700 is paid to Edward Kirton, Gentleman of the Robes to Prince Charles, for 'provision of robes for the Prince'.

20th John Lisle MP reports 'concerning diverse passages and proceedings of the army', that is to say the complaints of Waller and Cromwell against Manchester.

21st The Commons pass the ordinance appointing Sir Thomas Fairfax to overall command of the New Model Army.

22nd Information is laid before the House by one J. Bromwich alleging that one Major Ingoldsby is guilty of irregular dealings amounting almost to treason.

23rd The Committee once again orders Sir William Brereton to act on its orders to reduce Tong Castle, Lindsill Abbey and Shrawardine House.

24th A warrant is issued to the Constable of Tottenham (Middx.) to seize some of the horses of Captain Hemming's troop as security for the payment for quartering his men.

25th Montrose, the will o' the wisp, 'is believed to betwixt the head of Loch Ness and Lochaber'.

26th The Earl of Antrim, 'for whom the King had as little regard or kindness as for any man', is created a marquess as a matter of policy.

27th   Major-General Browne, tired at last of his command at Abingdon, asks to be relieved. Failing this he reports that 'we are in great want of gunpowder, match and bullet'.

28th   The worried Committee writes to the Governors of Reading, Aylesbury and Henley imploring them not to relax their vigilance in case the enemy makes a surprise attack.

29th   Sir William Waller, who has remained in London until this day organizing his force, is urged to action by the Commons.

30th   Treaty of Uxbridge is debated between the Royalist and Parliament commissioners, the terms of which are so harsh that Clarendon remarks 'that it would have been more reasonable to ask the King to abdicate'.

31st   Warwick at Holborn orders the speedy victualling of the frigates *Providence* and *Warwick* to enable them to continue their work in the west

February

1st   Waller arrives at Farnham.

2nd   Montrose defeats Argyll at Inverlochy.

3rd   This day the Royalist garrison march out of Belvoir Castle with the honours of war. Major Henry Markham is appointed governor.

4th   The ordinance appointing Fairfax to command the New Model Army is passed by the Lords.

5th   More logistics. The Committee of Coventry is ordered to assist Colonel Harley or Captain Giffard with the protection of a convoy of provisions despatched by Sir Samuel Luke between Warwick and Northampton.

6th   The Commons orders that Colonel John Fiennes' regiment of horse shall be paid without delay. To achieve this the Parliamentary commissioner is to take an exact muster and forward it to the House.

7th   The Commons expresses its thanks to one Captain Laurence Larran, who has not only preserved the fort at Dungannon but has also captured a ship valued at £500. He is rewarded by promotion to Lieutenant-Colonel and a cash bonus of £200.

8th   Upon the marching of Maurice toward Chester, Brereton is promised reinforcements this day.

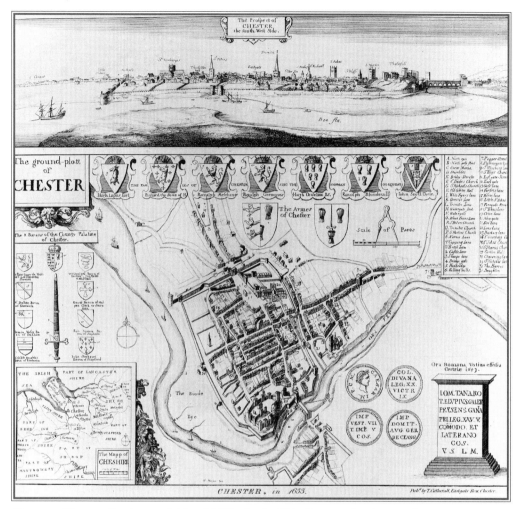

Chester stood firm as a Royalist stronghold until 1646 when Lord John Bryon was forced to surrender.

9th   The Committee of the Navy (Parliament) publishes its Prize Account this day for the period August 1644 to February 1645, a sum total of £23,593 11s 6d.

10th The Queen writes to Pope Innocent X: 'The particular knowledge I have of Seigneur Gregario Pizzari enables me to recommend him very strongly . . . he is well informed of the affairs of England . . . which renders him more capable to serve. . . .'

11th The Queen writes to Cardinal Spade: 'The long cognizance I have of your merit and friendly disposition on all occasions causes me to direct the Chevalier Digby to communicate to you the business . . . which I have with his Holiness.'

12th The Lieutenant of the Tower receives as prisoners Lord Brabazon, Sir James Weir and Sir Henry Tichborne.

13th The Committee writes a stiff letter to the Accounts Committee to speed up the collectors of prize goods so that quicker returns may be made.

14th Colonel Montague is ordered to continue the work of fortifying Bulstrode Whitlock's residence, Phyllis Court near Henley, as safely and expeditiously as possible.

15th The Recorder of London is ordered to draw interrogation out of the letters wherewith to examine the Countess of Banbury.

16th An apologetic letter from Brereton bewails the loss of Rawden House near Cirencester. 'I call all honest men to witness . . . who have observed my care and diligence that I have never done the least thing to prejudice the public safety. . . .'

17th Colonel Fox receives a commission from the Committee at Worcester to raise a troop of horse, receiving £70 weekly as its pay.

18th Fairfax arrives in London and visits the Commons where the members are impressed by his becoming modesty.

19th Maurice relieves Chester. A cheering letter from Montrose reaches the King.

20th Lieutenant-Colonel Mark Gryme reports to the Governor of Henley (Colonel Edward Montague) a case of embryonic trades unionism: a Captain Taylor and a Lieutenant Rowse came into the garrison and harangued the troops who thereafter mutinied and refused to march without their arrears of pay, which were duly and speedily paid.

21st Lord Wharton, Lieutenant-General Cromwell, the London Recorder and three others are appointed to interrogate the Irish prisoners in the Tower.

22nd Colonel Thomas Mytton takes Shrewsbury with a surprise night attack, the governor, Sir Michael Ernle, 'being sick of a consumption a long time is killed in his night shirt'.

23rd The Committee writes sternly to the Committees of Essex, Suffolk, Norfolk and Cambridge who are responsible for paying the Newport Pagnell garrison who are, as usual, in arrears.

24th   Captain Taylor and Lieutenant Rowse are arrested and 'referred to the examination of The Committee'.

25th   Despatched by the King on 22 February to relieve Pontefract, Langdale meets Rossitter in a sharp cavalry action at Melton Mowbray. The latter, outnumbered, is routed.

26th   The Committee replies to Massey's penitent letter regarding the loss of Rawden House and seems to infer that the blame is not all Massey's; it had intended to send reinforcements itself.

27th   Cromwell and Ireton, with three troops of Ironsides, join the ex-Manchester's horse in Sussex, forming a body of 2,000.

28th   Captain Taylor, examined by The Committee, contends he had no part in the 'pretended mutiny' and that Gryme had a grudge against him.

March

1st   Langdale relieves Pontefract Castle.

2nd   A new ordinance is issued to the committees of fifteen counties acquainting them with Parliament's required method of dealing with deserters, i.e. returning them to the colours rather than drastic punishment.

3rd   The Committee at Shrewsbury is kept in touch by a dispatch this day: Langdale's forces are gone north, Goring's army is more or less static about Weymouth and Derby and Yorkshire are to continue with Brereton.

4th   Prince Charles leaves Oxford for Bristol.
        Cromwell and Waller are instructed to proceed immediately into the west, 'all excuses set aside'.

5th   Venn is informed that the pay allocation to Windsor garrison is £60 per week until further notice.

6th   Prince Charles reaches Bath, 'where it was his intention to stay two or three days'.

7th   Twelve recruits, 'committing violence on the houses of the inhabitants', are hauled up before the Justices of St Albans and two of them are hanged.

8th   The combined forces of Cromwell and Waller reach Andover.

9th   Lord Fairfax receives a polite letter from The Committee stating that it has written to the Parliament commissioners

Charles, Prince of Wales, the future King Charles II, by William Dobson. The Prince was then about fourteen years old, the age he was appointed to the nominal position of Captain-General of the south-west of England with Lord Hopton as his military advisor.

with the Scots Army and to Leven himself requesting that they collaborate with him as much as possible.

10th Cromwell and Waller arrive at Amesbury.

11th Prince Charles receives the Commissioners of Somerset at Bath and finds nothing that was promised at Oxford has been done; 'of his Lifeguard not one man or horse, of his subsistence money not one penny'.

12th Waller destroys Colonel Sir James Long's regiment of horse near Trowbridge.

13th Maurice leaves Chester. Shortly after, Brereton re-imposes the siege.

14th Sir Thomas Fairfax's shortage of draught horses for his train of artillery causes Parliament to requisition them, a certain quota to each county.

15th   Colonel Ludlow is given command of the Lord General's Lifeguard and the troops of Major Duett and Captain Saville, which are to be quartered around Blackwater 'to preserve those parts from incursions of the enemy from Basing and Winchester'.

16th   A warrant is issued to Colonel Owen Rowe of London for the provision of 200 pikes, 200 muskets, 400 bandoliers, 200 swords and belts for the use of the Aylesbury garrison.

17th   Lieutenant-Colonel Grymes is ordered to remove his self-imposed tax from the town of Henley. Hereafter only the Parliament-appointed taxes should be levied.

18th   Ludlow is to be reinforced by the troops commanded by Captains Ramsey, Stevens and Bruce. Furthermore he is informed that the governor of Farnham Castle is alerted to their presence and possible needs.

19th   Waller appoints a rendezvous at Cerne Abbas this day and leaves Cromwell to proceed in that direction. Waller deviates towards Bristol in the belief that a bribe might open the gates thereof.

20th   With Goring in the West Country, one Royalist general at least was less than enthusiastic. 'I expect nothing but ill from the West' wrote Rupert to his friend Will Legge this day.

21st   This day the ship *Prosperous*, master Richard Thompson, is contracted into the service of Parliament.

22nd   Wood notes a skirmish involving one 'Phips, the rag man' with 20 horse and 'a party of Royalists from Borstall'.

23rd   From Marshfield Waller reports on the failure of the British plot: 'ye business failed through the faint heartedness of those that undertook it.'

24th   Ralph Bailey, gunner on the *Nonsuch*, was transferred to *Mere Honour* as master gunner following the death of the former master gunner, Robert Bacon.

25th   John Clarke of Dunkirk petitions Lord Digby, stating that one John Sandys had ordered a large number of arms for the King's service for which Clarke had pledged his credit to the sum of 7,753 florins; now Sandys and the arms are gone, and no one knows where. Clarke is being dunned for the debt, and states that His Majesty cannot expect further assistance if this debt is left unpaid.

26th   Waller reaches Downton 6 miles south of Salisbury and notes that Cromwell is en route from Ringwood to Dorchester.

27th   Waller reaches Ringwood this day. Major-General Holborne of the Taunton garrison, with 2,000 horse and foot marching toward the Cerne Abbas rendezvous, reaches Axminster.

28th   The Queen writes to Digby from Paris, chiding him that she has received no news from him: 'I fear you are as inconstant to your friends as you are to your mistresses.'

29th   Lord Jermyn, also in Paris, is still busy endeavouring to organize seaborne opposition to the Parliament. He writes to Digby, the King's principle Secretary of State, asking for blank signed commissions for 'we cannot have too many privateers at sea as long as this war lasts'.

30th   The Parliament appoints Sir John Wollaston, Thomas Adams, John Warner, Thomas Andrews, Francis Allen and John Dethicke, merchants of London, to be Treasurers at War for the securing of £80,000 for maintaining the New Model Army.

31st   Cromwell and Holbourne join at Cerne Abbas, despite Goring's efforts to prevent them.

April

1st   Fairfax's list of his officers for the New Model Army is submitted to the Lords, who object to no fewer than two colonels and forty captains on social or political grounds. The list is approved by a single vote.

2nd   Anticipating the passing of the Self-Denying Ordinance, Essex and Manchester resign their commissions.

3rd   The Self-Denying Ordinance is passed by the Commons.

4th   FORMATION OF NEW MODEL ARMY. Commander-in-Chief: Sir Thomas Fairfax. Major-General of the Foot: Phillip Skippon. Lieutenant-General of Horse is not at first designated, but at the last Oliver Cromwell is appointed. Lieutenant-General of Ordnance: Thomas Hammond.

5th   Skippon reviews the foot at Reading and harangues them.

6th   Easter Day. Fairfax reviews the horse at St Albans.

7th The Committee of the Navy is informed that a proportion of the beef and pork left over from last year's fleet is so salty that it is inedible. 'It was then thought fit to dispose of it to the best advantage of the State.'

8th Rupert arrives at Oxford for a consultation with the King.

9th Six hundred horse march to join with Colonel Rossiter from the York garrison, 'until further orders'.

10th A fortnight's pay is demanded for the horse of Northampton, Newport Pagnell and Aylesbury before they will march to join Massey.

11th Rupert attends Prince Charles's Council of War in the West.
Goring has orders to advance into Dorset with his horse and to send his foot and cannon to reduce Taunton.

12th Ill-will over the precedence between Sir John Berkeley and Sir Richard Grenville threatens to split the unity of the Royalist forces in the west.

13th The Committee writes a cordial letter to Leslie, thanking him for his assistance to Gloucester's Governor, Colonel Massey, and asking him to keep in touch.

14th Major Childe, commander of the Kent Trained Band, receives an urgent message to march back into the county 'on account of information just received of dangerous commotions in Kent which if neglected might cause dangerous affects'.

15th After Essex hangs thirteen Irishmen for the sole reason that they were Irish, Rupert retaliates by hanging a similar number of Parliament soldiers which causes a paper battle between the two of them.

16th Waller, who has by this time fallen back on Salisbury with his subordinate commanders, prepares to surrender his commission this day under the terms of the Self-Denying Ordinance.

17th An anxious letter is sent from The Committee to Lord Fairfax with regard to the ill feeling that has sprung up between the Scots and the people of Westmorland. It is afraid that the touchy Scots might not march south if further harassed, 'therefore take especial care that no affronts or discontents may be given them'.

18th Captain Nicholas, Captain Sadler and Captain Bernard are ordered to concentrate on Malmesbury and place themselves under the governor's orders.

19th   Sir Thomas Fairfax is instructed to send some horse if Major-General Browne sends foot to assist in the siege of Sherborne Castle.

20th   Cromwell is ordered to advance and to endeavour to sever the King's lines of communication with Rupert.

21st   More logistics. The Exchequer is ordered to pay Colonel William Legge, Governor of Oxford, £1,500 to purchase wheat for the garrison and the city.

22nd   Rupert routs Massey at Ledbury.

23rd   Cromwell is at Watlington.

24th   Cromwell forces the crossing of the Cherwell at Islip, driving back the Queen's regiment and taking its standard, powdered with the gold French fleur-de-lys.

      Bletchingdon House is tamely surrendered by Sir Francis Windebank.

25th   The Committees of Cumberland and Westmorland are given two alternatives: either pay the Scots Army or undertake the siege of Carlisle. They choose the latter and offer 3,000 foot and 600 horse, whereof 1,000 foot and 200 horse would be supplied by Westmorland, the rest by Cumberland.

26th   Massey storms and takes Evesham, which surrenders 'for want of men to defend the works'.

27th   Sir Henry Bard, Governor of Campden House (Gloucester), writes to Rupert, begging for a reprieve for Sir Francis Windebank, who has been sentenced to death for the surrender of Bletchingdon.

28th   Fairfax is ordered to take the New Model Army to succour Taunton.

29th   Cromwell summon's Faringdon House, the garrison of which repels both it and the attack which followed.

30th   Fairfax marches from Windsor to Reading.

      The King sends for Goring.

May

1st   The Commons recommends that £1,000 be provided for intelligence (i.e. shipping) and £500 'for extraordinary uses of the trayne'.

2nd   Sir Thomas Fairfax is notified of the advance of Rupert and Maurice on Oxford from Bradway.

3rd   Rupert and Maurice are at Stow-on-the-Wold this day.

4th   Sir Thomas Fairfax is notified that a Major Bridges claims to
         have intelligence that the Princes' real destination is
         Warwick.

5th   The claim proves false as Rupert and Maurice arrive at Oxford
         this day.

6th   The Royalist Western Army attempts to carry Taunton by
         storm. The garrison commander is Robert Blake.

7th   The Royalist Oxford Army leaves for the summer campaign.
         The Committee hastily writes to Fairfax with this news and
         tells him to wheel the New Model Army about and to send on a
         small force to relieve Taunton. This Fairfax does, entrusting
         Colonel Weldon with the latter task.

8th   A general rendezvous of the Royalists is held at Stow-on-the-
         Wold. Present at this time are 5,000 foot and 6,000 horse.

9th   By sheer weight of numbers and gun power the Royalists at
         Taunton force Blake and his men back into last ditch positions
         centred on the church and castle after an all day assault.
              THE BATTLE OF AULDEARN Montrose defeats Urny
         spectacularly.
              The King send Goring back to the West – a fatal mistake, as
         proved at Naseby – and starts his march north.

10th   Summoned to surrender at dawn, Blake replies shortly that he
         would first eat his boots. Hearing of Weldon's relieve force
         rapidly bearing down on them the Royalists withdraw to the
         jubilation of the Tauntonians.

11th   Having started his march north on 9 May, intending to relieve
         Chester and to attack the depleted Scots army, the King reaches
         Droitwich this day.

12th   A pamphlet is published this day in Oxford giving 'orders for
         preventing the plague in this city'.

13th   Clarendon states that 'at this time the King amused himself
         with reorganizing the Western Army'. If it was a genuine
         attempt, it must have offended more than it pleased. Goring
         was in overall charge, Grenville to be Major-General, Berkeley
         to concern himself solely with the Plymouth siege, and Hopton
         to be General of Artillery.

14th   The New Model Army reaches Newbury this day. Royalists take Hawksley House (Worcester).

15th   The indefatigable Committee, in the midst of all its worries, even finds time to concern itself with the numbers of the Norfolk Trained Band cavalry. It tells the deputy lieutenants 'it is a great temptation to the enemy to strike where little strength is'.

17th   Sir John Digby writes testily to his brother George: 'I presume that you have an account of the proceedings at Taunton, to be free with you that enterprise was so unhappily interrupted that I am quite out of countenance to relate the particulars.'

18th   On or about this day the King changes his mind about the hierarchy of the Western Army. Now Goring is to take as many men as can be spared to Northampton, while Hopton is to command in the West.

19th   Fairfax reaches Oxford but is unable to do much more that surround it and wait for the arrival of the siege train.

20th   The Committee reprimands one Captain Coleman: 'We are informed that your troop has lain six weeks at Hemel Hempstead whereby the county is burdened and the country neglected.'

21st   Lord Fairfax writes to Leven from York informing him of troop movements and the King's probable intentions.

22nd   The King reaches Market Drayton only to learn that the siege of Chester had been abandoned, only partially and temporarily as it later turned out.

23rd   Good news for the New Model Army. Fairfax is notified that £10,000 will be available if 'he do but send a convoy to Windsor to collect it next Tuesday'.

24th   Lord Fairfax writes to Leven, keeping him informed of the King's whereabouts: 'His forces lie in Cheshire, in dispersed quarters being clogged with many and great pieces of ordnance.'

25th   The King again orders Goring to march, but he makes plausible excuses not to do so.

26th   Colonel Vermuyden is told to note the Scots march into Westmorland and that he is to hold himself at instant readiness to march to Nottingham or those parts, to be in the best position to defend the Eastern Association.

27th   It is agreed that the forces to be raised by Sussex to reduce Basing House should be taken out of the garrisons of that county.

29th   Langdale having cut off Leicester, Rupert encircles the town. This is seen as bait to cause Fairfax to abandon the siege of Oxford.

30th   Rupert now sieges Leicester and bombards it from a vantage point, causing great breaches in the walls.

31st   Rupert's troops attempt to storm Leicester and are twice vehemently thrown back from the breach, but a party of horse from Newark, under Colonel Page, attacks the opposite undefended side and the town falls. The Royalists 'miserably sack the place without distinction of person or place'.

June

1st   Gaunt House, one of the ring of fortified manors round Oxford, surrenders on terms, after a three-day siege. Fairfax puts 200 men there as a garrison with a Colonel Moore as governor.

2nd   Five or six thousand Clubmen gather at Marshalls Elm, Somerset, to present a petition to Prince Charles complaining of 'the intolerable oppression, violence and rapine of Goring's men'.

3rd   The Prince replies to the Clubmen's petition by telling them that he has written to Goring expressing his displeasure but also stating that the Clubmen themselves are breaking the law by appearing in such numbers.

4th   The Royal army prepares to march south but as Langdale's horse refuses to, the idea comes to nothing.

5th   Having been instructed to leave Oxford, seek out the King and recover Leicester, Fairfax reaches Newport Pagnell this day.

6th   The Committee writes to Browne at Abingdon somewhat guerulousy that if he could convince them he needed his total of horse made up to 600 and it could be achieved cheaply, it would consider it.

7th   Colonel Vermuyden is ordered to hasten his juncture with Fairfax.

8th   Fairfax's council of war makes the destruction of the King's army its primary target.

9th The tug of war between Fairfax and his masters ends when Parliament gives him a free hand in the conduct of military operations.

10th Parliament finds a loophole in the Self-Denying Ordinance which allows Cromwell to command the horse at Fairfax's urgent request.

11th To illustrate the many cares with which The Committee was burdened, while Fairfax was approaching the fatal battle (Naseby), it was writing worriedly to the Governor of Chichester, telling him to improve his defences.

Oliver Cromwell.

12th The New Model Army reaches Kislingbury this day.

The Royalist army is taking its ease and the King is hunting at Fawsley Park, near Daventry, when the news reaches him that Fairfax is only 5 miles away.

13th Fairfax is reinforced by Cromwell. The Royalists commence withdrawal.

14th THE BATTLE OF NASEBY. The King's 'Oxford' army are annihilated by the New Model Army. *See separate account on pages 156–7.*

15th The King and Prince Rupert lead the broken remnants of their army to Ashby-de-la-Zouch this night.

16th The King arrives at Lichfield.

17th The King reaches Bewdley where he rests his survivors this night.

18th Fairfax takes Leicester.

The King arrives at Hereford 'with some disjointed imagination that he might . . . raise a new army'.

19th Digby writes to Ormonde regarding 'the unfortunate loss of a most hopeful battle'. With everlasting optimism he states that with the addition of Irish levies to the Western Army the loss would be offset.

20th Realizing that there was now no danger of a Royalist invasion of

Scotland, Leven plunges south and reaches Mansfield this day.

21st The Naseby prisoners, 4,000 strong with 50 captured standards, are paraded through London and camped in Tothill Fields.

22nd On or about this date the Clubmen of the locality 'come up against the walls of Lamport and discharge their muskets against it'. Sir Francis Mackworth charges and disperses them.

23rd Leven writes a sharp letter to Fairfax alleging that he was not kept informed of the progress of the negotiations for the surrender of Carlisle.

24th A letter is sent from The Committee to Fairfax ordering him to keep in constant communication with Leven and the Scots army.

25th The capitulation of Carlisle; Sir Thomas Glenham marches out and is escorted as far as Hereford by David Leslie.

26th Rupert arrives in Barnstable by water this day to consult with Prince Charles regarding the defence of the West.

27th David Leslie writes a joyous letter regarding the capitulation of Carlisle to Fairfax and states that he has put a Scots garrison to hold it, which little pleases the Parliament commissioners.

28th Fairfax resolves to relieve Taunton and reaches Marlborough this day.

29th The Marquess of Newcastle, in Paris, writes to a Captain Bushell at St Malo telling him not to wait as he did not know what his future movements might be.

30th Fairfax commences a forced march into the West Country. Amesbury is reached this day.

July

1st Fairfax and the New Model Army reach Bower Chalke, 7 miles from Salisbury. The King is at Abergavenny.

2nd THE BATTLE OF ALFORD. Montrose defeats Baillie.

3rd The King arrives at Raglan Castle. Fairfax interviews the Western Clubmen and speaks to them somewhere between Crewkerne and Blandford.

4th Joshua Sprigge, chaplain to Fairfax, is in Beaminster, which was burned down the previous year, 'a place of pittifullest spectacle one can behold, hardly a house not consumed with fire'.

5th The surprising news reaches Fairfax that Goring has abandoned

The Battle of Naseby
14 June 1645

The two armies spent the early morning of 14 June manoeuvring for position. Fairfax eventually settled for the Naseby ridge and made his dispositions there. Skippon, who marshalled the foot, drew it up after the Swedish method, with five regiments in the front line of three more.

Commissary General Ireton led the left wing of horse and Lieutenant-General Cromwell the right. The thick boundary of Sulby Hedges on the left was lined by 1,000 dragoons under Colonel Okey to enfilade any Royalist attack. The New Model Army's strength was not up to that which its creators had seen as desirable, but numbered at least 13,500 all arms.

Across the valley called Broad Moor, which was unenclosed – though patches of cultivated grain interspersed the bracken – was the gentle slope of Dust Hill where stood the Royalist army, destined to be the King's last battle array. Astley commanded the foot, Rupert the right wing of horse and Langdale the left. The King, magnificent in full armour, stationed himself on a point of vantage with his Lifeguard. Their total strength according to Clarendon was about 7,400 but this sounds a little on the low side.

The most nerve-racking time for a soldier is waiting for something to happen and it was probably for this reason that Fairfax withdrew his foot a few yards behind the crest of the ridge, bearing in mind, that many of them were inexperienced conscripts.

Perhaps at this stage Rupert thought that the New Model Army was in retreat, or perhaps he too was tired of waiting, for at about 10 a.m. the Royalist army commenced a general attack. Rupert's wing charged full tilt into Ireton's horse and after some hectic cut and slash work broke through the Parliament line and, as at Edgehill, plunged on joyously to pillage the baggage train instead of assaulting the exposed flank of Skippon's foot.

Cromwell's wing, despite the broken ground pitted with rabbit holes, steadily advanced and although Langdale's men fought with fierce valour they were less disciplined and outnumbered, and gradually gave way. It was at this time that the

the resumed siege of Taunton and is marching toward Yeovil. Marching toward Crewkerne, advance elements of the New Model Army clash with Royalist patrols.

6th A warrant is made by The Committee for the supply of 100 barrels of powder for York.

7th The Committee writes to Fairfax regarding Goring's withdrawal from Taunton: 'We desire you to attend the motions

much discussed incident of King Charles's personal participation took place. It was probably when Langdale's men were thinning out and heading for the rear that Charles took command of the reserves and prepared to charge home against Cromwell's flank. Would this surprise attack have turned the tide? Would it have resulted in the death of the King? Would such a death have been more honourable and preferable to a death on the scaffold? The answer must be forever surmise, for the King allowed himself to be deterred from his purpose by the intervention of the Earl of Carnwarth, who turned the royal horse's head. The moment was lost.

In the centre the foot regiments fought fiercely – a desperate struggle which swayed back and forth, yet could have only one result with such a disparity of numbers. During the affray Skippon was badly wounded but refused to leave the field, 'so long as there is one man that will stand'.

The only recorded instance of dragooners charging occurred at this point, when Okey, collecting his men from behind Sulby Hedges, led them against the unfortunate foot on the left while Cromwell decimated them on the right.

About this time Rupert managed to get a proportion of his men, mauled by the baggage guard, to return to the field. He was too late to save the day, the infantry and, one might think, his honour and reputation which had been sadly tarnished at Marston Moor.

Any attempt at getting the reserves to make a stand now was negated by the final volley from Okey's men. The Royalist survivors, who not unnaturally had had enough, fled from the field as fast as they could. The cavalry thundered in pursuit with considerable slaughter for 12 miles while the foot plundered the Royalist camp. The capture of the King's private correspondence, which revealed all his dealings with the Irish papists and others, was almost as valuable as the victory itself, and very shortly afterwards it was published by a gleeful Parliament.

It was not only the virtual obliteration of an army, but the end of a cause, the end of a reign, the kiss of death for a monarch.

For a full account of the battle see *Naseby, the Campaign and the Battle 1945* by Brigadier Peter Young (Roundwood Press, 1979) or *The Battle of Naseby and the Fall of King Charles I* by Maurice Ashley (Alan Sutton, 1993).

of Goring's forces and to hold constant correspondence with the Scots forces about Worcester.'

8th Colonel Richard Norton, Governor of Portsmouth, is instructed to forward money for the New Model Army by ship to Lyme Regis immediately unless he receives contrary instructions from Fairfax.

9th Digby, ever optimistic, writes to Henrietta Maria: 'We live here

The Retreat at Naseby, *a mezzotint by W. Giller from a painting by Abraham Cooper, mid-nineteenth century.*

in great disquiet until we hear how your Majesty hath digested the news of our late misfortune Naseby . . . of which we have already lost the sharp sense.'

10th   THE BATTLE OF LANGPORT. Fairfax and Cromwell defeat Goring.

Archbishop Laud is executed.

11th   Lord Littleton, Keeper of the Great Seal, is buried in the north aisle of Christ Church, Oxford, on or about this day.

12th   Both Houses nominate the Earl of Rutland, Lord Wharton, Sir Henry Vane and three others to be commissioners to be sent to Scotland to deal with all matters concerning the safety and welfare of both countries.

13th   A Mr Francis Allen is required to supply 100 barrels of powder and six tons of match to the New Model Army as it is running short of these precious commodities.

14th   The Scots are notified of the names of the Parliament commissioners 'to give satisfaction to your desires'.

15th   Colonel Richard Norton is again required to meet a convoy of provisions for Fairfax and with all diligence to 'assist Captain Potter in the despatch and shipping of same'.

16th   In an attempt to bolster the sagging morale of the Western Army Rupert leads the cavalry in a raid on the Parliament quarters at Wells.

17th   The logistical problems are manifest when a harassed Committee writes to the Navy Committee saying that while Pembroke has been supplied with 100 barrels of gunpowder, they have no bullet or match. Can the Navy possibly supply some?

18th   Rupert attempts to conciliate the Western Clubmen near Bristol and to persuade them to favour the King's cause, but without success.

19th   Another committee is appointed by Parliament to liaise with the Scots, this time with the Scots army, so eager are the two Houses to avoid misunderstanding with their allies.

20th   Communication is an issue not just for Parliament. In a letter to Sir John Berkeley, Lord Jermyn suggests establishing a packet boat service between Dartmouth and St Malo and offers to contribute towards the expenses.

21st   Rupert at Bath endeavours to revitalize the garrison and also addresses a meeting of country folk at Lansdown.

       This night he crosses Severn.

       Pontefract Castle surrenders.

22nd   Shaken out of his pleasant idyll at Raglan Castle by news of the defeat at Langport, the King meets Rupert at Crick for consulation. The latter returns to Bristol, which is the King's intended headquarters.

23rd   Bridgwater is taken by Fairfax. The loss of its considerable stocks of provisions and munitions is another nail in the Royalist coffin.

24th   The Commons appoint the next Sabbath as a day of thanksgiving for their military successes.

Ludlow Castle, Shropshire. Castle and town together were an important Royalist base during the war, the castle holding out until 1652 when it was slighted by the Parliamentarians.

August

1st Laugharne defeats Stradley on Colby Moor and drives the Royalists out of Haverfordwest, advancing on Carew Castle.

2nd Fairfax summons Sherborne Castle commanded by Sir Lewis Dyve who bade him defiance. The Duke of Richmond shows the King a letter from Rupert remarking on the King's present situation and in short making the point that 'half a loaf was better than no bread'.

3rd The King replies to Rupert this day, 'I know my obligations both in honour and conscience, neither to abandon God's cause, injure my successors, nor forsake my friends.'

4th The King, 'entertaining a new imagination that he might get into Scotland to the Marquess of Montrose', leaves Cardiff.

5th The King writes to Prince Charles from Brecknock directing him to go to France 'whensoever you find yourself in peril of falling into the rebels' hands'.

6th   The committees of Newport Pagnell and Northampton are required to send a troop of 100 horse to Bedford to meet a convoy of food for the Scots and escort it to Northampton.

7th   The King arrives at Ludlow Castle.

8th   Colonel Douglas sends a warrant to the constables of the parish of Sedgefield from Hartlepool requiring them to supply the Scots army with four draught horse teams and two teamsters to each draught.

9th   The Committee of Gloucester is ordered to provide the Scots army, which professes itself unable to march to Hereford because of a lack of gunpowder, match and bullet, 'as much of these commodities as you can spare'.

10th   Parliament, obviously anxious to please, assures the Scots that warrants have been issued 'to provide all their needs'.

11th   Sir James Livingstone vehemently denies the accusation of the Brancepath Committee that he has laid on them 'intolerable burdens' by his impositions. 'I defy any man in the county to prove this, except for the grass and hay which is within the command of the Castle.'

12th   The King receives 'a very cheerful letter from Prince Rupert in which he promises to hold Bristol'.

13th   The King reaches Ashbourne.

14th   Sherborne Castle surrenders to Fairfax.
       The King is at Chatsworth.

15th   THE BATTLE OF KILSYTH: Montrose again defeats Baillie.
       The King is at Welbeck.

16th   Lady Denham certifies to Parliament that her son-in-law, Stephen Soame, arrested as a delinquent, was resident at her house at Boarstall at the time he was alleged to be serving with the King.

17th   The King proclaims from Welbeck grace and pardon to all such of the City and County of York who should return to their natural allegiance at this time.

18th   The King is at Doncaster, where he raises 3,000 foot within 'who undertook within four and twenty hours to appear well armed and ready to march'.
       Montrose enters Glasgow.

19th   This night arrives the news that David Leslie is at Rotherham with all the Scots horse. This means only one thing to the King's advisers, and in a panic, not waiting for their new recruits, the Royalists remove to Newark.

20th   It transpires that Leslie is in fact, returning home with all speed to protect Edinburgh from Montrose and has no knowledge of the King's whereabouts. 'If the King had fallen upon me then he would have found me in a very ill posture to resist,' he comments.

21st   Basing House is besieged by Colonel John Dalbier 'the cunning engineer'.

22nd   All day long there is a general rendezvous of horse and a setting of quarters and guards of the New Model on the far side of Bristol.

23rd   Captain Blagrave's company from Reading joins Dalbier at Basing this day. Later a further 100 musketeers arrive from Southwark. Fairfax commences the final siege of Bristol.

24th   Antonio de Souza, the Portuguese agent, writes to Digby thanking him guardedly for the King's letter and also for past favours.

25th   Propositions are put forward by Colonel FitzWilliams and recommended by the Queen setting forth the concessions to be granted to the Irish Catholics for aid.

26th   A warrant is issued to one Alderman Avery to deliver 200 mortar shells, now in the custody of John Browne and also the gunpowder to the Committee of Hampshire for use against Basing House.

27th   The Earl of Warwick is notified that The Committee is only too willing to send 2,000 men after the King provided they are paid.

28th   The King arrives at Oxford.

29th   Prince Charles arrives at Exeter.

30th   Colonel Francis Thornhagh reports to The Committee for Colonel General Sydenham Poyntz regarding their military operations.

31st   The King sets out again to Worcester, his new intention being to relieve Hereford.

September

1st   Rupert makes a sally from Bristol in wet and misty weather but is beaten back by Colonel Rainsborough.

2nd   Upon receiving notice that the King's relief force is closing on Hereford the Scots besiegers lift the siege.

3rd   The ship *Blessing of Cramond*, captured in April 1644 when on a mission for Parliament and taken into Scarborough, is discovered intact at the fall of the town and ordered to be restored to her master, Captain John Kerse.

4th   The King enters Hereford 'and his majesty received with full joy into the city'.

5th   Montrose commences his march to the border to meet the King. The bulk of his army stay in Scotland; he travels with only 700 men.

6th   An ordinance is issued from both Houses appointing one Thomas Fauconbridge Comptroller of Excise with a salary of £500 per annum.

7th   Captain Henry Gardner, whose father Sir Thomas Gardner was Recorder of London, is killed at Thame while raiding.

8th   A simple fact like the granting of an annuity to Rupert's penniless brother the Elector Palatinate by Parliament is later to assume sinister connotations.

9th   After endless negotiation Fairfax realizes that Rupert has no real intention of surrendering Bristol and is only playing for time, so he determines to assault the city.

10th   After an all-out assault which is fiercely contested Rupert surrenders Bristol to Fairfax.

11th   The news about Bristol reaches Exeter 'and cast all men on their faces and damped all the former vigour and activity'. The King is now at Raglan again.

12th   The Committee writes rather threateningly to the Committee of Hampshire informing it that if Basing and Winchester are not blocked up, not only will the Sussex Committee not send reinforcements it will withdraw the troops already sent.

13th   THE BATTLE OF PHILLIPHAUGH. Montrose is decimated by David Leslie.

14th   The King writes a bitter letter to Rupert from Hereford

James Graham, Marquess of Montrose, attributed to Willem van Honthorst.

regarding his failure to hold Bristol, and revokes all commissions granted to his nephew. He also orders the arrest of Will Legge, Governor of Oxford, purely on the grounds of his friendship.

15th   Prince Charles writes to Sir Thomas Fairfax asking if he might be an intermediary in an attempt 'to restore a happy peace, and we might feel it a great blessing . . . to be an instrument in the advancing of it'.

16th   Resolved in the Commons this day that the sum of £1,128 17s 8d from the sale of hangings and plate from the sack of Bridgwater should be sent to Fairfax for distribution to the soldiers concerned.

17th   A penitent letter is sent from Rupert to the King regarding Bristol, 'if your Majesty had vouchsafed me so much patience as to hear me before you made a final judgement'.

18th   The Chancellor goes to Pendennis Castle on a pretext of investigating customs revenue but in fact to ensure that the frigate provided for Prince Charles's escape should be at instant readiness.

19th   The Committee instructs Colonel Carne to take charge of the forces for the reduction of Langford House in Wiltshire.

20th   Brereton storms Chester defences before dawn this day and takes the Eastgate suburbs.

21st   The King with an army of 4,000 men advances to the relief of Chester. Colonel General Poyntz, who is seeking to intercept the King, is hastily directed on to him by The Committee.

22nd   Despite these intrusions from the outside world Brereton hangs on like a bulldog, and continues to bombard the city wall at close range and makes 'a breach which ten men may enter'.

23rd   The King reaches Chester, Langdale being detached.

24th   THE BATTLE OF ROWTON HEATH. This is an overwhelming defeat for the King in an ill-managed and chaotic battle outside the walls of Chester.

25th   The King arrives at Denbigh Castle. The disaster at Rowton Heath is seconded by the news of the catastrophic defeat of Montrose at Philliphaugh which negates the King's optimistic schemes.

The Phoenix or King Charles's Tower, Chester from where the King watched the destruction of one of the last Royalist armies in September 1645.

26th   News reaches the King of the surrender of Berkeley Castle, Gloucestershire and Devizes, Wiltshire.

27th   Winchester Castle is besieged by Cromwell.

28th   Maurice 'waits upon the King with 800 horse'.

29th   Goring sends extravagant demands for personal agrandisement to the Chancellor.

30th   The Committee writes to Colonel General Poyntz returning grateful thanks for his services and voting him £500 and 'for the greater encouragement of those under your command £5,000.'

October

1st   The Committee chides the Committee of Southwark, saying that it was ordered that 145 recruits should be levied by impressment. These should have been at Reading the previous Saturday but not one man has yet been levied.

2nd   Sir Thomas Glemham is appointed Governor of Oxford.

3rd   Sandal Castle in Yorkshire is surrendered by the Royalist commander, Colonel Bonivant.

4th   The King is at Newark with 1,400 men.

5th   The King sends orders to Sir Gervase Lucas, Governor of Belvoir Castle, ordering him to accommodate Gerrard's horse, 300 strong.

6th   After a prolonged bombardment Lord Ogle surrenders Winchester Castle to Cromwell.

7th   Brereton gives £5 to one Timothy Widdowes who carried the tidings of the King's defeat at Chester.

8th   Cromwell arrives at Basing House complete with a heavy siege train.

9th   The question of cash arises again. Major Ennis is ordered to join Poyntz but protests that despite all The Committee's thunder his men's pay is so much in arrears that he cannot march until they are paid.

10th Lilburne, who was sent to Newgate Prison for speaking out against William Prynne and Speaker Lenthall, this day publishes his *England's Birthright*, which he had written in prison and in which he equates liberty of conscience with civil liberties.

11th Another preacher of new doctrines, one William Walwyn, publishes *London's Lamentable Slavery* this day. It is a sequel to his *Compassionate Samaritan* (published 1644). These two men, although dissimilar, later become partners in the Leveller movement.

12th The King is at Tuxford.
        Cromwell with little time to waste crisply summons Basing House to surrender. The Marquess of Winchester refuses equally crisply. The Parliamentary artillery, including the giant cannon royal (68 pounder), opens fire.

13th The King at Welbeck, north of Newark, this day calls a Council of War. Digby, the King's evil genius, is vehement for a march into Scotland to seek out the beaten Montrose.

14th The storm and destruction of Basing House are undertaken by Dalbier and Cromwell.
        Digby and Langdale are sent on detached service into Scotland for the King who is at Doncaster.

15th   Dalbier is detached to siege Donnington Castle.

       Digby wins, then loses a confused action at Sherburn in Elmet.

16th   Fairfax gains Tiverton and fortifies various strong points on the east side of Exeter.

       Rupert arrives at Newark despite the King's order to the contrary. His object is to clear his name over Bristol.

17th   Goring writes to Culpeper stating his intention to hold Exeter with 1,000 horse and all his foot. If the occasion arises he will use it as a strategic base.

       All Digby's scattered forces reform at Skipton.

18th   Poyntz, ordered by The Committee to siege Newark, reaches Warsop this day.

19th   Digby and Langdale reach Dumfries this day and being unable to contact or learn the whereabouts of Montrose abandon the expedition.

20th   At the court martial that Rupert has insisted upon, the Royal Council of War absolves him from any slur on his honour, ability or loyalty. The ill feeling between the King and his nephew is only erased on the surface.

21st   The unreliable Goring changes his mind about Exeter and retires on Newton Bushell.

22nd   Goring writes to Rupert that if Grenville will work with him he will perform any task required of him.

23rd   Rupert replies to Goring that Grenville will work with him and that in the circumstances he will leave the whole defence of the west in Goring's hand.

24th   With enemy forces closing in and men deserting by degrees Digby and Langdale take ship from Ravenglass.

25th   The Committee writes to the Committee of Hampshire stating with some asperity that the county had been assessed at 500 foot and 200 horse for the reduction of Donnington Castle. It is expected to report on 28 October latest.

26th   It is plain that the King's hostility to Rupert has not abated when he replaces Sir Richard Willis (one of Rupert's supporters) by Lord Bellasis to command Newark. This leads to a violent quarrel between the two factions.

A. THE OLDE HOVSE . B. THE NEW. C. THE TOWER THAT IS HALFE BATTERED DOWNE . D. THE KINGES BREAST WORKS . E. THE PARLIAMENTS BREAST WORK

Basing House, Hampshire. The house was besieged and battered by Parliamentarian forces in October 1645.

The ruins at Basing House.

27th   One order, among others, to delinquent commanders and committees this day shows the energetic and tireless Committee at its best when it tells Colonel Martin, 'This is to repeat our further order to march the regiment to Newbury. We anticipate your liveliest endeavour heretofore.'

28th   The Committee writes to the Eastern Association stating, 'We have received many and sad complaints of the state of the garrison at Newport Pagnell where the soldiers are in great arrear of pay.' It finishes with a note of veiled menace to pay them – now!

29th   The King's replacement of Willis arouses angry passions among Rupert's supporters. Unprecedented scenes occur when they come into the Royal presence and demand satisfaction. Not receiving it they depart in high dudgeon for Belvoir Castle.

30th   This day Henrietta Maria writes to Pope Innocent X: 'My wishes will always be for the increase of the Catholic religion and for the service of your Holiness.'

31st   Parliament ordains a warrant for 500 swords and bandoliers for 'such as are engaged for the service against Newark'.

November

1st   Poyntz and Rossiter join forces and occupy Shelford.

2nd   Gerrard writes bitterly from Belvoir Castle to Ralph Skipwith at Oxford stating that all of Rupert's party has received pass to leave the country. 'A generous, excellent reward,' he comments.

3rd   Poyntz delivers a formal surrender demand to the Governor of Shelford House, Colonel Phillip Stanhope, who returns a defiant answer. The house is stormed and 140 of its defenders are slaughtered.

4th   The King, having travelled overnight from Newark with 400 horse, stays briefly at Belvoir and sleeps at Codsbury.

5th   The King is once again at Oxford.
     Bolton Castle, famous seat of the Scropes, is surrendered by Colonel Henry Chaytor after the garrison has been reduced to eating horseflesh.

6th   A circular letter from The Committee is sent to seven counties demanding to know the state of the garrisons in their charge and the numbers.

7th   The King writes to Prince Charles from Oxford instructing him to take ship to Denmark and 'not to delay one hour'.

8th   The King is compelled to relieve Gerrard of his command by popular demand and replaces him with Astley. As a sop to his pride Gerrard is created baron which infuriates many who feel themselves more deserving.

9th   Poyntz summons Wiverton, commanded by Sir Robert Therrill. Shocked by the massacre at Shelford, Therrill's wife persuades him to surrender.

10th   Fairfax is approached regarding ordinance left in Poole by Waller. He is asked if he does not require it, might the Hampshire Committee use it?

11th   Parliament is heartily glad to offer Rupert and his adherents safe conduct passes to leave the country, nominating Yarmouth, Dover, Rye and Southampton as exit ports. The passes are valid for fourteen days.

12th   The Speakers of both Houses write to the Scottish Estates bitterly complaining that Scots garrisons have been placed in Carlisle, Tynemouth, Hartlepool, Stockton, Warkworth and Thirlwall without consent of Parliament.

13th   The articles of disgarrisoning Welbeck, Bolsover and Tickhill are agreed and are signified to Poyntz.

14th   The Parliamentary army treasurers are ordered to despatch £30,000 to Fairfax. It must be shipped at Portsmouth and thence to Weymouth.

15th   Apparently not all the recruits are willing, for Colonel Jephson's horse is ordered to escort the draft from Reading to within one day's march of Bristol, there to join Skippon's regiment.

16th   Beeston Castle which has been besieged for a year surrenders this day.

17th   Poyntz and Rossiter camp at Bottesford preparatory to reducing Belvoir Castle.

18th   A strange, terse minute is made in The Committee's proceedings: 'Major-General Browne must make the best use he can of Mr Blakeby for the public use.'

19th   There is more trouble at Abingdon. The Committee notes that, 'unless an establishment be made for the maintenance of the garrison it will be impossible to keep a force there.'

20th   Lord George Goring writes from Exeter to Prince Charles that for health reasons he must absent himself from his command and repair himself to France. Without waiting for a reply he travels to Dartmouth and boards the first available ship, so quitting the Civil War in which he has performed so long.

21st   Lack of cooperation always infuriates The Committee. The committees of Hertfordshire and Bedfordshire are castigated for not sending their quota of horse and dragoons to Newport Pagnell.

22nd   Poyntz storms the outworks at Belvoir and takes them after a bloody struggle. The defenders retire into the castle and Poyntz is driven to besiege it.

23rd   The Commons sends a letter to Rupert saying that unless the Prince makes use of its concessions to leave England within fourteen days they will be cancelled.

24th   Sir Robert King's messengers to The Committee has been taken prisoner by the Banbury garrison.

25th   Berkeley Castle is saved for posterity by an order of the House of Lords over-ruling The Committee: 'The Castle must not be defaced, slighted, demolished through any pretence whatsoever at your peril seeing Lord Berkeley hath suffered so deeply already.'

26th   The final siege of Newark is undertaken by the Earl of Leven and the Scots army.

27th   Sir Richard Grenville advises Prince Charles to send to Parliament treating for peace on his own behalf, 'to sit still, a neuter between King and Parliament'.

28th   Brereton reports to The Committee: 'The besieged in Chester remain obstinate and do not seem inclinable to embrace any overtures.'

29th   Some of the Merchant Adventurers are ordered to present themselves to the Commons concerning interdicting trade to Worcester.

30th   The Militia Committee at the Savoy requests an advance of £10,000 for the payment of the City of London forces recently sent out for the public service.

*Sir William Brereton,
commander of the
Parliamentarian forces in
Cheshire.*

December

1st Sir Thomas Fairfax is notified that Abingdon has been held by the London auxiliaries who will return home on 16 December. Can he replace them?

2nd The Committee writes to the Committee of Nottingham relating that it has seen a letter addressed to one of its members regarding the condition of its county and the catalogue of its wants and woes. Its members had not, it wrote, considered it their province and had passed it on to the Commons who in turn had referred it to the appropriate committee.

3rd Captain Davies is ordered to take charge of the garrison in Burley House in Rutland during the absence of the governor, Colonel Waite, who is to attend a committee of the House of Commons.

4th The committees of Northumberland, Lancashire, Salop and Stafford are ordered not to withdraw their forces from Chester as 'it will not now be a work of either much time or difficulty to reduce it'.

5th   The King contacts Parliament saying that if it would send safe conduct passes he would send commissioners 'who would make particular propositions to them'.

6th   'Money is the sinews of war.' A committee of members of the Commons comes to the Guildhall to attend a meeting of the Common Council to ask for a loan of £30,000 to pay the Scots army. After a debate the council agrees to guarantee this money at the rate of 8 per cent.

7th   The King writes even more urgently to Prince Charles to make his escape without delay.

8th   Divers warrants are issued this day. A number of carts are to be requisitioned for the purpose of transporting uniforms from Reading to Portsmouth.

       Sir Michael Wharton's house, chamber and stables are to be searched, likewise the prisoners in the Tower, by 'Mr Beck, Mr Prynne and whoever they may take to assist them'.

9th   The Speakers of the two Houses write to Sir Thomas Glemham, Governor of Oxford, acknowledging the receipt of the King's message and promising a speedy reply.

10th   Brereton opens fire on Chester with a heavy mortar. An eye witness notes: 'The great grenadoes like so many demi-phaetons threaten to set the city if not the world alight.'

11th   The papers found on the Tower prisoners (*see* 8 December) are sent to the Committee for Examinations and Mr Banks, the Clerk to the committee, attends the meeting to give necessary information.

12th   Colonel General Poyntz is ordered to send Colonel Haynes' regiment back to the Eastern Association rather than take upon himself the cost of paying them.

13th   The London Militia Committee is ordered to provide fifty dragoons as a convoy for a provision train which is to be sent to those besieging Newark.

14th   An order from the Lord High Admiral says the ship *The Globe* is to be fitted out and victualled ready for sea with all speed so that she may not lay in the river longer than necessary. A postscript states that the crew of *The Globe*, *Adventure* and *Crescent* are all unpaid and should be paid without delay.

15th Colonel Whalley is warned that it is reported that Lord Astley (formerly Sir Jacob) with Sir John Campsfield and 1,000 horse are advancing on Chester. If this is proved correct he is to take two regiments 'and prevent an interruption of the siege'.

16th The Earl of Leven is notified by The Committee that a convoy is on its way to Newark with provisions and money.

17th The fifty dragoons accompanying the Newark convoy (*see* 13 December) are ordered to march as far as Grantham. For this they will be paid by the Militia Committee.

18th Colonel John Birch, with a volunteer force, advances over the ice-bound countryside to make a surprise attack on Hereford. The dispirited Royalist garrison makes only a token resistance and the governor, Sir Barnabas Scudamore, makes his escape over the frozen River Wye.

19th Provisions are finding their way into Newark. Poyntz and Rossiter are ordered to make the blockade total.

Newark, showing the fortifications around the town. The strategically placed Royalist base was strongly defended throughout the war.

20th   The search of Sir Michael Wharton's effects proves fruitless for he is discharged this day (*see 8th December*).

21st   Stores and ammunition now depleted, Colonel Sir John Mallory surrenders Skipton Castle on terms to Parliament.

22nd   A certificate is issued by Colonel John Fox to the Earl of Denbigh certifying that Major Reginald Fox, 'now lying sick and lame at Warwick', has lost everything in Parliament's service.

23rd   One James Croft of Bristol, 'well affected towards Parliament in whose service he has borne arms', petitions for the return of six kilderkins of tin and twenty bales of calves' skins which he had consigned to France. The ship had been taken by the Parliamentary man-of-war *Fellowship* and was to be sold as a prize.

24th   The Committee chides the Committee of Salop. The garrison of Oswestry is very much in arrears of pay and it is the responsibility of the latter commission to pay up.

25th   Parliament replies to the King's proposals of 5 December regarding new proposals. It says it is pointless. It will send him a number of Bills for the Royal Assent. Then and only then could there be peace.

26th   Although the weather is 'fitter for a fire than a march', Prince Charles goes from Truro to Bodmin.
    The King writes again to Parliament proposing a personal treaty.

27th   Prince Charles goes to Tavistock.

28th   Ship captains Bowen and Batten are alerted that there are reported to be two Royalist ships at Roven laden with munitions.

29th   A pass is issued by the King for Sir Peter Killigrew to come to Oxford 'without let or molestation' to convey letters to Westminster with the monarch's answers.

30th   Brereton reports the complete encirclement of Chester.

31st   An account by Thomas Smith and John Hill, collectors of prize goods. The contents of the *Golden Sun*, taken by the Parliarmentary warship *Garland*, master Captain Owen, fetch £789 0*s* 1*d*. The state's share is £411 10*s*.

Events Leading up to the Second Civil War and After

From 5 May 1646 to 30 January 1649

On 5 May the end of the First or Great Civil War came when the King calmly surrendered his person to the Scottish army at Southwell.

Anyone less self-delusory than Charles would have admitted total defeat and escaped to the Continent to plot and plan for another day. Although he did admit in a conversation with Rupert that had he been a mere soldier or statesman he might have considered himself ruined, he was totally convinced that God would not suffer his anointed to be overthrown. So with sublime confidence, if not arrogance, he went to Scotland. Unfortunately he found that the Scots regarded him somewhat in the nature of a viable political pawn and when they became convinced that he regarded them in the same light, and that far from granting them their cherished ambitions of imposing the Presbyterian Church on England he was in fact only interested in splitting the alliance between the Scots, and the army and Parliament, they despaired of getting a satisfactory settlement. Baillie wrote, 'The King's madness has confounded us all'. In the end, tiring of the monarch's delaying tactics, the Scots virtually sold him to his enemies, not for thirty pieces of silver it is true, but for the first heavy instalment of Parliament's war debt.

But despite their possession of the King, all was not well in the ranks of the victors. While the conflict was still raging they were united in a common cause against a common enemy. Lacking this singleness of purpose a wide gulf was opening between the two factions of the reforming party. First there were the Presbyterians who wished to replace the detested and intolerant Anglican Church with their own brand of Christianity, which was equally narrow and repressive. Far more open-minded but equally vehement were the Independents who believed that it was the right of every congregation in the country to choose freely its own style of worship. They felt that the Presbyterian mode was as distasteful as the Anglican. The Presbyterians were dominant in Parliament but their opponents were powerful in the country and particularly in the army.

As in all wars, once victory is won the first thing to be considered redundant is the army that was the instrument of that victory. Ostensibly on a point of reducing public expenditure, but in fact because Parliament was becoming afraid of the army's potential under its popular and trusted commanders Fairfax, Cromwell and Ireton, it decreed the armed forces must be reduced to modest proportions instead of the massive strength of 22,000 that it now was.

Parliament was greatly indebted to the military both in terms of the victory and in the matter of back pay – the foot were owed for eighteen weeks, the horse for forty-three. However, it made the soldiers only a beggarly offer; it declared that a six-week payment should discharge the debt. Not unnaturally the soldiers held meetings to grumble over the shabby way they had been treated. These meetings resulted in the hammering out of proposals of their own to make England a place fit for patriot heroes to live in and the foundation of a committee that was virtually the army's own Parliament which they called the Grand Council.

Thus the cause for which Pym and Hampden had struggled and which had been strengthened by war was now split asunder by peace.

At first Parliament imagined it had full control of the situation and ordered the army to disband as directed. The army's answer was a declaration most likely drawn up by Ireton which requested payment of arrears, guarantees against future conscription, and pensions for war widows and disabled soldiers. Parliament rejected this with disdain and again ordered it to disband. Instead the army concentrated at Newmarket and declared that until its demands were met it would not disband.

At this point a remarkable change of partners took place. The army began to look to the King, and the Presbyterians to their brothers in religion – the Scots. Possession of the King's person became all important to Cromwell and Ireton. Some historians say this was because they were fearful for Charles' safety, others say because they saw in him a valuable bargaining counter. On 3 June 1647 on the orders of Cromwell, Cornet George Joyce with 400 Ironsides rode to Holmby House where the King was negotiating with the Parliamentary commissioners and took over. Next morning Joyce intimated with great respect that His Majesty should leave. When asked where his warrant for such a move was, the cornet nodded at his 400 men. It was enough.

Cromwell, Ireton and Fairfax met the cavalcade at Childerley near Newmarket. After discussion the King wrote to both Houses instructing them to accept the reasonable terms of the army. It has been suggested that had all parties been reconciled at this time a new Golden Era might have been the future. But the King was insincere in his dealings with Cromwell as with the Parliament, and the army was hardly likely to be reconciled with Parliament either. Parliament proved as intractable as Charles had been in times past, its only answer being to continue with its demobilization plans.

Fairfax's answer was simple and direct. He occupied London with the army and subdued Parliament in August 1647. But all was not well even now, for there arose dissensions in the army itself. A conservative body consisting of the more level-headed officers like Fairfax and Cromwell wanted a restoration of the traditional form of government with inbuilt safeguards. But others under John Lilburne preached an embryo communist doctrine. They believed all men were created equal therefore all men should be entitled to equal wealth, equal influence and equal opportunities. They were called 'Levellers' because of these revolutionary principles.

Oliver Cromwell thought this path led only to anarchy so when Lilburne and his followers refused to return to their units he saw it as mutiny and treated it as such.

In the middle of all this turmoil it was not unnatural that the King, fearing for his life, escaped from Hampton Court where he was domiciled. With his usual sublime optimism he did not make straight for the Continent but only to the Isle of Wight, to Carisbrook Castle, exchanging one prison for another. But from the comparative safety of this retreat, he commenced to weave the familiar web of intrigue and negotiation with anyone who might seem useful. Eventually the Scots, who had shown themselves to be hardly trustworthy, entered into an engagement in the latter half of December 1647. They agreed to put the King back on the throne by force of arms, in return for which they required the abolition of the Independents and the Anglican Church, and the establishment of Presbyterianism for a trial period. Pockets of Royalist resistance, which were impatiently waiting for a opportunity to reverse the decision of the 1642–6 struggle, were to rise up

Carisbrooke Castle, Isle of Wight. Charles was held captive here from November 1647 to autumn 1648.

all over the country as soon as the Scots crossed the border. Thus even the New Model Army would be swamped by the sheer impossibility of being everywhere at the same time.

Royalist hopes flamed high in those early months of 1648 and it looked as though the strategy could not fail. It was only through their own impatience that it did. The insurrections that were to saturate the country were triggered prematurely. Under the iron hands of Cromwell and Fairfax they were contained or suppressed by the time the laggard Duke of Hamilton crossed the border, and Cromwell was free to give him his undivided attention. On 16–17 August 1648 he smashed the duke with his customary thoroughness at Preston.

The result of this Second Civil War had the opposite effect from that which the King anticipated. Although Parliament was still negotiating with Charles to preserve the fragmentary remains of the old government, the army, particularly Cromwell, had soured on the King. His apparently sincere and friendly negotiations were seen for what they were, only procrastinations to make time while he negotiated their overthrow with their enemies. No satisfactory agreement could be reached with such a man, whose half truths and deceit would eventually lure them all into a quicksand of intrigue and mutual suspicion. The senior officers met and agreed that 'Charles Stuart that man of blood, should be called to account for that blood he hath shed'.

Early in December, Cromwell ordered Colonel Thomas Pride to purge Parliament of the Presbyterian factor. Forty-five were arrested as they came to take up their seats and many more were turned away. In the end only seventy members, the majority of whom were Independents, took their appointed places. Nevertheless, they claimed the full authority of the Commons, although the common folk with devastating wit gave them the popular and slanderous name that has gone down into history – the Rump. The power of the army was behind them, giving them sufficient authority both to try the King and to execute him. It is not the purpose here to defend or execrate this deed, merely to record it. Uncommitted readers will form their own conclusions speedily and certainly those committed will take little notice of these views.

1646

January

9th   Cromwell surprises Lord Wentworth's cavalry at Bovey Tracey, south-west of Exeter, and cuts them to pieces.

15th   The Prince of Wales and his council decide to reorganize the Western Army. Hopton is in general command, with Wentworth commanding the horse and Grenville the foot. The army now totals almost 2,000 foot and 3,000 horse.

19th   Fairfax storms Dartmouth and sieges Exeter.

February

3rd   Byron surrenders Chester.

10th   In the hope of relieving Exeter, Hopton occupies Torrington.

14th   Fairfax, leaving a brigade to contain Exeter, arrives at Chumleigh this day.

16th   THE BATTLE OF TORRINGTON. Bad weather prevents an advance from Chumleigh until early morning this day when Fairfax draws up his army to assault Torrington. The Parliamentarian Council of War, having reconnoitred the Royalist position, decides to attack next day, but when other patrols report, as darkness falls, that Hopton seems to be on the point of retiring, the attack is made immediately.

   The Royalists fight with unexpected ferocity; a Parliamentary officer records: 'The service was very hot . . . it was maintained on both sides for some while.'

   After about two hours Fairfax's men are inside the town and a general action ensues in the dark streets. Suddenly the darkness is split asunder by a vivid flash and a giant explosion as some desperate soldier fires the large powder magazine stored in the church, killing 200 Parliamentary prisoners immediately. The falling debris causes many casualties among the contestants in the streets, Fairfax himself having a narrow escape.

Lord Byron, Royalist Governor of Chester during the siege of 1645–6.

March

2nd   As the crumbling Western Army staggers westward the Prince of Wales and his council realize the imminence of the end and they sail for the Scilly Isles.

6th   Fairfax offers such generous terms to Hopton that he dare not make them known to his men.

12th   Even Hopton realizes by this date that what men he has left are so demoralized that further resistance is impossible. He accepts the terms, which action results in the end of the army in the west.

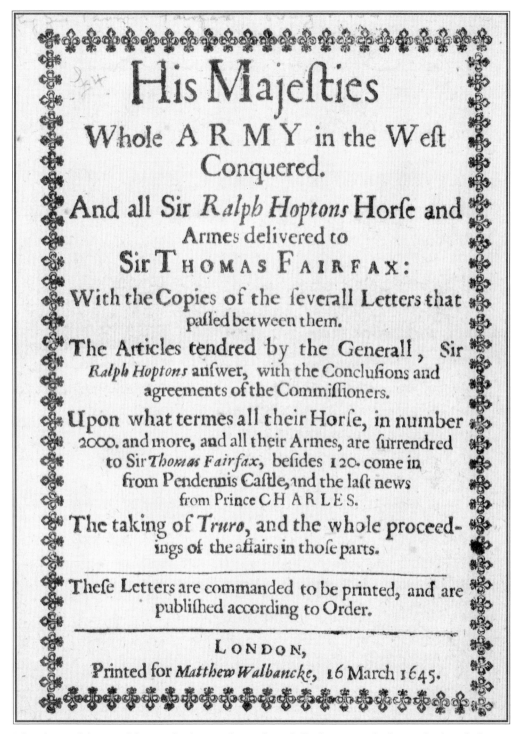

His Majesties

Whole ARMY in the West Conquered.

And all Sir *Ralph Hoptons* Horse and Armes delivered to

Sir THOMAS FAIRFAX:

With the Copies of the severall Letters that passed between them.

The Articles tendred by the Generall, Sir *Ralph Hoptons* answer, with the Conclusions and agreements of the Commissioners.

Upon what termes all their Horse, in number 2000. and more, and all their Armes, are surrendred to Sir *Thomas Fairfax*, besides 120. come in from Pendennis Castle, and the last news from Prince CHARLES.

The taking of *Truro*, and the whole proceedings of the affairs in those parts.

These Letters are commanded to be printed, and are published according to Order.

LONDON,
Printed for *Matthew Walbancke*, 16 March 1645.

The title page of the terms of the surrender, drawn up by Fairfax and offered to Hopton after he capitulated completely in March 1646. Two months later the King surrendered to the Scots.

The pitched stone court of Raglan Castle, which took the brunt of the Parliamentarian bombardment of 1646.

	21st	Cornered by Brereton and Morgan, Astley surrenders the last Royalist army at Stow.
April	*9th*	Berkeley surrenders Exeter on similar excellent terms.
	27th	The King in disguise leaves Oxford for the Scots camp at Newark.
May	*5th*	Charles surrenders to the Scots at Southwell.
June	*24th*	The surrender of Oxford on terms by Glemham.
July	*31st*	Holles attempts to send six New Model Regiments to Ireland but is thwarted.
August	*16th*	Pendennis Castle surrenders at last.
	19th	Raglan Castle is surrendered by the veteran Marquess of Worcester, leaving Harlech as the last Royalist stronghold.

Pendennis Castle, Falmouth, Cornwall: the last English mainland base to fall to the Parliamentarians.

1647

January	*30th*	Charles is handed over to Parliamentary representatives by the Scots.
March	*16th*	The surrender of Harlech Castle.
	30th	A moderate petition from the army is declared seditious by the Commons.
May	*31st*	Cornet George Joyce of Fairfax's Lifeguard is ordered to safeguard the train of artillery at Oxford and then to secure the King's person at Holmby House.
June	*4th*	Joyce removes the King from Holmby House.
	10th	A general rendezvous of the army takes place on Triploe Heath. Parliamentary commissioners visit Triploe and are told very definitely that the army will not disband without satisfaction.
	14th	The declaration of the army asserts its right to oppose Parliament in defence of its rights.
July	*26th*	Rioters in the City force the Speakers of both Houses and the leading Independents to leave London and seek the protection of the army.
August	*6th*	The New Model Army enters London.
		'Heads of the Army Proposals' are presented to Parliament. Largely Ireton's work, they quite moderately advocate religious tolerations, a bi-annual Parliament and a kind of limited monarchy.

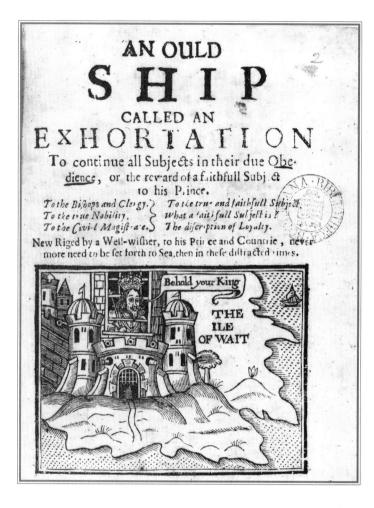

Charles I in Carisbrooke Castle, Isle of Wight, 1648, as depicted by a Royalist broadsheet of the time.

Oct–Nov		The General Council of the army meets in Putney Church in London.
October	18th	The army extremist pamphlet *The Case of the Army Truly Stated* is presented to Fairfax.
	30th	The Levellers' 'Agreement of the People' presented to the Council results in uproar.
November	11th	The Council breaks up. The King escapes from Hampton Court, whence he travels to Carisbrooke Castle.
December	26th	The King signs the engagement with the Scots.

1648

March

13th Sir Thomas Fairfax becomes 3rd Lord Fairfax of Cameron on the death of his father.

23rd Colonel Poyer, Governor of Pembroke Castle, declares for the King after a dispute over arrears of pay.

April

28th Langdale takes Berwick.

29th Sir Phillip Musgrave surprises Carlisle.

May

11th Cromwell joins Horton and commences to siege Pembroke and Chepstow Castles.

Chepstow Castle, Gwent. Chepstow held out for the King during the First Civil War to become a major Royalist stronghold during the Second.

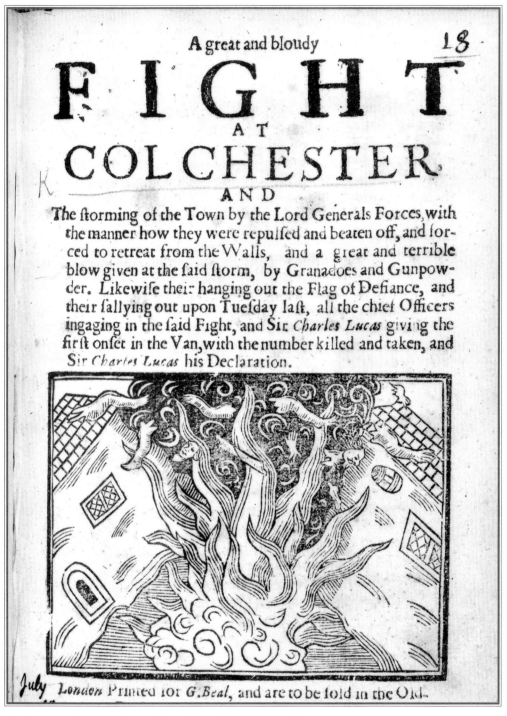

A great and bloudy

FIGHT

AT

COLCHESTER,

AND

The storming of the Town by the Lord Generals Forces, with
the manner how they were repulsed and beaten off, and forced to retreat from the Walls, and a great and terrible
blow given at the said storm, by Granadoes and Gunpowder. Likewise their hanging out the Flag of Defiance, and
their sallying out upon Tuesday last, all the chief Officers
ingaging in the said Fight, and Sir *Charles Lucas* giving the
first onset in the Van, with the number killed and taken, and
Sir *Charles Lucas* his Declaration.

London Printed for *G.Beal*, and are to be sold in the Old.

An illustration from a pamphlet describing the siege of Colchester in 1648.

| 21st | Revolt in Kent. Rochester is seized. |

| 26th | Dartford and Deptford are taken by Royalists. |

| 27th | The fleet is in the Downs mutiny, its officers being mainly Presbyterian. Fairfax musters his army on Hounslow Heath. |

| 30th | Fairfax's army reaches Eltham. |

| 31st | The army reaches Gravesend. |

June

| 1st | Ignoring Rochester, Fairfax reaches Malling this day and travels thence to Maidstone. Although the attack is premature, he seizes the town after bitter street fighting. |

| 3rd | The Earl of Norwich, who had commanded at Maidstone, arrives this day at Blackheath and seizes Bow Bridge, hoping that the City will rise for the King. However, he is disappointed. |

| 4th | Norwich retreats on Colchester which has been garrisoned by troops under Sir Charles Lucas, Sir George Lisle and Lord Capel. |

| 9th | Norwich and his Kentish Royalists reach Colchester. |

Colchester, a scene of conflict between the combined Royalist forces of Lisle, Lucas and Norwich and Parliamentarian troops led by Fairfax, June 1648.

James, 1st Duke of Hamilton,
by an unknown artist after
Van Dyck.

11th	Fairfax crosses the Thames at Tilbury and advances on Colchester.
13th–14th	Fairfax attempts to storm the town but is roughly handled by the determined defenders.

July

8th	The Duke of Hamilton belatedly crosses the border with a raw army of 3,000 horse and 6,000 foot.

Pembroke Castle was a major Parliamentarian base throughout the First Civil War, but changed hands during the Second to become an equally important base for the Royalists. Cromwell finally reclaimed the castle after a prolonged operation from May to July 1648.

11th   Poyer surrenders Pembroke Castle to Cromwell, freeing Cromwell for service in the north.

14th   Fairfax, having forwarded siege arrangements, summons Colchester but receives a derisive answer, stating that a ready cure for his gout is at hand.

Scots cavalry clashes with Lambert's near Penrith.

15th   Lambert falls back to Appleby.

Hamilton awaits reinforcements at Kirkby Thore, eventually being joined by another 6,000 foot.

27th   Lambert is joined at Barnard Castle by forward elements of Cromwell's army.

August

7th   Hamilton continues to advance and Lambert to fall back steadily before him, reaching Knaresborough this day.

12th   Cromwell joins Lambert at Wetherby. He now commands 2,500 horse and dragoons, 4,000 foot, plus another 1,600 foot and 500 horse out of Lancashire.

The Battle of Preston
17–19 August 1648

As Cromwell continued his advance on Preston it became clear that Langdale lay between the Parliamentarians and their next objective. Langdale himself rode into the town and warned Hamilton of the imminent danger and the urgent need to get his widely dispersed army into close battle array.

Unfortunately for the Royalist cause Hamilton, perhaps smiling indulgently, dismissed his warning as exaggeration and the approach of the Parliament army as merely a probing attack. On the morning of 17 August Langdale got his men together and commenced retiring on Preston. His rear guard was soon engaged by forward units of the New Model Army. Langdale again reported to Hamilton and found that the Scots were badly over extended. Baillie and his foot were engaged in crossing over the Ribble en route southwards, Callendar and the horse were still at Wigan, while Monro's troops were an even greater distance northward.

No great soldier, Hamilton might even now have saved the day by decisive action, but with all the stubborness of a weak man he still declined to believe the danger as great as it was. Langdale went back to his command presently to bear the weight of Cromwell's attack with the skill born of long experience, lining the hedges with musketeers and blocking the sunken lane leading from Longridge to Preston.

The Royalists fought fiercely and, owing to the soft nature of the ground which impeded the Ironsides, they held their position and then when the weight of numbers told fought from hedge to hedge. At first the retreat was orderly but once beyond the

16th   The Scots army being seriously short of provisions is foraging far and wide. This day a dangerous gap has opened up between the foot at Preston and the horse at Wigan. Langdale's force way out on the left is moving southwards from Settle.

16th–17th   Cromwell, without knowing the precise location of the Scots, decides to march on Preston. This night sees him camped in the grounds of Stonyhurst Hall, east of Preston.

17th–19th THE BATTLE OF PRESTON. Cromwell defeats the allied Scots and Royalists. *See separate account above.*

19th   The Scots reel back towards Warrington where they hope to hold the line of the River Mersey, but Cromwell traps them at Winwick.

20th   Baillie is ordered by Hamilton to surrender the foot while Hamilton retreats with the horse.

protection of the enclosures and hedges on the expanse of Ribbleton Moor where the New Model Army's cavalry could be used to advantage, the retreat became a rout, Langdale's survivors being pushed right into town. Hamilton, by now able to realize the extreme danger, made an effort to make a stand on Preston Moor. But when the choleric Callendar came up and asked what madness was this, standing on the open moor, he wavered and agreed to a far more complex plan which he had neither the time, nor his troops the cohesion to fulfil.

Very shortly Hamilton, with a small Lifeguard, was cut off from his troops on the other side of Ribble. Showing some decisiveness at last he ordered the rear guard horse to escape northwards while he and his small party swam the Ribble with their horses. By leading several charges against scattered bodies of enemy horse that tried to block his passage, Hamilton showed that while he was no strategist, at least he was not a coward.

With the area north of the Ribble cleared of Scots, Cromwell turned his attention to Preston Bridge, which was held by two Scots brigades. They held on stubbornly for two hours giving Baillie time to put his foot in a defensive posture around Walton Hall. By this time darkness had fallen with forward elements of the New Model Army across the bridge looting the Scots' wagon train.

About 4,000 of Hamilton's men had been taken and 1,000 killed. Again influenced by Callendar, Hamilton decided not to stand and fight and the dawn of 18 August saw the Scots army in full retreat. The scheme was to join with Middleton and his horse, but this again was bungled, the two bodies taking different roads. Altogether Preston was the biggest fiasco that could have been imagined and worthy more of the title of tragi-comedy than that of a battle.

25th	Lambert catches up with the Scots cavalry at Uttoxeter and they too surrender.
28th	Colchester surrenders to Fairfax, the garrison having eaten all the available horses, cats and dogs. The execution takes place by firing squad of Sir Charles Lucas and Sir George Lisle.

September

22nd	Cromwell goes north and meets Argyll, once more in power, and concludes an agreement with him.

Oct–Nov

	While Cromwell is dallying at the siege of Pontefract Castle, Holles re-opens negotiations with the King, widening even further the gulf between army and Parliament.

November

16th	The King flatly rejects a new treaty, irked by the restrictions it places on the monarchy.

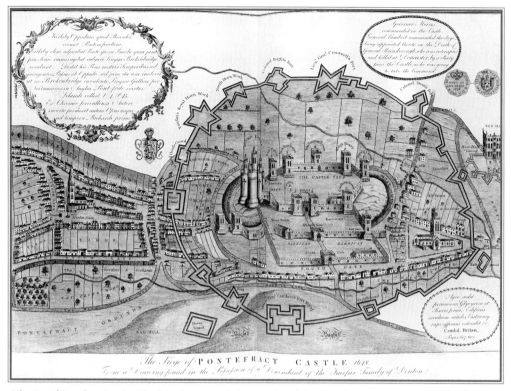

The siege of Pontefract Castle. After being in a state of almost continual siege from August 1644 to July 1645, the Royalist garrison at Pontefract Castle finally surrendered on 21 July.

20th   A remonstrance is presented to the Parliament by the army demanding the King be brought to trial but is ignored.

29th   The army takes matters into its own hands and sends units of the New Model Army to the Isle of Wight and for the second time the King is taken into custody.

30th   The King is moved to Hurst Castle.

December

5th   A crisis is precipitated by the Presbyterians' declaration that they wish to carry on negotiations with the monarch.

6th   PRIDE'S PURGE. The army's answer to the Presbyterians is sharp and effective. Colonel Pride, whose foot regiment is backed by Colonel Rich's horse, surrounds the Commons' house. Assisted by Lord Grey of Groby he denies access to 240 Presbyterian members and detains 39 who offer violence.

23rd   The King is taken to Windsor.

25th   A final attempt to reach an agreement with the King fails.

1649

6th The so-called Rump Parliament sets up a High Court to try the King.

8th Of the 136 nominated commissioners, 53 meet to discuss the High Court proceedings. When Fairfax understands that Cromwell and his followers are determined to execute the King he leaves the gathering horrified.

The King's death warrant. Among the signatures are those of Cromwell (first column) and Ireton (second column).

The Rump Parliament of 1649 satirized.

20th The King's trial commences.

27th The King is sentenced to death by John Bradshaw and his tribunal, as a tyrant and traitor who had for his own ends not hesitated to shed the blood of his own people.

30th The King is executed in Whitehall.

February

5th Prince Charles is proclaimed King (Charles II) by the Scottish Estates.

7th The monarchy is abolished and replaced by a Council of State.

March

15th Cromwell is appointed to command in Ireland.

30th After careful assessment of the logistical position Cromwell accepts the command.

Fairfax as the King's executioner, c. 1649.

A contemporary Dutch engraving of the execution of Charles I.

John Lilburne, Leveller, 1641.

May

Leveller mutinies. In the early months of the year pamphlets and agitation are urged on by the evocative Lilburne until mutiny is sparked off when Captain Thompson leads 200 troopers in open revolt at Banbury. Fairfax and Cromwell sternly and efficiently deal with these mutinies.

July

10th   Cromwell leaves London for Ireland. Travelling through Wales, he arrives in Dublin on 15 August. He stays until June 1650.

The Third Civil War 1650–1

The cause of the Second Civil War is complex even when explained in a simplified way. In comparison the cause of the so-called Third Civil War is easily explained as simply an invasion by the rightful King backed by his Scottish subjects to restore the monarchy and to terminate the republic.

The background, however, may deserve some examination. After Charles I's death, the monarchy and the House of Lords were officially abolished. They were replaced by a Council of State consisting of forty-one members including Fairfax, Cromwell and Bradshaw. It became treasonable to proclaim Prince Charles, or anyone else, king.

The Scots were not prepared to go along with this republicanism and remained a monarchy. King Charles II was proclaimed King on 5 February 1649. The new King was not in the least like his father. He was shrewd, cynical and believed that the end justified the means. He immediately began to weigh up the chances of regaining the throne in England. Invasion from Ireland, Scotland and even the chance of Montrose doing it for him all presented themselves as possibilities. The troubled affairs in Ireland were, as always, complex. But the appointment of Oliver Cromwell as Lieutenant of Ireland put paid to any hopes Charles II might have had of using Ireland as a base for an invasion.

Charles was encouraged by the unsettled state of England. There had been a resurgence of the Levellers and the emergence of two more groups: the Fifth Monarchy, who believed that the time of God's personal rule was at hand, and the Diggers, who maintained that the English soil should belong to those who tilled it.

In March 1649 commissioners from Scotland had waited upon Charles II with the same terms as they had tried to impress on his father. At that time he had not wanted to commit himself, wishing to wait and see what materialized, but now a year later he received a new deputation of Scots and after weeks of discussion and manoeuvring he signed the Treaty of Breda on 1 May 1650. With a stroke of his pen he had abandoned Montrose and Ormonde and had undertaken to impose the Presbyterian Church in England when he gained his throne. The Scots would never have allowed him to land unless he had agreed to do this, let alone crowned him King at Scone.

The Scots had not bound themselves to support Charles in an attempt to gain the throne by force of arms. However, by the mere fact that the King was permitted to land the Third Civil War was made inevitable.

1650

March

23rd   Montrose lands at Kirkwall on the Orkney Islands with a nucleus of Danish and German mercenaries. He recruits 1,000 Orkney volunteers.

April

12th   Montrose lands in Scotland, takes Thurso and Dunbeath Castle and marches on Dunrobin Castle which closes its gates against him.

27th   Montrose, awaiting reinforcements confidently at Carbisdale, is lured from his strongpoint by Colonel Strachan and his command cut to pieces.

May

21st   Montrose is hung, drawn and quartered at Edinburgh.

Montrose is paraded through the streets of Edinburgh before his execution, 21 May 1650.

June

1st Cromwell returns from Ireland.

13th It is obvious that the Scots intend invading England, so Parliament decides to anticipate this stroke by a counter-stroke and to invade Scotland before its one-time ally is prepared. This day Fairfax is voted to command the army with Cromwell as his deputy.

20th Parliament announces its intention of invading Scotland. Fairfax, who thought he was to command an army to defend England, refuses to countenance such an act of aggression against a people who had a Solemn League and Covenant with his country.

23rd Charles II arrives in Scotland, and as a matter of expediency takes the Solemn League and Covenant.

26th Fairfax refuses to countenance the invasion and resigns his commission. Cromwell is appointed to command, with Charles Fleetwood as deputy.

July

19th Cromwell concentrates his forces at Berwick.

22nd He crosses the border.

Berwick in the early seventeenth century, from the town plan by John Speed.

26th   Cromwell is supplied by sea at the only reasonable harbour before Edinburgh, a small town called Dunbar which he reaches this day.

29th   Cromwell draws up facing David Leslie's strong fortification stretching from Leith to Edinburgh.

30th   Cromwell writes to the president of the Council of State that he is withdrawing to Musselburgh because of the pouring rain and short rations.

31st   Major-General Robert Montgomery makes a surprise attack with 1,000 horse on the camp at Musselburgh. Despite an initial success they are driven off with casualties.

August

1st   Cromwell falls back to Dunbar where the men are issued tents.

12th   He returns to Musselburgh intending to cut Leslie's lines of communications.

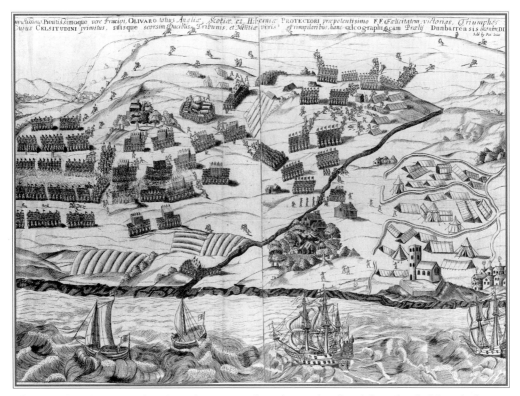

The Battle of Dunbar, 3 September 1650. This engraving shows the Scottish and English cavalry (far left) and pikemen (centre left) in fierce combat. At the top of the picture the Scottish cavalry can be seen fleeing up the hill – without a shot fired.

The Battle of Dunbar
3 September 1650

It can be seen that for once Cromwell had been out-manoeuvred by Leslie. When the New Model Army fell back on Dunbar the enemy general posted himself on Doon Hill two miles from the town, in an almost unassailable position which would enable the Scots commander to advance on the town, fall on Cromwell's rear or even to bar his retreat on Berwick as he wished.

It was strategically a classic situation, seemingly only needing the *coup de grâce*. But Cromwell was no ordinary tactician, and Leslie was answerable to the Kirk. The ministers wanted a swift result, so Leslie at their bidding descended the hill and took up a position along the Brox Burn. This is a shallow stream, ordinarily fordable but now swollen by rainfall, running between steep banks, which higher up formed a formidable obstruction but declined as it progressed towards the sea. By the time it reached Broxmouth House it was hardly an obstacle at all. The movement of the Scots army of 6,000 foot and 16,000 horse took all day on 2 September.

Cromwell and Major-General 'Honest John' Lambert reconnoitred the enemy position and simultaneously spotted the flaw in the Scots' position. Sandwiched between the hill and the burn, Leslie's left was cramped, with little room to manoeuvre, while there was nothing on the right to impede cavalry. At the Parliamentary Council of War that night Cromwell put his idea to the commanders: 'If we beat their right wing we hazard their whole army for they would be in great confusion . . . for they have not great room to traverse their regiments. . . .' Cromwell had no more than 3,500 foot and 7,500 horse. Outnumbered by two to one this was a

13th   Cromwell occupies Braid Hill in order to threaten the Queensferry road.

27th   The campaign develops into a chess game with adroit move and countermove. Cromwell moves to cut Leslie's communication with Stirling, only to be countered.

September

1st   The English army is back at Dunbar 'shattered, weary and discouraged'. Cromwell has definitely lost the first round. In all his attempts to make Leslie stand and fight he has been out-smarted.

2nd   On the previous night Leslie has cut Cromwell's lines of communication and is now presenting only two alternatives: either Cromwell must fight on Leslie's terms or evacuate by sea under the Scots fire.

daring plan which by the law of averages could not be expected to succeed.

During the night the troops went to battle stations. Against the low ground by Broxburn House, Cromwell stationed six veteran regiments of horse under Fleetwood and Lambert. 'He rid all night . . . on a little Scots nag, biting his lips until the blood ran without receiving it, his thoughts busily employed to be ready for the action,' wrote an eye witness.

After a night of wind and rain all was ready. The leading horse regiments were backed up by the foot of Monck, Pride and Overton. At 4 a.m. on 3 September the first attack went in. The over-confident Scots were unprepared for such audacity, they had seen their overnight position as merely a jumping-off point for an easy victory. Nevertheless they rallied and 'the enemy made a very gallant stand and there was a very hot dispute between their horse and ours', reported Cromwell later. Meanwhile Monck had led his foot against the massed infantry of the enemy centre.

While this was falling out the wily Cromwell at the head of the Ironsides, supported by Pride's foot, had crossed the burn and fell upon the Scots in a flanking attack. Eventually by inclining to the left they were completely outflanked. 'I never beheld a more terrible charge,' wrote an officer. 'Our foot making the Scots give ground for upwards of three-quarters of a mile.' At this the Scots' left wing, without a shot fired, fled. Although a number of regiments stood their ground, and died where they stood, the vast majority of Leslie's great army fled into the red rays of the rising sun, casting away their weapons as they ran. Cromwell had achieved the well nigh impossible and broken Leslie's army which had had the advantage of both the ground and numbers. No wonder the Ironsides sang Psalm 117 as they re-formed: 'O praise the Lord . . . For his merciful kindness is great toward us. . . .' The pursuit went on for eight miles. . . .

3rd	THE BATTLE OF DUNBAR. Cromwell launches a surprise early-morning attack and defeats Leslie and his Covenanters. *See separate account above.*
4th	Lambert is sent with six regiments of horse and one of foot to Edinburgh. Cromwell goes after Leslie, who with several thousand survivors of Dunbar has taken refuge in Stirling.
17th	The English army arrives at Stirling. Cromwell has no wish to break his strength against the fortifications of the lofty castle so withdraws to Edinburgh.

December

24th	Edinburgh Castle surrenders on easy terms.

George Monck, Duke of Albemarle, who fought with Cromwell, Pride and Overton at the Battle of Dunbar.

1651

January

1st   Charles II is crowned King of Scotland at Scone with Bruce's golden circlet, having endured public humiliation by confessing all his sins, his father's and mother's too.

Charles II, crowned king in Scone, Scotland, 1651.

By June Cromwell had been reinforced and now commanded ten regiments of horse, fifteen regiments of foot and two regiments of dragoons. Leslie, unabashed by his defeat and still based at Stirling, was ready to try again and was recruiting Highlanders successfully. Colonels Kerr and Strachan, survivors of Dunbar, were recruiting at Glasgow. Colonel Edward Massey, hero of Gloucester who was Parliamentarian but not Cromwellian in sympathy, joined Charles with a contingent of English Royalists. Thus the Royalist army, Scots and English, were perhaps 15,000 foot and 6,000 horse.

June

25th   Cromwell, who has been ill since February, is well enough to take the field this day.

August

1st   Cromwell while sieging Perth hears that after a long period of ineffective manoeuvres which wasted men and achieved no advantage the Royalist army has plunged south.

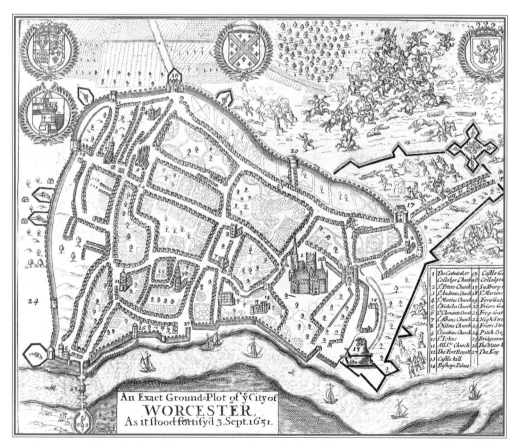

'An Exact Ground-Plot of the City of Worcester, as it stood fortified 3 Sept. 1651.'

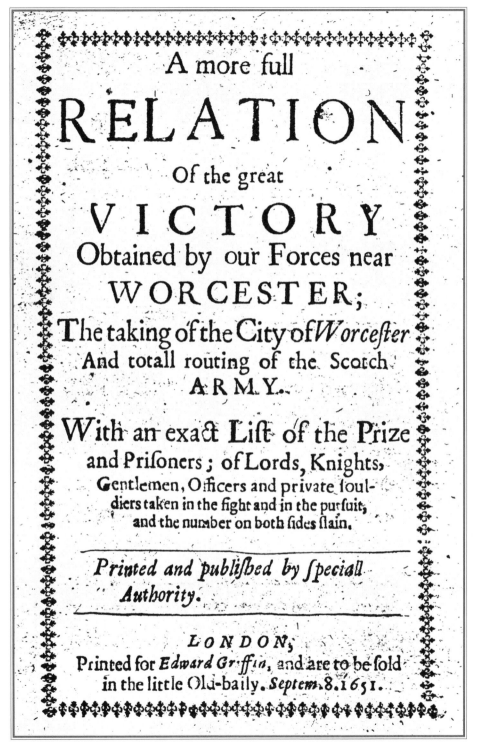

A more full

RELATION

Of the great

VICTORY

Obtained by our Forces near

WORCESTER;

The taking of the City of *Worcester*
And totall routing of the Scotch
ARMY.

With an exact Lift of the Prize
and Priſoners; of Lords, Knights,
Gentlemen, Officers and private ſoul-
diers taken in the fight and in the purſuit,
and the number on both ſides ſlain.

*Printed and publiſhed by ſpeciall
Authority.*

LONDON,
Printed for *Edward Griffin*, and are to be ſold
in the little Old-baily. *Septem.* 8. 1651.

'A more full Relation of the great Victory Obtained by our Forces near Worcester; . . .'

The Battle of Worcester
3 September 1651

On 2 September Cromwell had completed his reconnaissance of the enemy position, for although his army numbered 28,000 against the Royalist 16,000, the majority of whom were Scots, it was not his nature to leave anything to chance. It was his intention to operate from both sides of the River Severn and to that end he had assembled a mass of bridging material, the basis of which was 'twenty great boats'.

Very early in the morning of 3 September Fleetwood set out from Upton but owing to the necessity of towing the boats against the current he did not reach the River Teme until well after midday. Both the Teme and Severn were to be bridged, within pistol shot of one another. The overall plan was for General Deane to force the well-defended crossing at Powick Bridge – the first encounter in the Civil War and part of the last – while Fleetwood used the pontoon bridge. They were opposed by Major-General Robert Montgomery's brigade and the fighting was very bitter all along the Teme front. When Cromwell saw how desperate the resistance was and how little headway even his seasoned troops were making, he demonstrated the soundness of his bridge-building scheme by marching three brigades across to overwhelm the enemy.

He was opposed by Colonel Pittscottie's fanatical Highlanders, dour, tough and desperate, who held the Parliamentary attack for a while but eventually were pushed back from hedge to hedge by the weight of numbers. Their forced withdrawal left Colonel Keith's flank vulnerable – he was defending Powick Bridge – and soon, their ammunition expended and discouraged by the wounding of Montgomery, the Scots were streaming back on Worcester completely routed. It is hard to imagine why Major-General Dalziell's brigade in reserve was not committed when it could be seen that the pressure on the river front was too great.

2nd Perth surrenders. Cromwell orders that Monck with 5,000–6,000 men should remain behind to take Stirling and that Lambert with 4,000 horse should advance at once to join Rich and Harrison on the border to harrass the Royalists in any way they might.

8th Charles reaches Penrith.

15th The Royalists are at Wigan. After a spectacular forced march Lambert joins Harrison and Rich.

This, the first phase of the battle, took a little over two hours. King Charles, observing that Cromwell had seriously weakened his right wing to succour the left, now launched a double attack on the Parliamentary positions at Red Hill and Perry Wood. Both of these attacks were successful and, had Leslie's cavalry seconded them instead of refusing to move from the safety of Worcester's defences, Cromwell's position might well have become desperate, despite his careful planning. As it was the issue was in doubt for some while, the Parliamentary troops giving way all along the line until the advent of Cromwell and his three brigades who had recrossed the river.

By this time the impetus of the Royalist attack had lost its power: they were running short of powder and shot, the Duke of Hamilton, leader of the Perry Wood attack, was shot in the leg, and they retreated on the city in considerable disorder. This marks the second stage.

The third and last phase was one of chaos, cowardice and feats of individual bravery. The Parliamentary guns played on the city and soon all but one of its gates were in enemy hands. On Castle Mound Sir William Hammond, Colonel Drummond and Lord Rothes made a determined last stand until they were offered terms by Cromwell in person. Sir Alexander Forbes refused to surrender Fort Royal so the Essex militia took it by storm and turned its guns on the city it was meant to defend.

Meanwhile Dalziell's brigade surrendered without firing a shot, while Leslie, whose cavalry had turned the tide at Marston Moor, was still inactive and could only stare at the carnage 'as one amazed and bereft of his senses'.

The charge up Sudbury Street led by the Earl of Cleveland diverted the attention of the victors long enough for the King to escape through St Martin's Gate. It was a complete and total disaster for the King; his army had suffered between 2,000 and 3,000 dead and very few officers of consequence escaped Cromwell's net.

Cromwell wrote his dispatch to the House when he was 'so weary and stiff and scarce able to write', but it was for him, 'a very glorious mercy and as stiff a contest for four or five hours as I have ever seen'.

22nd Charles enters Worcester, the Loyal City, as its inhabitants called it.

25th Robert Lilburne routs the Earl of Derby who had returned from the Isle of Man to join the King at Wigan.

24th Lambert meets Cromwell at Warwick.

27th They reach Evesham this day.

28th Lambert is detached to cross the Severn by Upton Bridge, dispersing the Royalist guard at that point.

An eighteenth-century reproduction of the oak chest carved with a scene of Charles II's escape at Boscobel, 1651.

	29th	Cromwell invests Worcester.
September	*3rd*	THE BATTLE OF WORCESTER. Cromwell's army, reinforced by militia and other bodies, numbered about 28,000 strong. The Royalists are decisively defeated. *See separate account on pages 212–13.*
October	*13th*	Charles II flees the country.

Epilogue

Hugh Peters, Cromwell's chaplain, addressing the militia told them, 'When your wives and children shall say unto you, where have you been and what news: then shall you say you have been at Worcester, where England's sorrows began and where they have happily ended.' It was indeed so, for the Civil Wars that had run their wearisome and destructive course for nine years were ended. Now Charles Stuart, King of Scotland and England, was a penniless refugee who would never again return to gain his throne by force of arms but only in God's good time at his countrymen's request.

Select Bibliography

Contemporary Histories, Memoirs and Tracts

Archer, Elias. *The Marching of the Red Trained Bands*, London, 1643

Atkyns, Richard and Gwyn, John. *Military Memoirs*, ed. Peter Young and Norman Tucker, Longmans, 1967

Birch, Colonel John. *Military Memoir* by Roe, his secretary, ed. J. and T.W. Webb, Camden Society, 1873

Bulstrode, Sir Richard. *Memoirs*, 1721

Calendar of State Papers: Domestic

Calendar of State Papers: Venetian

Calendar of State Papers: Ireland

Calendar of the Committee for Compounding

Calendar of the Committee for the Advance of Money

Commons Journals 1625–60

Carlyle, Thomas. *Cromwell's Letters and Speeches*, ed. S.C. Lomas, 3 vols, 1904

Clarendon, Edward, Earl of. *The History of the Rebellion*, ed. W. Dunn Macray, 6 vols, Oxford, 1888

Clark, T.S., ed. *Life of James II*, collected out of Memoirs written by his own hand . . . 1816

Coe, Richard. *An Exact Dyarie*, London, 1644

Dillon, Lord. 'On a list of Officers in the London Trained Bands 1643', *Archaeologia*, 1890

Drake, Edward. *The Diary of the Siege of Lyme Regis*, contained in full in *Civil War in Dorset*, ed. A.R. Bayley, 1910

The Life and Letters of Sir Lewis Dyve. ed. H.G. Tibbutt, Beds. Historical Records Society 1948

Hamper, William, ed. *The Life, Diary and Correspondence of Sir William Dugdale*, 1827

Hopton, Ralph, Lord. *Bellum Civile*, ed. C.E.H. Chadwyck Healey, Somerset Record Society, 1902

Hutchinson, Lucy. *Memoirs of the Life of Colonel Hutchinson*, ed. C.H. Firth, 2 vols, 1885

'The Journal of Prince Rupert's Marches', *English Historical Review*, 1898

Luke, Sir Samuel. Journal, I.G. Phillip, 3 vols. Oxfordshire Record Society, 1947

——. *Letter Books 1644–45*, ed. H.G. Tibbutt, Historical Manuscripts Commission

Tracts Relating to Particular Battles and Sieges

Cropredy Bridge: 'A Full and Exact Relation . . . .', Thomas Ellis 1644

Edgehill: Sir Richard Bulstrode, 'Memoirs and Reflections' 1721

Dunbar: C.H. Firth, 'Transactions of the Royal Historical Society', Vol. XIV

Marston Moor: 'A Full Relation of the late Battle . . . obtained at Marston Moor within five miles of York. . . .' by Captain Stewart, printed London, 1644

First Newbury: 'A True Relation of the Late Expedition . . . . with a description of the fight at Newbury', 1643, *see Bibliotheca Gloucenstris*

Second Newbury: Sir Edward Walker, 'Historical Discourses for both battles'

W. Money, 'Battles of Newbury'

York: 'True Intelligence from the English and Scottish Army now besieging York' by Simeon Ashe and William Goode. There were a number of 'True Intelligences' from these gentlemen who were chaplains to the Earl of Manchester. Printed in London, 1644

Worcester: 'Boscobel or His Majesty's most miraculous preservation', T. Blount

Miscellaneous Tracts

'A Perfect Table of 299 Victories since the King attempted to enter Hull' by Essex and Fairfax 1646

'The Yeare of Jubilee or England's Releasement', a summary of Fairfax's achievements from Naseby to the late reduction of Oxford, by S. Sheppard 1646

'England's Remembrances: or a catalogue of all or most of the Several Victories and strongholds obtained by Parliament' 1645

News-sheets of the Period

Certaine Informations

Mercurius Aulicus

Mercurius Britannicus

Mercurius Civicus

The Moderate Intelligencer

A Perfect Diurnal

Perfect Occurrences

The Scottish Dove

The Spie

The Weekly Account

Recent Publications

Adair, John. *Roundhead General*, MacDonald, 1969

——. *Cheriton, 1644*, Roundwood Press, 1973

——. *A Life of John Hampden the Patriot*, MacDonald, 1976

Andriette, Eugene A. *Devon and Exeter in the Civil War*, David & Charles, 1971

Ashley, Maurice. *The Battle of Naseby and the Fall of King Charles I*, Alan Sutton, 1993

——. *The English Civil War*, Alan Sutton, 1992

Atkin, Malcolm. *The Civil War in Worcestershire*, Alan Sutton, 1995

Bayley, A.R. *The Civil War in Dorset, 1642–1660*, Taunton, 1910

Broxap, E. *Great Civil War in Lancashire 1642–51*, 1910

Coate, Mary. *Cornwall in the Great Civil War*

Eddershaw, David. *The Civil War in Oxfordshire*, Alan Sutton with Oxfordshire Books, 1995

Emberton, Wilfrid. *Love Loyalty, The Great and Perilous Siege of Basing House*, 1972

Everitt, A.M. *The Community of Kent and the Great Rebellion 1640–60*, Leicester University Press, 1966

Firth, C.H., ed. *The Memoirs of Edmund Ludlow*, 1894

Hollings, J.F. *Leicester during the Great Civil War*, 1840

Johnson, D.A. and Vaisey, D.G. *Staffordshire in the Great Civil War*

Kingston, A. *Hertfordshire during the Great Civil War*, 1894

——. *Newark on Trent, the Civil War Siege Works*, Royal Commission for Historical Monuments

Phillips, John Roland. *Memoirs of the Civil War in Wales and the Marches*, 2 vols, London, 1874

Porter, Stephen. *Destruction in the English Civil War*, Alan Sutton, 1992

Rushworth, John. *Historical Collections 1618–1701*, 7 vols, 1659–1701

Register of the Privy Council of Scotland

Sherwood, Roy. *The Civil War in the Midlands 1642–1651*, Alan Sutton, 1992

Sprigge, Joshua. *Anglia Rediviva*, 1647

Stanford, C. Thomas. *Sussex in the Great Civil War*, 1910

Symonds, Richard. *Diary*, ed. C. Long, Camden Society, 1859

Tennant, Philip. *Edgehill and Beyond: The People's War in the South Midlands*, Alan Sutton, 1992

Twentyman, M.S. 'Account of Siege of Newark' in Brown's *History of Newark*, 1907

The Thomason Tracts, a unique collection of tracts and news-sheets collected by George Thomason 1640–61, now in the British Museum

Vicars, John. *England's Parliamentarie Chronicle*, 3 vols, 1643–6

Walker, Sir Edward. *Historical Discourses on Several Occasions*, 1705

Warburton, Eliot. *Memoirs of Prince Rupert and the Cavaliers*, 1849

Washbourne, J. *Bibliotheca Gloucestrensis*, a collection of pamphlets, London, 1823

Wedgwood, C.V. *Montrose*, Alan Sutton, 1995

Wenham, Peter. *The Great and Close Siege of York*, Roundwood Press, 1970

Wharton, Sergeant Nehemiah. *Letters*, ed. by Sir Henry Ellis, *Archaelogia*, 1853

Whitlocke, Bulstrode. *Memorials of English Affairs*, 1682

Wood, Alfred C. *Nottinghamshire in the Great Civil War*, Clarendon, 1937

Wood, Anthony. *Life and Times, 1632–1695*, ed. Andrew Clark, Oxford, 1891

Wroughton, John. *The Civil War in Bath and North Somerset*, Victor Morgan, 1973

Young, Peter. *Edgehill 1642*, Roundwood Press, 1967

——. *Marston Moor 1644*, Roundwood Press, 1970

——. *Cavalier Army*, Allen & Unwin, 1974

Young, Peter and Emberton, Wilfrid. *Sieges of the Great Civil War*, Bell, 1978

Young, Peter and Holmes, Richard. *The English Civil War 1642–51*, Eyre Methuen, 1974

Young, Peter and Toynbee, Margaret. *Cropredy Bridge 1644*, Roundwood Press, 197

Index

Many minor references have been omitted.

Abbey-cum-hir 135
Aberdeen, Battle of 124
Abingdon 109, 120, 122, 136, 140, 142, 171, 173
Adwalton Moor, Battle of 67, 90
Aldbourne 77, 78, 101
Alford, Battle of 155
Alton 87–8
Andover 22, 24
Anglesey 82–3, 85
Antrim, Earl of 141
Appleyard, Lt-Col 103
Argyll, Earl of 142, 195
Arundel 87, 88, 89, 93
Arundel, Lady 62, 63
Arundel, Lord 68
Ashburnham, John 8, 53, 94, 96, 100
Assheton, Col 40, 100
Astley, Sir Bernard 127, 130
Astley, Sir Jacob (later Lord) xvii, 29, 156, 171, 175, 184
Aston, Maj-Gen Sir Arthur 46, 57, 61, 74, 125, 134
Aston, Sir Thomas 78, 100
Auldearn, Battle of 151
Axminster 125, 133
Aylesbury 27, 46, 106, 122, 147, 149

Bacon, Robert 147
Bailey, Ralph 147
Baillie, Robert 155, 161, 177, 195, 196–7
Balfour, Sir William 8, 43, 101, 122, 124
Ballard, Maj-Gen 56
Bamfield, Col Joseph 87
Banbury 41, 114, 128, 130, 137, 172, 201
Bankes, Sir John 136
Bard, Col Sir Henry 103, 150
Barnstaple 75, 113

Basing 147, 163
Basing House 71, 83, 84–5, 103, 113, 117, 123, 124, 127, 132, 133, 162, 167
Bastwick, Dr John 33
Bath 65, 83, 85, 97, 117, 131, 159
Bath, Earl of 33, 34, 38
Beacon Hill, Battle of 121
Beaminster 103, 155
Bedford, Earl of 4, 35
Beeston Castle 171
Bellasis, Lord 168
Bellasis, Sir John 102
Belvoir Castle 53, 142, 171, 172
Berkeley, Justice 76
Berkeley, Sir John 33, 54, 112, 149, 151
Berkeley Castle 166, 172
Birch, Col John 125, 175
Birmingham 58, 59
Bishops' Wars 2
Blackburn 47, 54
Blake, Lt-Col (later Admiral) Robert xxii, 109, 113, 135, 151
Bletchingdon House 150
Blewett, Capt Francis 107
Blount, Thomas 21
Bodmin 120, 121
Bohemia, Queen of 24
Bolingbroke Castle 81
Bolles, Col 88
Bolton 55, 58, 109, 170
Booth, Sir George 65
Boswell, Sir William 18, 97
Bovey Tracey 181
Braddock Down, Battle of 53
Bradshaw, John 199, 201
Brentford 44, 45, 49

Brereton, Sir William xxii, 58, 59, 64, 65, 69, 82, 89, 137, 144, 146, 165, 167, 172, 174, 176, 184

Bridgnorth 39, 99

Bridgwater 65, 66, 159, 165

Bristol 57, 69, 70, 71, 77, 90, 163, 165, 168

Bristol, Earl of see Digby

Brooke, Lord 35, 38, 54

Broughton Castle 41

Brown/e, Col John 37, 38, 56

Browne, Maj-Gen 100, 106, 112, 113, 115, 122, 136, 140, 142, 150, 153, 171

Bushell, Thomas 94

Buttercram 107

Byron, John, Lord xvii, 8, 11, 13, 35, 37, 78, 85, 89, 93, 95, 117, 119, 137, 181

Byron, Sir Nicholas 39, 43, 94

Byron, Sir Richard 72

Byron, Sir Thomas 24

Caldecote House 37

Callendar 196–7

Cambridge 34, 122, 144

Campsfield, Sir John 131, 175

Capel, Arthur, Baron xvii, 82, 85, 191

Carbery, Earl of 74, 77

Carew, Sir Andrew 75

Carisbrook Castle 179, 188

Carlisle 150, 155, 171, 189

Carnarvon, Robert, Earl of xviii, 68, 79

Carnwarth, Earl of 157

Caskieben, Laird of 20

Castle Dore, Battle of 122

Cavendish, Gen Charles 58, 63, 70, 71

Cawley, William 51

Chalgrove Field, Action at 66, 67, 92

Chaloner, Mr 68

Chandos, Lord 27, 110

Charles I, King (main references) 1, 34, 35, 71, 90, 92, 114–15, 119, 126, 130–1, 137–8, 156–7, 160, 174, 176, 177–80, 184, 187–8, 195, 196, 197, 199

Charles II
    as Prince of Wales 6, 15, 24, 42, 45, 82, 149, 155, 165, 170, 174, 181, 184
    as King 199, 201, 204, 209, 212–13, 214

Charles Louis, Elector Palatinate 4, 14, 19, 24, 163

Chatsworth 86

Chaytor, Col Henry 170

Chepstow Castle 189

Cheriton, Battle of 101, 102–3, 137

Cheshire 26, 59, 64, 152

Chester 69, 86, 117, 144, 146, 151, 152, 165, 172, 173–4, 174, 175, 176, 181

Chichester 51, 52–3, 89

Cholmley, Sir Hugh 22, 25, 128

Cholmley, Sir Richard 133

Chowbent 48

Chudleigh, Maj-Gen James 61

Cirencester 27, 54, 76, 144

Cleveland, Earl of 115, 213

Colchester 191–2, 195

Constantine, William 75

Conyers, Sir John 13, 69

Cooper, Mayor Edmund 95, 123

Cooper, Sir Anthony Ashley 121, 127, 132, 135, 136

Corbridge, Action at 96

Corfe Castle 66, 135

Cottington, Lord Francis 18, 55

Coventry 34, 142

Crane, Sir Richard 109

Crawford, Maj-Gen Lord 87–8, 134

Croft, James 176

Cromwell, Capt 62

Cromwell, Oliver xxii–xxiii, 6, 30, 34, 62, 63, 75, 81, 119, 128, 135, 137–8, 144–50 passim, 154, 156–7, 158, 166, 167, 178–80, 181, 189, 193, 194, 195, 199, 200, 201, 204–7, 210, 212–13, 214

Cropredy Bridge, Battle of 112, 114–15, 137

Culpeper, John, Baron 9, 35, 88

Cumberland 39, 150

Cumberland, Earl of 33

Dalbier, Col John 162, 167, 168

Dalziell, Maj-Gen 214–15

Dartmouth 80, 172, 181

Deane, Gen 214

Denbigh, Earls of 59, 98, 100

Derby, Countess of 45, 99, 106, 109

Derby, Earl of 39, 45, 48, 57, 58, 61, 213

Dering, Sir Edward 11, 12, 13, 18, 96

Devizes 166

Devon 30, 39, 98, 112, 126

Digby, George, Earl of Bristol 4, 9, 11, 29, 33, 148, 154, 157–8, 167, 168
Digby, Sir John 46, 152
Dodding, Col 40, 121
Doddington, Sir Francis 115, 122
Doncaster 161, 167
Donnington Castle 131, 132, 168
Dorchester 65, 66, 71, 74, 89, 114, 133
Dorset 56, 128
Dorset, Earl of 6, 38
Dover 35
Dover, Earl of 96
Downs mutiny 191
Drogheda 16, 134
Drummond, Col 215
Dunbar, Battle of 205, 206–7, 210
Dunbeath Castle 203
Dungannon 142
Dunrobin Castle 203
Dunster 65, 66
Durham 2
Dyve, Sir Lewis 80, 83, 133, 160

Edgehill, Battle of 40, 42–3, 49, 63, 69
Edinburgh 2, 86, 203, 206
Elgin, Lord 123
Ellesmere 94
Erle, Sir Walter 84, 101, 106, 141
Ernle, Sir Michael 144
Essex 120, 144
Essex, Robert, Earl of xxiii, 4, 17, 30, 34, 37, 38, 40, 42–3, 44, 45, 49, 59, 71, 75, 76–7, 78–9, 80, 81, 89, 92, 109, 110, 117, 120–8 passim, 130, 132, 148, 149
Evesham 150
Exeter 45, 56–7, 75, 106, 107, 112, 117, 163, 168, 181, 185
Eythin, Lord 118

Fairfax (father and son) xxiii–xxiv, 67, 90, 115, 189
Fairfax, Lord Ferdinando 22, 25, 46, 62, 98, 102, 117, 134, 136, 145–6, 149
Fairfax, Sir Thomas 26, 27, 53, 58, 64, 81, 89, 95, 98, 99, 101, 106, 110, 113, 118–19, 120, 139, 141, 142, 144, 146–7, 148, 150–65 passim, 168, 171, 173, 178, 180, 181, 184, 188, 191, 192, 193, 195, 197, 201, 204

Falkland, Lord 9, 79
Faringdon House 150
Farnham 46, 83, 85, 86, 87, 88, 102, 139, 141, 142
Fielding, Col Richard 39, 43, 61, 63
Fiennes, Col John 37, 67, 142
Fiennes, Col Nathaniel 37, 65, 67, 69, 70, 77, 89
Finch, Lord 4
FitzWilliams, Col 162
Five Members plot 9, 10, 13, 48–9
Fleetwood, Gen Charles 204, 207, 212
Forbes, Sir Alexander 213
Ford, Sir Edward 87, 93
Fortescue 43
Forth, Patrick Ruthven Earl of 41, 103, 132
Fox, Col John 139, 144, 176
Fox, Maj Reginald 176

Gage, Col Sir Henry 120, 123, 124, 129, 132, 133, 140
Gainsborough 69, 70, 71, 89
Gardner, Capt Henry 163
Gell, Sir John 58, 85, 90, 99
Gerbier, Sir Balthazar 16
Gerrard, Baron 167, 170, 171
Glemham, Sir Thomas xviii, 113, 155, 166, 174, 184
Gloucester 55, 72, 74, 75, 76, 92
Godolphin, Sidney 54
Goodwin, Col Arthur 37, 46
Goring, Lord George xviii, 33, 36, 58, 64, 119, 121, 122, 127, 139, 141, 149, 151, 152, 153, 155–6, 158, 166, 168, 172
Gosport 34
Gould, Col William 65, 95
Grantham 58, 63, 175
Greene, Father Thomas 11
Grenville, Sir Beville 38, 68
Grenville, Sir Richard 120, 121, 124, 126, 149, 151, 172, 181
Grey, Lord, of Groby 47, 51, 66, 196
Gryme, Lt Col Mark 144, 145, 147
Gurney, Sir Richard 9, 30, 34

Halton Castle 69
Hamilton, Duke of 180, 192, 193, 194–5, 213
Hammond, Sir William 213
Hammond, Thomas 148

Hampden, Col John xxiv, 1, 2, 9, 26, 31, 66, 67, 79, 90, 92, 178

Hampshire 83, 117, 162, 163, 168, 171

Hampton Court 10, 11, 15, 179, 188

Harcourt, Chevalier 82, 86

Harlech 184, 187

Hartlepool 161, 171

Haselrig, Sir Arthur 7, 9, 52, 67, 103, 108, 125

Hastings, Henry 28

Hastings, Sir William 127

Haverfordwest 74, 77, 160

Hawarden Castle 84, 87

Haynes, Capt James 134

Hemel Hempstead 152

Hemyock Castle 99

Henderson, Sir John 51, 53, 56, 58, 81

Henley 141, 142, 147

Henrietta Maria, Queen 8, 11, 13, 14, 16, 19, 54, 55, 64, 65, 66, 67, 69, 106, 107, 112, 143–4, 148, 162, 170

Henrietta, Princess 112, 117

Herbert, Lord 58, 59

Herbert, Sir Edward 9

Hereford 61, 65, 163, 175

Hertford, Earl/Marquess of 33, 37–8, 65, 66, 68, 69

Highnam 58

Hobart, Sir Miles 62, 141

Hoghton Tower 55

Holborne, Maj-Gen 135, 136, 148

Holland, Earl of 16, 17, 22, 31, 40, 58

Holles, Denzil 9, 12, 185, 195

Holmby House 178, 187

Homebridge 98

Hopton Heath, Battle of 58, 90

Hopton, Sir Ralph (later Baron) xviii, 16, 17, 33, 36, 39, 45, 48, 53, 54, 56–7, 61, 64, 67–8, 69, 75, 79, 80, 85, 86, 87, 88, 93, 96, 100, 102–3, 109, 120, 126, 137, 151, 152, 181, 182

Hornby Castle 81, 113

Hotham, Sir John 12, 21, 23, 29, 33, 64, 139

Hotham, Capt John (son) 67, 139

Howley House 67

Hoyle, Thomas 123

Huddleston, Col 80, 121

Hull 12, 19, 21, 22, 23, 29, 30, 31, 33, 72, 75, 80, 81, 90, 92, 139

Hungerford, Sir Edward 58, 62, 64, 67

Huntingdon 121

Hutchinson, Col John 51, 61, 62, 67, 72, 77

Hyde, Edward 15, 46, 49

Inchiquin, Lord 98

Ingoldsby, Maj 141

Inverlochy 142

Irby, Sir Anthony 62

Ireland/Irish 1, 6, 11, 12, 19–20, 57, 63, 72, 76–7, 85, 86, 87, 123, 136, 137, 149, 162, 199, 200, 201, 204

Ireton, Commissary Gen Henry xxiv, 28, 29, 156, 178, 187

Isle of Wight 34, 179, 196

Islip 109, 150

James, Duke of York (later King) 21, 42, 52, 82

Jephson, Col Sir William 8, 123, 140, 171

Jermyn, Lord 97, 98, 148, 159

Jersey 21

Johnson, Thomas 20

Jones/Joyce, Capt 108

Joyce, Cornet George 178, 187

Keith, Col 214

Kent 13, 21, 22, 31, 35, 69, 83, 191, 122, 133, 149

Kerr, Col 210

Killigrew, Sir Peter 53, 176

Kilsyth, Battle of 161

Kimbolton, Lord 4

Kineton 40, 42–3

Kingston 11, 45, 72

Kingston, Earl of 69

Knaresborough 112, 134, 136, 193

Knyveton, David 85–6

Lambert, Maj-Gen John 47, 119, 193, 195, 206–7, 212, 213

Lamport 155

Lancashire 39, 40, 47, 54, 61, 193

Lancaster 57, 58, 90

Langdale, Marmaduke, Baron xx, 96, 145, 153, 156–7, 167, 168, 189, 194–5

Langport, Battle of 158, 159

Lansdown, Battle of 68

Larran, Capt Laurence 142

Lathom House 98–103 *passim*, 106, 109, 121

Laud Archbishop William 1, 4, 94–5, 96, 97, 98, 158

Launceston 51, 53, 61, 120

Ledbury 150

Lee Bridge 82

Lea/Lay, Capt 85

Leeds 53

Legge, Col William xx, 98, 147, 150, 165

Leicester 26, 28, 31, 34, 37, 36, 77, 153, 154

Lenthall, William (Speaker) 25, 63, 64, 72, 74, 167

Leslie, Maj-Gen David 119, 137, 149, 155, 162, 163, 205, 206–7, 210, 213

Levellers movement 167, 179, 188, 200, 201

Leven, Alexander Leslie, Earl of 2–4, 106, 107, 110, 118, 172

Lichfield 61, 154

Lilburne, John 46, 167, 178–9, 200

Lilburne, Col Robert 134, 213

Lincoln 26, 30, 34, 82, 85, 120

Lincolnshire 56, 106

Lindale 80

Lindsey, Earl of 26, 29, 30, 41

Linsay, Earl of 119

Lisle, Sir George xx, 78, 131, 191, 195

Littleton, Sir Edward (Lord) 4, 24, 107, 158

Liverpool 81, 89, 110, 129, 132, 137

Livingstone, Sir James 161

Lloyd, Sir Richard 84

London 20, 40, 49, 69, 70, 71, 72, 74, 78, 187, 188, 191

Londonderry 19

Long, Col Sir James 146

Lostwithiel 122, 123, 124, 126, 137

Lucas, Sir Charles xx, 119, 191, 195

Lucas, Sir Gervase 167

Lucas, Sir John 35

Ludlow 22, 161

Ludlow, Col 135, 137, 147

Luke, Sir Samuel 61, 142

Lunsford, Col Thomas 8

Lyme Regis 75, 93, 97, 98, 99, 106, 107, 108, 109, 110, 117, 132–3, 139

Maidstone 18, 31, 191

Maitland, Lord 119

Mallory, Col Sir John 176

Manchester 31, 38, 39, 40, 47, 64

Manchester, Edward, Earl of xxiv, 81, 82, 106, 109, 110, 118, 128, 130–1, 137–8, 148

Mandeville, Lord 9

Marlborough 46, 155

Marshall, Stephen 14

Marshalls Elm 33, 153

Marston Moor, Battle of 112, 113, 118–19, 137

Martin, Col Henry 71, 136, 170

Mary, Princess 4, 13, 14, 16–17, 18

Massey, Lt-Gen Edward 58, 59, 72, 76, 92, 120, 140–1, 145, 150, 210

Maurice, Prince xx–xxi, 34, 54, 59, 65, 68, 69, 75, 80, 82, 85, 89, 107, 110, 131, 144, 146

Melcombe Regis 72, 112

Meldrum, Sir John 33, 66, 89, 98, 99, 100, 129

Melton Mowbray 145

Middleton, Sir John 114–15, 121, 122, 124, 126, 195

Middleton, Sir Thomas 66, 84, 85, 135, 137

Milford Haven 66, 77

Modbury 53, 55

Moleyn, Michael 99

Monck, Gen 207, 212

Monmouth 27, 59

Monmouth, Earl of 23

Monro 196

Montgomery Castle 135, 137

Montgomery, Maj-Gen Robert 205, 214

Montrose, James Graham, Marquess of xxi, 123, 124, 141, 142, 151, 155, 161, 163, 165, 201, 203

Moore, Col 40, 100, 110, 153

Musgrave, Sir Phillip 80, 189

Mytton, Col Thomas 94, 144

Nantwich 38, 89, 93
    Battle of 95

Naseby, Battle of 154–5, 156–7, 158

New Model Army 131, 133, 134, 138, 141, 148, 156, 194–5, 206–7

Newark 56, 72, 97, 98, 99, 100, 172, 174, 175

Newbury 127, 152, 170
    First Battle of 77, 78–9, 92
    Second Battle of 128, 130–1, 133, 135, 137

Newcastle 44, 96, 127

Newcastle, William, Duke of xxi, 46, 47, 55, 59, 67, 71, 72, 75, 81, 83, 86, 96, 106, 107, 113, 118–19, 155

Newport, Sir Richard 39
Newport Pagnell 80, 83, 170, 172
Nicholas, Secretary 18, 22, 24, 25, 97
Nicholas, Sir Edward 106
Nichols, Anthony 65, 74
North Scarle 70
Northampton 37, 42, 149, 152, 161
Northampton, Earl of 58, 115, 128, 130
Northumberland 2, 173
Northumberland, Earl of 28, 29
Norton, Col Richard 71, 113, 117, 123, 133, 157,
    159
Norwich Cathedral 13
Norwich, Earl of 191
Nottingham 34, 35, 51, 61, 62, 67, 72, 77, 173

Ogle, Lord 167
Ogleby, Lord 121
Okehampton 54
Okey, Col 156–7
Onslow, Sir Richard 11
Orkney Islands 203
Ormonde, James Butler, Marquess of 16, 57, 76–7,
    82–3, 83, 86, 154
Ormskirk 41, 121
Oxford 35, 37, 38, 41, 42, 43, 47, 48, 51, 52, 59,
    74, 108, 152, 153, 166, 184
Oxford University 34, 37, 48, 54, 55, 67

Page, Col 153
Paulet, Capt 107
Paulet, Lord 93, 110, 126
Pembroke 74, 77, 159, 189, 193
Pembroke, Earl of 16, 34
Pendennis Castle 165, 184
Pennington, Isaac 34, 69
Pennington, Sir John 29
Pennyman, Sir William 59, 74
Percy, Henry 74–5
Perth 210, 212
Philliphaugh, Battle of 163, 165
Pink, Dr Robert 34
Pittscottie, Col 214
Pizzari, Gregario 143
Plymouth 46, 53, 54, 79–80, 85, 89, 95, 124, 125,
    126, 151
Pollard, Sir Hugh 8, 33

Pontefract 46, 53, 134, 145, 159, 195
Poole 72, 74, 75, 77–8, 82, 84, 85, 89, 125, 126,
    127
Popham, Col Alexander 33, 59–61, 64, 67
Portland 72, 109, 127, 134
Portland, Earl of 34
Portsmouth 33, 34, 36, 93, 101, 140, 157
Powick Bridge, Skirmish at 38
Poyntz, Col Gen Sydenham 162, 165, 166, 170,
    171, 172, 174, 175
Preston 41, 47, 54, 58, 81, 89, 121
    Battle of 180, 194–5
Pride, Col Thomas 180, 196, 207
Prynne, William 167, 174
Pym, John 2, 6, 9, 12, 48–9, 74, 87, 92, 137, 178

Radway 42
Raglan 59, 155, 159, 163, 184
Rainsborough, Col 134, 163
Ramsey, Sir James, 43
Rawden House 144, 145
Reading 42, 59, 61, 108
Rich, Col 195, 212
Richmond, Duke of 12, 63, 134, 160
Rigby, Col Alexander 40, 80, 85, 89
Ripple Field, Battle of 59, 90
Robartes, Lord 113, 123
Rochester 35, 191
Roe, Father Alban 11
Romsey 56
Rossiter, Col 145, 149, 170, 171, 175
Rothes, Lord 215
Roundway Down, Battle of 69
Rowe, Sir Thomas 16, 18, 19, 24, 25, 75
Rowse, Lt 144, 145
Rowton Heath, Battle of 165
Rupert, Prince xxi–xxii, 13, 14, 29, 31, 34, 36–7,
    42–3, 44, 45, 49, 53, 54, 58, 59, 61, 66, 69,
    70, 78–9, 92, 100, 109, 110, 112, 113, 117,
    118–19, 132, 137, 140, 147, 149, 150, 153,
    154, 156–7, 159, 163, 165, 168, 171, 172
Ruthin, Col William 46, 48, 51, 53, 56
Rutland, Earl of 69, 158
Rye 17, 171

Sackville, Sir John 34
St Albans 43, 145, 148

Salisbury 56, 57, 127

Salop/Shropshire 39, 55, 141, 173–4, 176

Saltash 52, 53

Sandal Castle 167

Sandys, Col Edwin 34, 35

Savile, Lord 4, 26, 53, 67

Savile, Sir William 95

Saye and Sele, Lord 4, 17, 25, 37, 38, 41

Scarborough 113, 163

Scotland/Scots 1–2, 19, 44, 55, 69, 77, 86, 92, 119,
        127, 134, 137, 149, 158–9, 163, 171, 172,
        174, 177, 179–80, 184, 187, 188, 194, 195,
        196–7, 201, 203–7, 209, 212–13

Scudamore, Sir Barnabas 175

Seacroft Moor, Battle of 58

Selby 102

Sevenoaks 34, 69

Shelford 170, 171

Sherborne 33, 35, 36, 37, 59–61, 150, 160, 161

Sherburn in Elmet 168

Shrewsbury 37, 39, 144, 145

Shuttleworth, Col 40, 61

Skippon, Maj-Gen Phillip xxiv, xxvi, 10, 24, 49,
        123, 130, 148, 156–7

Skipton 47, 112, 168, 176

Smith, Sir John 43, 103

Somerset 29, 31, 33, 53, 55

Somerset House 58

Sourton Down, Battle of 61

Southampton, Earl of 35, 134

Southsea Castle 35

Southwell 177, 184

Stafford 58, 93, 173

Stamford, Earl of 31, 51, 53, 56

Stamford Hill, Battle of 64

Stapleton, Sir Phillip 19, 22, 25, 43, 79

Starkie, Col 40, 55

Stawell, Sir John 33, 66

Stewart, Lord John 103

Stidcombe House 98, 99, 106

Stirling 207, 210, 212

Stow-on-the-Wold 78, 151, 184

Strachan, Col 203, 210

Strafford, Earl of 2, 4, 6

Stratton, Battle at 64

Strode, Col William 9, 52

Stuart, Lord Bernard 115, 131

Sudeley Castle 75, 110

Sunderland, Lord 79

Swansea 64

Swayne, Col Arthur 126

Sydenham, Col Francis 98, 126, 133

Tadcaster 18, 46, 118

Tate, Zouch 135, 138

Taunton 65, 113, 135, 136, 148–52 passim, 155,
        156

Tavistock 45, 117, 176

Taylor, Capt 144, 145

Therrill, Sir Robert 171

Thurland Castle 80, 85

Tichborne, Sir Henry 144

Tippermuir, Battle of 123

Tiverton 122, 168

Torrington, Battle of 181–4

Turnham Green 45, 49–50

Twysden, Sir Roger 18

Vane, Sir Henry 6, 20, 69, 72, 136, 158

Vane, George 134

Vaughan, Sir George 68

Vavasour, Sir William 79, 136

Venn, Col John 8, 44, 133, 140, 145

Verney, Sir Edmund 43

Wakefield 53, 59, 64

Wales/Welsh 38, 58, 59, 66, 92

Walker, Sir Edward 103, 107

Waller, Edmund 41, 65, 68

Waller, Sir William xxvi, 22, 24, 33, 35–6, 46, 47,
        51, 52–3, 56, 57, 58, 59, 61, 63, 64–5, 66,
        67–8, 68–9, 70, 71, 72, 74, 80, 81, 83, 84, 85,
        86, 87, 88, 89, 90, 93, 100–1, 102–3, 109,
        113, 114–15, 125, 127, 128, 130–1, 132, 133,
        141, 142, 145, 146, 147, 148, 149

Walwyn, William 167

Wardlaw, Col James 79, 95

Wardour, Sir James 21, 62, 63, 64

Wareham 85, 98, 121, 122, 125

Warrington 41, 59, 64, 65, 81

Warwick, Admiral the Earl of 4, 21, 29, 45, 48, 85,
        86, 87, 96, 106, 109, 110, 112, 142, 174

Welbeck 120, 161, 167, 171

Weldon, Col Anthony 139, 151

Wells 159

Wem 82

Wemyss, Col James 86, 115

Wentworth, Col Henry 39, 78

Wentworth, Viscount 1, 181

Were, Col 97, 98–9, 106, 123–4, 125, 126

Westmorland 149, 150, 152

Weymouth 72, 112, 113, 125, 129

Wharton, Lord 17, 144, 158

Wharton, Sir Michael 174, 176

Wigan 41, 47, 58

William of Orange, Prince 4, 6, 16–17, 19

Willis, Sir Richard 94, 168, 170

Willoughby, Lord 69, 70, 71

Wilmott, Lt-Gen Lord 43, 46, 61, 69, 115, 120

Winceby, Battle of 81

Winchelsea 17

Winchester 47, 101, 102, 166, 167

Winchester, Marquess of 94, 167

Windebank, Sir Francis 4, 150

Windsor 11, 44, 145

Wood, Anthony 48, 63, 65, 67, 147

Worcester 37, 38, 55, 152, 172

    Battle of 212–13, 214

Wormleighton 42

York 17, 19, 95, 96, 106, 107, 109, 110, 112–13, 115, 117, 118-19, 123, 152, 161